D1028282

Building Respected Companies

The current financial crisis has clear macroeconomic roots, but the dominant view of the firm has made the crisis deeper and more devastating. Over the past few decades, maximizing shareholder value has become the firm's main objective. Chief executives have been keen on this because their economic incentives have been clearly associated with stock market performance. Unfortunately, this has driven many CEOs to make terrible decisions based on short-termism and greed. In this way, the firm has become the object of anger, criticism and cynicism. In *Building Respected Companies*, Jordi Canals argues that we must address this problem by developing companies that truly serve society, not just their shareholders in the short term. This requires a new perspective of what a firm is, what the purpose of the firm in society should be and what the role of the board of directors and senior executives should be.

JORDI CANALS is the Dean and Professor of General Management at IESE Business School. His areas of interest are corporate governance, globalization and corporate strategy. He is the author of several books, including *Universal Banks* (1996) and *Managing Corporate Growth* (2000). A Fulbright Fellow, he was a research fellow at Harvard Business School and a guest scholar at The Brookings Institution and the World Bank. He was also a member of the task force on corporate governance in Spain (2002–3).

Endorsements

"Leadership must raise the aspirations of organizations and nurture their teams to deliver extraordinary performance. This must be achieved with the vision of building a globally respected corporation as recognized by all its stakeholders. Dean Canals brings out the essence of building a globally respected corporation and the role of leadership and governance in nurturing it." Dr. Narayana N.R. Murthy, Chairman, Infosys Technologies.

"A solid corporate reputation offers firms better growth and performance perspectives, and helps manage better current and future risks. This book offers a rich perspective on the role of chief executives in leading and developing corporate legitimacy, respect and admiration in society". César Alierta, Chairman, Telefonica.

"The current financial crisis hopefully acts as a catalyst not only for structural reforms but for mindset changes of business leaders. Jordi Canals' book articulates that only "values create value" and good leaders need to act accordingly. We need leaders with a long term view who help companies make a positive contribution to the common good of society and who clearly put character as the main criteria in the selection of good leaders. May the readers of this book contribute with their behaviour to positively change the business world." Franz Haniel, Chairman, The Haniel Group and Metro Group.

"This thoughtful book is no opportunistic response to recent events. Jordi Canals has been asking profound questions for many years: What exactly are companies for? How should CEOs be judged? Can short-term and long-term objectives be reconciled? What is the commercial value of something called respect? Here he suggests sage and workable answers to these and other highly topical issues." Sir Martin Sorrell, CEO, WPP.

"The global financial crisis and related corporate turmoil provide a compelling case for rethinking the purpose of companies. Using the crisis as a launching point, Jordi Canals presents a new vision of the company which is responsive to all its stakeholders while fulfilling its role as a responsible member of society. His work integrates diverse issues of corporate history, economics, corporate governance, and management practice, in a straightforward manner. This book will be useful not just for leaders on the verge of a crisis, but more importantly, for any business leader in search of inspiration on how to create respected, enduring enterprises." Victor Fung, Chairman, Li&Fung Group.

"As a CEO of a consumer goods company whose mission is 'bring health through food to as many people as possible', I am totally aligned with Jordi Canals' opinion that beyond profit, firms have a role to play in society. I welcome this book because it explores the notion of corporate reputation and leadership both in a visionary and pragmatic manner. This is not just a theoretical issue: we all sometimes wonder what purpose we have and why we get up and go to work every morning." Franck Riboud, Chairman and CEO, Danone.

Building Respected Companies

Rethinking Business Leadership and the Purpose of the Firm

JORDI CANALS

CAMBRIDGE
UNIVERSITY PRESS

CAMBRIDGE UNIVERSITY PRESS
Cambridge, New York, Melbourne, Madrid, Cape Town, Singapore,
São Paulo, Delhi, Dubai, Tokyo

Cambridge University Press
The Edinburgh Building, Cambridge CB2 8RU, UK

Published in the United States of America by Cambridge University Press,
New York

www.cambridge.org
Information on this title: www.cambridge.org/9780521192101

First published 2010

Printed in the United Kingdom at the University Press, Cambridge

A catalogue record for this publication is available from the British Library

Library of Congress Cataloguing in Publication data
Canals, Jordi.
  Building respected companies : rethinking business leadership and the
  purpose of the firm / Jordi Canals.
    p. cm.
  Includes bibliographical references and index.
  ISBN 978-0-521-19210-1
  1. Corporate culture. 2. Social responsibility of business.
  3. Leadership. I. Title.
  HD58.7.C3467 2010
  658.4′08–dc22
  2010008749

ISBN 978-0-521-19210-1 Hardback

Contents

Figures

Tables

Preface

The current debate around corporate governance, leadership and corporate reputation has its roots in the business scandals in the United States and Europe during the last technology bubble at the turn of the century. The current financial crisis introduces new dimensions to this debate and is spreading the conviction that some corporate policies and individual behaviours must change in the business world.

Today, several influential voices support the thesis that capitalism must be reinvented. The G-20 summits in Washington in November 2008 and London in April 2009; the proposals for a new international financial architecture; the current redesign of financial regulation in the United States and the European Union; the scandals around executive compensation systems in Europe and the United States; and the increasing government intervention in the financial system and other industries around the world are examples of relevant voices and policy actions that point to a new direction in the balance between governments and the private sector. Most of those actions focus their attention on the government's role in the economy. This is an important reflection. Nevertheless, the effort to rethink what went wrong with the Western economies over the past few years needs to take into account the notion and purpose of the firm and the role of business leadership.

Beyond the usual explanations for the current financial crisis – the credit boom, the savings glut and the collapse of real estate – there is abundant evidence to suggest that many firms have lost their sense of mission and purpose in society. Moreover, the financial crisis reveals the poor quality of business leadership. Leadership is not an exact science, but it appears that many business decisions focused exclusively on the short term and were not made in the most professional way; the financial leverage in many firms went beyond prudent advice; compensation systems went out of control; and sound ethical principles were replaced by sheer opportunism and self-interest. As a result, some companies have gone bankrupt or are on the brink of collapse. A key question is what their boards and senior managers did or did not do to drive their firms to this desperate state. There is a widespread belief that the quality of business leadership can and should be improved, and that corporate reputation must be restored. How should this challenge be tackled?

This book wishes to offer some new perspectives on what a firm is, what business leadership is about and how good corporate governance and leadership can help develop better companies.

THE CURRENT CORPORATE GOVERNANCE DEBATE

In Western countries, many governments would like to make corporate governance rules mandatory, thus intensifying the degree of government intervention in business. The Sarbanes-Oxley Act of 2002 is a case in point. It was passed by the US Congress following a spate of corporate scandals during the technology bubble in the late 1990s and introduced a system of corporate governance mechanisms, including inflexible rules that did not help prevent the current economic crisis. The intention was good, but the final outcome rather mediocre. The current debate over executive compensation in the United States and Europe is suffering from the same weaknesses: a strong appetite for government intervention and some proposals to limit compensation which have been designed without considering the wider context of corporate governance, and the duties and responsibilities of board members and senior executives.

This debate makes chief executives and senior managers unhappy. They feel that its implicit aim is to curb management's power in favour of shareholders. They argue that this approach may not be desirable because neither shareholders nor even directors themselves have a sufficiently thorough knowledge of the company's situation and challenges, as there is a limit to the amount of time they can devote to the firm. Giving shareholders and board direct-ors more decision-making power to the detriment of senior manage-ment may stifle entrepreneurship, and regulators may be taking a step in the wrong direction.

It is very unlikely that these discussions about governance will help firms escape the current crisis or minimize the risks and costs of a new one. The reason is that though those issues are important, they do not get to the root of the problem. Moreover, the nature of the current financial crisis points toward other, deeper roots, such as a poor understanding of the firm's operations, deficient internal control mechanisms, mediocre risk management systems, the com-bination of ambitious financial goals and leverage with risky com-pensation incentives and, more importantly, poor leadership at the top. An indispensable first step toward improving the firm's govern-ance is rethinking what a firm is, what its purpose is, what society expects from firms, and what roles and responsibilities board direct-ors and senior executives should have.

THE FIRM'S PURPOSE

This book aims to rethink the firm's purpose, and explore how firms can become respected institutions through better leadership and governance. We consider firms to be vital institutions for society and believe we cannot afford to see them and their reputation crumble. Better regulation can help. But what drives corporate performance – beyond good luck – is the quality of leadership and management dis-played by the board of directors and the senior management team: the goals they set, the strategy they adopt, the speed and effectiveness of its execution and, more importantly, the quality of the people they work with and how they engage them.

By redefining the purpose of firms and business leadership, this book aims to shift the debate over corporate reputation and gov-ernance from the regulatory perspective toward the firm's mission and purpose. It also examines how companies can become respected institutions and how the senior management team – and not only the board of directors – can play a key role in this process. Though external control mechanisms, including product markets, capital markets and government regulation, have an influence in improving corporate governance and performance, we view these forces as insufficient on their own. Just as a train cannot move without a locomotive, long-term corporate performance will not improve through regulation alone. It needs good leadership: an effective board of directors and a competent CEO.

Companies have a purpose and a role in society, and today firms are more important and relevant to society than ever. They are social institutions that must be profitable and efficient, but short-term profits are not their only final goal. Firms exist to offer goods and services that customers want to buy. Society grants firms a licence to operate as such because they make a contribution to the common good in this specific way. If firms do a good job, they will not only generate profits in the process, but also will invest in people development, physical capital and technology. It is imperative that we rethink the notion of the firm, what its purpose is and what role it should have in society. Unless we reframe this notion, opportunism and short-term views will dominate any debate about the firm.

BUSINESS LEADERSHIP

Good leadership and governance are the engines that drive the development of successful firms that fulfil their role in society. But governance goes well beyond regulation; it requires a more comprehensive approach. The company's CEO and the senior management team play a key role and must assume certain responsibilities in the governance process. In reality, the board of directors and the executive committee are like the company's lungs: a company cannot operate effectively in the long run if one of its two lungs is not working at full capacity. That is why the design of good corporate governance mechanisms cannot be limited to the structure and functions of the board of directors, or the measures taken to ensure that the shareholders' meeting works properly. Good governance mechanisms should also consider the leadership that the chief executive and senior executives provide. Leadership requires professionalism, innovation, initiative, integrity, team building and a shared culture and values, all of which come from the character and experience of CEOs and senior managers, not from external regulation.

FIRMS AS RESPECTED INSTITUTIONS

A more solid understanding of the firm and good business leadership will contribute to transforming the firm into a respected institution. Traditionally, a firm's reputation was based on its products, technology, brand or corporate culture. Today, we know that those qualities and attributes help a great deal. Respected firms develop many of those dimensions, integrate them and take them to a new level. By adopting this integrative perspective, companies may become more respected institutions in society, not only because they solve economic problems but also because they think in the long term, create sustainable human environments, invest in human capital and professional development, foster innovation and meet other challenges that are crucially important to society. Companies can and should be respected institutions. They are organizations with a distinctive economic mission, but they also have a purpose in society that is not confined to the economic goals.

The assumptions outlined above also provide potential answers to today's financial crisis. The current economic turmoil has been partially fuelled by an idea of firms as pure profit maximizers in the short term, on many occasions without connection with the firms' long-term performance, as well as by the notion of business leaders as agents focused only on delivering such results. The design of some economic incentives that link pay to performance in some risky ways for the company's long-term success was considered to be the key factor for senior managers to deliver the expected short-term results. The current crisis has proven those wrong, with the effect of putting the firm's reputation in jeopardy. This is very unfortunate, because firms are vital institutions in a dynamic, prosperous and fair society. For this reason, it is necessary that we make sure that companies could be perceived as respected institutions. This is why it is more important than ever to rethink what firms are, what purpose they have, what society expects from them, and what business leaders should do to effectively address this huge challenge that firms and society face.

Acknowledgements

The roots of this book lie in courses and programmes on general management and corporate governance for MBA students and senior executives that have been taught at the IESE business school over the past ten years. Discussions with students and executives both inside and outside the classroom were extremely helpful in shaping the concepts presented in this book. My deepest gratitude goes to each one of them. Over the years, the work and interaction with senior managers and boards of directors added new perspectives to the ideas discussed in this book on some of the toughest challenges boards and senior leaders must face. The experience of serving on the task force on corporate governance set up by the Spanish government (2002–3) and the interaction with regulators also helped shape some of this book's ideas from the viewpoint of public policy.

This book is based on a previous one that I initially wrote in Spanish, *En busca del equilibrio* (Prentice Hall, Madrid, 2008), although it includes new sections, concepts and cases. I deeply appreciate IESE professors Antonio Argandoña, Jose M. Campa, Joan E. Ricart and Juan C. Vázquez-Dodero for their help and guidance in reviewing the manuscript partially or totally. Their suggestions greatly improved the book. Three referees made extremely useful comments on how to improve the book and make some arguments stronger and clearer. I am very grateful to them. Paula Parish, Cambridge University Press Management Editor, did a terrific job in guiding me through the process of improving the draft. Any remaining mistakes are mine only.

I am also very grateful to Assumpció Cabré, Miriam Freixa, Mónica Mestres and Andrea Rocamora for their most helpful contribution to this book, while dealing efficiently with their usual, daily activities at IESE.

Part I Corporate crisis, leadership and governance

I Financial crisis: a leadership crisis?

I. AN ACCELERATED RACE TO THE TOP

On 15 April 2009, Oswald Grübel, UBS's chief executive, unveiled a financial loss of SFr2bn (€1.3bn) for the Swiss bank in the first quarter of 2009. With this figure, UBS's total writedowns, dating back to the beginning of the financial crisis in August 2007, reached around €37.8bn. After the technology bubble burst in early 2000, UBS had launched an impressive global expansion process, becoming one of the darlings of the investment banking industry. Its growth was phenomenal, its profitability was very high and its business model was admired by many competitors. At a time when other major investment banks, such as Morgan Stanley and Merrill Lynch, were experiencing severe problems, UBS seemed to have developed the capabilities to overtake them. The incredible trading floor of the recently built UBS regional headquarters in Stamford, Connecticut, was a symbol of the bank's new power in the United States: it was considered the largest trading room in the world. It aptly reflected UBS's ambitions to become one of the world's top investment banks by the end of the decade.

Unfortunately, in June 2007 UBS was being closely watched not for its ambitions, but for some hints that a deep crisis was brewing. The sudden replacement of Peter Wuffli, UBS's chief executive, with Marcel Rohner, came as a big surprise inside the bank. Wuffli had been the architect behind UBS's expansion; he had developed a business model that combined the investment banking and wealth management teams in a new, more efficient way. Nevertheless, the news that UBS's investment banking division had accumulated around $76bn exposure to toxic assets related to the troubled US housing market made investors very uneasy. When the markets for those assets collapsed in mid-2007, UBS was unable to sell them; this failure sent shockwaves internally and around the world, raising an alarm about the bank's financial position. Since this was a bank that had grown very quickly over the past few years, had escaped the technology bubble relatively unscathed and had a reputation for being managed well, the news came as a big shock to everybody.

This marked the beginning of the unravelling of UBS's investment banking division. The roots of its problems were complex and interrelated. UBS started to take more aggressive risks in 2005, when its top managers decided to run an internal hedge fund to take advantage of the growth opportunities in alternative investments. The decision seemed to put UBS in the same league as other top investment banks, which had already been developing their own internal hedge funds; it could help UBS close the gap with its peers in the fixed-income division. However, executing the decision was complex. In order to attract top people for that division, UBS had to design a special compensation system, with a more generous pay mechanism for senior employees who could generate new business with higher margins – by taking more risks. At the same time, UBS had to fund the new division. Since it was unable to raise all the required capital externally, UBS had to put up about $3bn to fund the new business. The goal was to run a unit that could operate at about twenty times its capital, with leverage up to $70bn.

The newly created hedge fund and the traditional fixed-income division accelerated UBS's activity by piling up mortgages and slicing and packaging them into specialized credit securities. As the housing and credit bubbles gained momentum, UBS's traders started to accumulate higher risks. For a bank known for its risk management control systems and the prudence of its lending operations, the crisis that had developed in less than two years was truly embarrassing. By June 2007, UBS held more than $20bn of different CDO (collateralized debt obligations) tranches. A few weeks earlier, the bank had tried to sell CDOs to determine the price that potential buyers would give those assets. In one day, the bank lost $50m. In October

2007, UBS revealed its first losses of $4.4bn. It was truly disappointing news.

In twelve months, UBS's reputation was severely damaged. Once one of the fastest-growing investment banks in the world, with the credibility of an innovative business model, it now represented every unwise strategy investment banks had adopted: extreme risk taking, dysfunctional compensation systems, excessive leverage, poor risk management systems and the concentration of investments in low-quality sub-prime CDOs. Furthermore, the top management team was taking too many risks without providing detailed information to the board of directors; and the board of directors was not fully aware of the bank's increasing financial leverage and risk.

It is true that UBS's quick expansion occurred in the context of a growing world economy that showed important financial imbalances in the United States and other key countries: a huge credit bubble in many countries; external imbalances (both surpluses and deficits) that were driving savings away from China, Japan and Germany into voracious spenders like the United States and Britain; and an increasingly deregulated financial system. But it would be ludicrous to say that the financial crisis that began in 2007 was unleashed by some of the factors that dominated the world economy after the technology bubble in the late 1990s and the sudden reversal of expectations. As we see in UBS's fall, recent corporate crises have their origins in strategic mistakes, reckless decision investments, mediocre risk management, dysfunctional control systems and too much leverage, a powerful cocktail that became even stronger when adulterated with destructive drops of greed. From a leadership perspective, we can observe in this and other corporate crises senior business leaders' negligence in making decisions without fully informing their boards, boards of directors forgetful of their duties and responsibilities, and the focus on short-term profits.

In this chapter, we shall explore some of the problems that have plagued companies in recent years and that have contributed to a deterioration of corporate reputation. We will map out the symptoms and diseases and argue for the need to rethink the notion of the firm, the role of CEOs and senior managers, and the concept of corporate governance.

2. THE CHANGING SOCIAL PERCEPTION
OF COMPANIES

In the late 1980s, a wave of deregulation and privatization swept the European economies. It was propelled by a similar wave unleashed in the United States in the early 1980s; this wave's influence extended beyond North America and Western Europe and shaped policies in Latin America, Asia and even Africa. State-owned companies were privatized, markets were deregulated, government intervention was pulling out from many industries, and faith in market economies and private enterprise seemed limitless. Corporate growth and share price maximization became popular, and globalization sparked international business expansion. Moreover, the fall of communism reinforced these trends. It looked like the market economy was unstoppable and that the business world was heading toward unlimited growth.

Two decades later, the business outlook was strikingly different. By mid-2009, the global economy was tanking, the huge credit bubble that developed in the early and mid-2000s had burst, corporate growth had disappeared, profits were sinking, powerful US investment banks had collapsed or gone bankrupt, and confidence in the business world and senior executives was quickly diminishing. In the 1990s and in most of the current decade, corporate growth and empire building were the fads that dominated the business world. Now, the current economic downturn is pressuring companies to perform for survival; but it is also forcing business leaders, scholars and regulators to rethink the role of companies, markets and governments and to reconsider the roles of senior leaders in companies and society.

The boom of the 1990s helped generate new management practices and saw the emergence of the charismatic CEO, unafraid of breaking the rules. For some years, strong economic growth seemed to prove those policies right. Nevertheless, the violation of basic management principles brought many companies to their knees, seriously harming their reputations. Many corporate crises were attributable to a disregard for sound financial management, speculation around IPOs, excessive leverage, senior executives' rule breaking and the lack of an effective system of corporate governance. In fact, many failing companies offered good products and services, and the new financial landscape gave them almost immediate access to capital markets. And yet, at the heart of the crisis was the role played by CEOs.[1] Corporate growth was the driving engine of decision making, regardless of whether it made sense or not. Governance was poor. Many companies lacked a sensible balance of power between the CEO and the board of directors. CEOs became celebrities on a par with top athletes or movie stars. Investment banks were the paradigm of this collective behaviour: aggressive risk-taking policies, excess investment, rashness, empire building, ballooning executive compensation and conflicts between the board and the CEO.

The purpose of this book is to reflect on the roots of the deterioration of corporate reputation over the past decade, the role of senior executives and board members in this process, and what needs to be done to rebuild respected companies. The underlying thesis is that the current notion of the firm as an economic organization whose purpose is to maximize its market value in the short term – and to be achieved by giving senior executives some economic incentives linked with performance – is an oversimplification that has opened the door to a game of incentives with adverse effects for the firm in the long term. Too often, this game has allowed strategies based on opportunism, self-interest and a lack of integrity. Confidence in

---

[1] Khurana (2002) offers a fascinating account of this transformation.

corporations will return if we rethink the notion of the firm, what society expects from companies, and how board members and senior leaders become stewards in this very important social institution. Unless there is a new sense of what companies are for, what they should achieve, and how their contribution to society should be defined, we may survive the current crisis, but we will be sowing the seeds of a new one.

The role of CEOs and senior business leaders in corporations and their wider impact on society is this book's second major topic. We will explore the transition from the shareholder-dominated governance system that prevailed in the West from the second half of the nineteenth century to the system dominated by CEOs, which began in the United States after World War I and in Western Europe a little later. The historian Alfred Chandler (1977) described this as a transition from investor capitalism to managerial capitalism. It is not only that CEOs accumulated a lot of power in the 1980s and 1990s, when many became empire builders and boards of directors were not particularly active; but in a period of strong economic growth, the sometimes reckless actions of many CEOs passed unnoticed. Not until the technology bubble burst in the early 2000s were some disastrous business decisions revealed. At the same time, with capital markets deregulation in the USA and Europe in the late 1980s and 1990s, financial markets started to get the upper hand in the way investors looked at companies and their decisions. Unfortunately, investment banks and other advisory firms started to get a stronger influence on boards of directors' decisions, sometimes bypassing or sidelining the interests of shareholders in the long term. CEOs became more powerful, but as far as they could please financial markets.[2] Unfortunately, the current financial crisis has revealed the weaknesses of this model of corporate leadership.

A similar phenomenon occurred more recently when the global economic growth recovered strength by 2004, although that

[2] For a historical description of the increasing role of financial markets and their impact on business leadership, see Davis (2009).

time the reckless behaviour was concentrated in financial institutions – more particularly, investment banks. CEOs and senior executives embarked on a remarkable spree of trading in dubious assets and reckless lending that was clearly lacking in prudence and good judgement. The temptation of generating rapid business growth and high short-term results was irresistible, but it was at the expense of long-term growth and survival. Moreover, the sense of mission that those senior executives had was not clear, beyond their own self-interest. The outcome is that by the end of 2008 the leading US investment banks had disappeared or, in the case of Goldman Sachs and Morgan Stanley, had chosen to be transformed into bank holding companies. Moreover, the subsequent financial meltdown had pushed the global economy to the brink of collapse.

The survival of the company as a respected social institution requires a redefinition of the role of the CEO and senior leaders in organizations; what their functions are; and what shareholders, employees and society at large should expect from them. All in all, we have to transform management into a more respected profession (Noria and Khurana 2008) whose appeal transcends the ability to make money.

The role of the board of directors and, in general, the notion of corporate governance must also be rethought. Corporate governance can never be a perfect substitute for entrepreneurial initiative or personal integrity, but it can bring some balance to the decision-making process and help CEOs avoid making imprudent judgements or rash decisions about specific business situations. Moreover, good governance can help improve corporate reputation.

Corporate governance is sometimes described as a balance of power among shareholders and CEOs or directors, as a means of managing conflicts of interest. There have been attempts to improve corporate governance by reforming board regulations or changing board structure and composition. These factors must be considered, but they are not as decisive as policies and initiatives to ensure that the board of directors works as a team, or that the CEO and top managers lead by example. The widespread adoption of governance codes has helped solve some problems by setting down in writing the best ways to structure the functions and powers of a company's governing bodies. This is an important step, but, as we shall see, it is not the essence of governance.

Good business leadership and governance have a very important effect: they help build respected companies. In a business world that seems focused on financial engineering and deal making, the value of institutions and people who can be trusted is priceless. Excellent corporate governance and business leadership must go beyond simply fulfilling legal requirements and move toward fostering long-term success and respect among all stakeholders.

3. CORPORATE CRISIS: SOME DRIVERS

We will begin the discussion by exploring certain dimensions and characteristics that we can observe in corporate crises in recent years (see Table 1.1). Although each crisis is different, they all highlight problems of corporate leadership and governance.

3.1 The explosion of corporate scandals

The general trend in the world economy during the 1990s – aside from regional setbacks, such as the Russian and Southeast Asian crises – was one of growth. The United States, in particular, experienced a spectacular economic expansion, driven by investment in information technology (IT).

Encouraged by the overall health of the world economy and the supposedly unstoppable power of IT to generate new industries and markets or redefine existing ones, both traditional and new-economy companies started to plan for growth. The so-called new economy – 'new' in the sense that it was founded on a more efficient use of information and enhanced connectivity between companies and customers – created a new market: the market for corporate growth. Senior executives began drawing up overly optimistic business plans. Consultants mined the rich seam they had discovered

Table 1.1. *Business leadership and governance: some challenges*

– Explosion of corporate scandals
– Emergence of the charismatic CEO
– Boards and CEOs
– CEOs' compensation
– Institutional investors

in executives' fixation on growth at any price. Investment banks, already swimming in cash, leapt at the enormous business opportunities these growth plans offered. And the media started to treat corporate CEOs as if they were Hollywood celebrities. The bubble expanded rapidly, thanks to a combination of mutually reinforcing factors.

Against the background of strong growth and the race to satisfy capital markets whose expectations were rising, many companies lost their sense of proportion. Some of the best-known corporate crises, such as Enron, AIG, Lehman Brothers and General Motors in the United States, or RBS, Vivendi, Fortis and Ahold in Europe, are multidimensional. Before disaster struck, some of the executives involved, such as Ken Lay or Jeff Skilling of Enron, Bernie Ebbers of MCI, Fred Goodwin of RBS or Hank Greenberg of AIG, were considered extremely talented business leaders.

The financial crisis afflicting today's global economy has its roots in the monetary flood that followed the bursting of the technology bubble, when central banks fought to avoid a recession. Interest rates were brought down, and liquidity injections made credit easily available. This financial context paved the way for a booming real estate industry; banks and other financial intermediaries encouraged people to buy homes by providing highly attractive conditions. Quick securitization of these sub-prime mortgages followed, banks' earnings ballooned, and the seeds of the current crisis took root. In 2008, Lehman Brothers and Bear Stearns collapsed; Merrill Lynch was acquired by Bank of America, bringing huge new problems for the acquirer; Citigroup's universal banking model was in deep crisis; and Goldman Sachs and Morgan Stanley chose to abandon their investment bank status and become holding banks. The European side of the drama in financial services includes well-known names such as RBS, Fortis and UBS. This unprecedented turmoil in the banking world has shaken the foundations of the financial services industry, the reputations of the major players and the pillars of a well-functioning market economy.

These crises also point to a failure of leadership and the eroding role and responsibilities of CEOs. They reveal a spectacular lack of professionalism in handling problems and making decisions; a disdain for shareholders and employees; an almost exclusive concern for the company's short-term stock price; and a lack of ethical behaviour. Above all, these failings demonstrate that professionalism and integrity are essential qualities for a chief executive.

3.2 The emergence of the charismatic CEO

Until the end of the 1990s (with the exception of a handful of names in the United States), CEOs in Europe and the United States did not enjoy celebrity status. They were in much the same category as lawyers, doctors or consultants. The profession of CEO had a prestige of its own, but its members were not media darlings.

Then, slowly but surely, a personality cult grew up around the figure of the CEO, fuelled by major restructuring, the irresistible growth of the technology bubble and the rise of new companies such as Yahoo!, Amazon and eBay, whose market value quickly outgrew that of traditional firms, such as banks or consumer product companies. In particular, in the United States, CEOs such as Jack Welch, Sandy Weill and Jeff Bazos, until then practically unknown outside their company or industry, became household names. Their entrepreneurial exploits were chronicled with the same passion as a Ryder Cup victory. Almost overnight, skilled professionals with a vital role to play in society were presented to the public as opinion makers and world-conquering visionaries. Many were blessed with success. Others were less fortunate.

Independently of CEOs' achievements, people's perception of the CEO's role in business and society underwent a sea change. At the same time, a market developed for CEOs with charisma and other, often controversial characteristics. As Khurana (2002) showed in his study of the CEO job market, the pendulum has swung from one extreme, where professional excellence and honesty were key, to the other, where priority is given to charisma and leadership ability, as perceived by financial analysts and public opinion. In some cases, boards of directors have looked for the impact a certain type of charismatic CEO can have on capital markets and public opinion – rather than results. What the CEO plans to do about the company's customers and employees or the results he or she expects to achieve in the medium term seem to be, for some boards, lesser considerations. (For ease of use, from now on we will use the term 'he', 'him' or 'his' as opposed to 'he or she', 'him or her' and 'his or her'.)

3.3 Boards and CEOs: in search of balance

CEO turnover in large companies has increased significantly in recent years. As a result, public company CEOs' average term of office has decreased.

Recent years have seen the end of a tradition in many industries by which a company's CEO came from within the industry or, very often, from within the company itself. When Carly Fiorina was named chief executive of Hewlett-Packard in 1998, she had no experience in most of the company's business units. As in many other companies, the idea of continuity, or the company's long-term prospects, seems to have fallen by the wayside, and the notion of the CEO as a professional committed to the service and long-term development of the firm has disappeared.

A number of factors may explain this. The first is the role of capital markets (Davis 2009). As long as a company's market value is increasing, investors tend to focus on other issues. However, as soon as a company performs below expectations, investors start to question the CEO and his strategy. At certain times in recent history, this questioning has been manifested by threats of a leveraged buy-out or a hostile takeover. Such mechanisms may help keep the management team disciplined, but they are not always effective and are difficult to put into effect.

Rather than go to this extreme, the board may choose to fire the CEO and seek a replacement. This is one of the board's functions. The difference today is that boards tend to be less patient than they used to be. They expect the CEO to deliver results quickly – and if he does not, they get rid of them. The emergence of a CEO job market, actively promoted by headhunters, has simplified the task of finding a replacement.

Unsatisfactory performance is not the only reason for a CEO's dismissal. CEOs may also be fired because their triumphs and blunders are so much more public today than they were in the past. Transparency is more than just a financial reporting requirement; it shines a spotlight on the work of any executive, broadcasting his successes and failures to the world.

Thus, episodes such as the departure of Carly Fiorina from Hewlett-Packard in May 2005, after months of persistent rumours about her differences with some of the directors, or the protracted wrangling between Michael Eisner and the board of Disney over the company's future, which lasted until 2005, are not merely a consequence of sub-par performance; they also reflect a shift in the relationship between the CEO and the board of directors.

In fact, in their last few years as CEO, both Eisner and Fiorina exercised total control over the executive function – even over the board of directors. In the end, however, their attitudes about certain investment decisions and their views about the direction of the business not only stirred unrest among the directors but also sparked a reaction against what the directors considered a break with the best practices of the past.

These and other episodes show that striking a balance of power between the CEO and the board of directors is not simple. It demands a clear separation of responsibilities, accountability for actions, space for disagreement and the common sense to realize that the CEO needs the board and vice versa. The balance of power in corporate governance should not be used to frustrate the other side's wishes; instead, it should ensure that decisions are based on the best ideas available from all sides, so as to obtain the best results.

An imbalance of power between a board of directors and a CEO can be highly disruptive. As time goes by, disagreements are magnified as both sides become mutually distrustful and quick to take offence. The end often comes sooner than expected, as every chance to restore harmony is wasted. Witness the persistent and eventually fruitless efforts by Philip Purcell, former CEO of Morgan Stanley, and Hank Greenberg, former CEO of AIG, to hold onto their jobs in 2005. In both cases, the balance of power between the CEO and the board of directors had been shattered. The same pattern could be observed in the autumn of 2007 with the removal of Charles Prince and Stan O'Neal as CEOs of Citigroup and Merrill Lynch, respectively, after those investment banks revealed heavy losses. We saw other dimensions of this saga with the US government forcing the resignation of Rick Wagoner, CEO of General Motors, in March 2009, because he was considered to be the main obstacle to executing a deep change in the company's priorities.

These CEOs had been in control of their companies for a long time. But instead of seeking a common ground with the board, very often they tried to impose their views in opposition to the board. Despite the enormous influence the CEOs had on the directors and the important role they had played in their companies over the years, the directors came under such pressure from investors and public opinion that in the end they had to ask their CEOs to resign.

The moral of the story is that today, under the influence of capital markets, boards of directors have been reaffirmed in their responsibilities and, at the same time, are expected to be more proactive in protecting shareholders' interests. Essentially, CEOs seem to have become weaker compared to boards of directors, while boards of directors are more exposed to shareholder pressure with respect to business performance and strategic decision making.

3.4 CEO compensation

A key issue in the relationship between CEOs and boards of directors is CEO compensation. Just as there has been a surprising increase in the visibility of the CEO and the goal of maximizing shareholder value in the short term, there has also been remarkable growth in CEO compensation, especially in the United States. As Warren Buffett put it, 'In judging whether Corporate America is serious about reforming itself, CEO pay remains the acid test. To date, the results are not encouraging' (from 'Letter to shareholders of Berkshire Hathaway', February 2004) .

In part, this trend reflects the notion of helping companies achieve their financial targets by linking executive compensation to those targets. The main problem appears when some of those targets are not under the control of senior managers. The increasing compensation packages also highlight that companies are willing to reward executives who achieve extraordinary results for shareholders in a given time frame. Nevertheless, what seems to be good for shareholders in the short term – increased return on their investment in the firm – may not be the best for shareholders and the firm alike in the short term.

CEO's compensation, like that of other professionals, cannot be based on guesswork. Numerous factors must be taken into account: the firm's challenges, industry-specific characteristics, the proportion of fixed and variable compensation, the pay of other CEOs in the same industry, the pay structure within the firm, and any profit-sharing mechanisms, to mention but a few.

During the last technology bubble, stock options became a very popular element of CEO compensation in listed companies; this strategy was thought to link pay very closely to performance. In the context of stock market euphoria and rapid economic growth, as experienced in the late 1990s, and in the absence of strong boards of directors, CEO pay skyrocketed, even to the point of causing public alarm. In most cases, there was probably no unjust or illegal enrichment on the part of the CEOs. Yet the astronomical figures cited in some instances put CEOs more on a par with Hollywood stars than with other professionals.[3] Unfortunately, executive compensation followed very similar patterns over the past few years, in particular in the investment banking industry, when the current financial crisis was in the making.

Unfortunately, this greater public awareness of CEO compensation has not been matched in many cases by executives' performance. The sympathetic appreciation of the CEO's challenges and its critical importance for corporate, economic and social well-being has disappeared. Thus, criticism has forced boards of directors to retake control of the situation and be much more proactive in negotiating CEO pay packages.

The impression in society at large that some CEOs, particularly in the United States, are paid too much raises doubts as to whether today's boards are actually capable of laying down new rules on these matters (Bebchuk and Fried 2004). Nevertheless, we live in an imperfect world, and what is right for one company may not be right for another. Also, governments should not intervene in these matters; it is up to boards of directors to work out the best solution, and to shareholders to approve it. Nevertheless, the lack of prudence by CEOs and boards of directors and, in many cases, the deficient professional competence displayed by boards of directors in this area has created a widespread opinion that boards have not been able to tackle the challenge and will not fix the problem that society has with executive compensation, in particular, investment banking.

---

[3] Executive compensation is an extremely complex topic and has become one of the thorniest areas in corporate governance. For an interesting exchange of contrasting ideas in this area, see Bogle (2008) and Kaplan (2008).

This helps explains why some official proposals in the United States, the United Kingdom or Germany to set caps on executive compensation for bankers deserve serious consideration, even though these regulations could be rather inefficient in dealing with that complex problem.

The effects of government intervention in fixing executive compensation will be small. In this, as in so many other areas of corporate governance, the important thing is that directors and shareholders think seriously about the criteria to be applied, the performance variables to be measured, the best means of assessing them and how these variables can be translated into a specific pay and benefits package. It also brutally highlights the need for information transparency.

The case of Richard Russo, former chairman of the US Securities and Exchange Commission (SEC), is illustrative. Russo was forced out of his post in 2003 after details of his compensation deal were made public. The central issue was not how much he made, which was certainly very substantial, but the lack of transparency in the pay negotiation and the backseat role taken by SEC directors in the face of a powerful and apparently very effective CEO. The dismissal of John Thain, former CEO of Merrill Lynch and one of the senior executives in Bank of America in January 2009, is also related to his former firm's hidden losses and his compensation package.

A procedure to keep executive pay under control requires prudent corporate governance mechanisms: a compensation committee in the board of directors, clear and specific contracts with CEOs, pay for real business performance – not just expectations – transparency toward shareholders and a sense of fairness in relation with other employees in the same firm. Here, too, transparency is an advantage for companies, particularly listed ones. It enables shareholders to know more about how the company's managers are paid and how compensation relates to performance. But transparency is not enough if society perceives that there is a break with fairness in the way a CEO is paid. This has and will have terrible effects on corporate reputation.

3.5 Institutional investors

During the years that Chandler (1977) described as the era of managerial capitalism in the United States, capital markets wielded a growing influence over the economy. The increase in market liquidity, the greater availability of savings instruments, the growing diversity of financial instruments available to companies, the securitization of financial institutions' assets, and a riskier attitude toward securities investment turned the US financial markets into an international model of how the financial system can drive economic growth.

In this context, institutional investors (mutual funds, investment funds and so forth) usually kept a low profile. Naturally, they monitored the companies' progress and assessed their situation and future prospects. But they did not interfere in the work of managers or the board of directors. Institutional investors understood that their comparative advantage lay in attracting customer savings and selecting good investments, not in actually managing the investees. Furthermore, if those investment firms got involved in managing investees, there could be conflicts of interest between the funds and the companies they managed, or between the funds and other customers. Lastly, more active efforts by investment firms to manage investees could have asymmetrical consequences. As long as everything went well for the company, nobody was likely to notice the positive differentiating contribution the institutional investor was making; but if things went wrong, the firm's reputation could suffer, diminishing its ability to generate new business.

The errors associated with the technology and financial bubbles and the corporate governance crises in large public companies have raised many serious questions about the role of institutional investors in governance. In other words, can a shareholder who keeps silent on crucial matters of corporate governance, despite owning a significant percentage of the capital, be a good shareholder? Should such ownership not demand more decisive action? Some institutional investors have responded to this question by showing a greater willingness to participate in the board of directors and accept responsibility.

However, improved corporate governance depends not only on the commitment of institutional investors, but also on the overall design of the various corporate governance mechanisms. In any case, the changes we have seen in recent years indicate that institutional investors are genuinely concerned about this situation. Every board must now channel this will to cooperate in order to avoid the undesirable situation where the board of directors is dominated by a minority of shareholders who pursue their own interests to the exclusion of the interests of the company as a whole. As we will discuss in the next section, corporate governance reform alone may not be enough to get out of the current corporate crisis.

4. THE ROLE OF CORPORATE GOVERNANCE

The expectations that the different corporate stakeholders and society at large place on companies have changed dramatically in recent years. Some of the expectations are contradictory. For example, investment funds have demanded that their investee companies obtain the best possible financial results in the short term. Usually, these funds have custody of the savings of thousands of citizens and company employees, who sometimes suffer as a result of the pressure that those funds put on companies to deliver short-term financial results.

CEOs and senior managers are also subject to contradictory expectations. On the one hand, they are supposed to have entrepreneurial initiative and identify new growth opportunities for the company. On the other hand, they are swiftly punished if they fail to deliver the desired short-term results. To reap, one must sow. It is ironic, therefore, that the average term of office for CEOs has been steadily decreasing in recent years. Boards of directors and shareholders have grown impatient with their CEOs. Largely as a result of this, CEOs have started to see their job as detecting opportunities not only for the company but also for themselves, with a view toward actions that will increase their market value in the short term, rather than the value of the company in the long run.

The rift between the expectations of shareholders and top management is not unbridgeable, but it is deeper today than ever before. At the root of the problem lies not just the separation of ownership and control (shareholders and managers), but expectations on either side that ultimately run counter to companies' interests and prevent them from contributing to society to the extent that society expects and needs.

Many of these shortcomings can be attributed to weaknesses in the system of corporate governance. As a first approach, we shall define corporate governance as the processes, rules and institutions that shape how formal authority is exercised in a company, how key institutions (the board of directors, the shareholders' assembly and the board of management) work, and how decision making operates. The purpose of good governance is the firm's long-term success and survival.

Corporate governance is beset by certain problems associated with the structure of modern companies, in which investors become shareholders, delegating the task of management to professional managers. The classic problem of the separation of ownership and control (Berle and Means 1932) is that managers' incentives may not be aligned with shareholders' interests. Consequently, there have to be mechanisms to allow the company's owners to achieve their objectives and effectively supervise management by using incentives and defining rules of behaviour for the management team.

When searching for solutions to this leadership challenge, we must explore the role of corporate governance. Today's political leaders talk about tougher regulation. The responsibilities of board members, CEOs and senior managers are under scrutiny. Disputes between shareholders and boards of directors, shareholders' confrontations with powerful CEOs and excessive executive compensation are important topics that shape the discussion of corporate reputation and governance. Shareholders and governments would like to see better corporate governance mechanisms in place in order to avoid future corporate crises, although they may not agree on how to make reform work.

4.1 Regulation

Some investors and governments believe that better regulation could improve the quality of governance. They would like to make corporate governance rules mandatory, thus intensifying the degree of government intervention in business. The Sarbanes-Oxley Act of 2002 provides a clear case. It was passed by the US Congress following some corporate scandals during the stock market bubble in the late 1990s. It introduced a more formal – and, in some areas inflexible – system of corporate governance mechanisms, with some clearer rules of conflicts of interest, that unfortunately did not help prevent a new crisis in 2007–8. The current debate on regulating executive compensation may suffer from the same weakness. It is an important topic, but trying to control it by sheer regulation, out of the wider context of corporate governance and the duties and responsibilities of boards of directors, may create more problems instead of helping solve the current ones. Good governance needs clear and well-defined frames where the different pieces and mechanisms fit together in a coherent way.

A softer approach to regulation is the design of codes of good governance. The first major step in this direction was the Cadbury Report (1992) in Great Britain.[4] This report defines corporate governance, distinguishes between good governance and effective

---

[4] Codes prepared in different countries also had some effects. The 2002 Sarbanes-Oxley Act in the United States, the Higgs Report in Great Britain, the Aldama Report in Spain and the Cromme Code in Germany, among others, are some of the landmarks in the history of good corporate governance and the formation of a solid set of ideas on the subject.

leadership, proposes specific improvements to the way governing bodies operate (the board of directors, in particular) and establishes a fundamental principle of corporate governance and corporate governance reform: comply or explain. This principle allows companies to define their own corporate governance mechanisms, but at the same time requires them to justify any deviation from accepted codes of practice.

The Cadbury Report did not translate directly into law, but that was not its purpose. It did, however, slowly bring the issue of corporate governance and the role of corporate governing bodies to the forefront of the debate in business and society. The corporate scandals mentioned earlier highlighted the need for effective mechanisms to improve corporate governance and counter the CEO's influence over the board of directors.

In general, the regulatory approach to corporate governance is not the panacea. Regulation can prevent management from making some big mistakes, but it has only limited impact. Regulation is like the tracks that keep a train firmly connected to its route. By themselves, however, they cannot carry a train to its destination. Regulation may also be compared to road signs. If they are well designed, they can prevent accidents. But good drivers are also imperative for ensuring that the traffic flows smoothly and that every vehicle reaches its destination. In this case, regulation performs the function of a railroad track or road signs: it is there to avert major mishaps. Tighter regulation can certainly prevent the abuse of shareholder rights. But it cannot guarantee the company's long-term success and survival as an organization. In other words, it has no bearing on the company's long-term success, which should be top management's primary objective.

For a company to survive in the long term, investors' interests must be protected. But firms also need good decision-making mechanisms; an entrepreneurial spirit that drives managers to detect and exploit business opportunities; attractive human resource policies to attract and retain talent and prepare for top management succession when necessary; a sense of innovation that balances the need to preserve what is good against the search for what is better; and investment in specific capital and technological assets to enable it to acquire distinctive competencies. Essentially, companies must seek competitive advantages that can be sustained in the long term (Porter 1996).[5] Shareholders who expect managers merely to maximize the share price in the short term so that they can sell their shares at a profit are either irresponsible or completely unaware of how a company works.

4.2 Shareholders and boards of directors

Most shareholders would like to have a more direct and stronger control over the board of directors. Some of them want to participate more directly (through electronic voting, for example) not only in shareholders' meetings, but also in important business decisions that are today still the prerogative of board members. Other shareholders, such as institutional investors, while in favour of increasing shareholder power, do not want to become actively involved in governance or in supervising the company's top management. They do not view this as their primary job. The crux of the problem is that too many shareholders do not trust the top management team of the companies in which they have invested; confidence has been missing for too long.[6]

Senior business leaders are not pleased with this debate. They believe that its implicit aim is to curb the power of top management in favour of shareholders. They argue that this approach is undesirable for several reasons. First, legal reforms place greater responsibility

---

[5] As we will see in detail in more Chapter 4, corporate governance needs to take into consideration basic notions of business strategy, for which both the board and the CEO should be held responsible. This idea shifts the debate on corporate governance from a legal perspective – still dominant today – to a more integrative approach.

[6] Cadbury (2002) offers a good analysis and some excellent suggestions on how to improve the quality of governance by changing the relationships between the board and shareholders.

on CEOs but also curtail their formal powers. Second, neither share-holders nor even directors themselves have a sufficiently thorough knowledge of the company's situation and challenges, since there is a limit to the amount of time they can devote to it. To give share-holders and directors more decision-making power to the detriment of top management is, in their view, a step in the wrong direction. In short, they believe that the closer supervision that shareholders would like to exercise over boards of directors and top management will actually stifle entrepreneurship and undermine the capacity for change and innovation that is essential to the business world.

In a nutshell, there is no basic agreement on how to improve firms' governance. As a result, efforts to make headway have focused on important yet partial aspects of the problem. Bringing independ-ent nonexecutive directors onto boards of directors, protecting minority shareholders, ensuring the proper function of the general shareholders' meeting and identifying directors' conflicts of inter-est are undoubtedly important issues, and taking them into account may help improve corporate governance. Nevertheless, no strong empirical evidence suggests that these are effective mechanisms. Moreover, the nature of the current financial crisis points to other problems, such as a poor understanding of the firm's operations, defi-cient internal control mechanisms and mediocre risk management systems.

4.3 Good governance and ethics

Unfortunately for firms, those discussions about corporate govern-ance may not help end the current crisis or minimize the risks and costs of a new one. The reason is that though the aforemen-tioned ideas are important, they do not go to the root of the current corporate crisis. What drives corporate performance and behav-iour is not regulation but the quality of leadership and manage-ment displayed by the board of directors and the top management team, the goals they set, the strategy they want to develop and its implementation.

Successful firms also require good leadership, both in the board of directors and in the top management team, entrepreneurial management and integrity. Companies that want to be respected as social institutions must comply with regulatory guidelines and common governance practices, but their success entails more than simply meeting those legal requirements. For this reason, finding a pathway out of the current crisis involves thinking again about the nature of the firm and the purpose of leadership.

Good leadership also requires ethics, personal integrity and service to the common good of the firm and society. A shared view of ethics, widely accepted by different people – a view that embraces respect for the dignity of the person, personal integrity, the notion of justice and the duty of loyalty – is indispensible. Ethics is a necessary condition for a healthy society, a dynamic economy and good governance.

Nevertheless, ethical behaviour cannot be imposed on boards of directors or business leaders. The law may give some rights special protection, but to be effective, ethical values must be lived and put into practice whether the law requires it or not. Without such action, even the most sophisticated regulations or the best governance practices will be little more than worthless papers, which disloyal directors will tear up at the first opportunity. Consider this: some of the companies involved in scandals were apparently in full compliance with legal requirements. The problem was not a lack of regulation but unethical behaviour. Boards and business leaders who do not respect clients or employees cannot build respected firms.

5. RETHINKING THE NATURE OF THE FIRM: REFRAMING THE ROLE OF CEOS

The current corporate crisis goes beyond the financial meltdown or the credit crunch; it is related to how some companies – and, indirectly, investment banks and capital markets – have operated over the past few decades. In most circumstances, markets are extremely efficient mechanisms, as long as the main players are well behaved.

When top managers make assumptions or pursue goals that pose a threat to the long-term existence of those firms, we must reflect on what is wrong with those goals and assumptions. In particular, we must rethink the firm's nature and purpose, business leaders' roles and responsibilities, and how firms can become respected institutions through better leadership and governance. We need healthy, solid and respected firms because they are vital institutions for individuals and society.

We argue that firms have a wider societal purpose that goes beyond economic efficiency. Firms exist to offer goods and services that customers want to buy, and to do so in an efficient way. They are social institutions that must be profitable and efficient, but short-term profits are not their only objective. Respected firms not only generate profits in that process but also invest in people's development; create healthy, human environments; feel responsibility for the communities in which they operate; and understand that companies can be effective drivers of change and progress in society. If the business world is going to move past opportunism, malpractice and short-term views, then rethinking the notion of the firm is indispensable. It is vital to reassess what the firm's purpose is – beyond profit maximization – and what role it should play in society. In this process, we need to take into account that firms need to have an economic, ethical and social performance that could be sustainable in the long term.

The widespread adoption of good governance practices and codes of corporate governance is an important trend, but, again, it is insufficient for improving corporate governance. Those good practices, that include some formal mechanisms of governance, control and supervision, may help governance improve.[7] But the excessive emphasis on them tends to overlook the fact that a company is a

---

[7] BBVA, Nestlé, Novartis and Santander, among other international companies, have defined very clear principles that inspire their codes of good governance. They could be a reference for many other firms. They are described in their annual reports and websites.

group of people whose activity is oriented toward producing goods and services to satisfy customers' needs, generating economic value along the way. A firm is a living organization driven by effectiveness, innovation, passion and leadership, not by regulation. The company is a very complex institution, one that can neither be controlled nor managed by an outside agent, such as a regulator or an institutional investor. For this reason, we must think deeply about the conditions and approaches that may help improve the companies' long-term success. This final outcome depends on different factors, but the quality of leadership and corporate governance is one of them.

Good leadership and governance are key engines that drive the development of successful firms. But governance goes well beyond regulation and requires a more holistic approach that includes the functions of both the board of directors and the top management team. They are like the company's lungs: a company cannot operate effectively in the long run if one of its two lungs is not working at full capacity. That is why good corporate governance cannot be limited to the structure of the board of directors, or the measures taken to ensure that shareholders' meetings work properly. Good governance should also consider the quality of the leadership that the chief executive and the senior management team provide.

The development of respected companies should be a long-term objective for senior managers. Good leadership and governance should have a clear goal: contribute to the firm's success in the long term and help turn the company into a respected institution. The firm's goals include economic goals, which are the distinctive objective of the company; but they go beyond economics as well. Economic performance is the outcome of strategies and their execution, policies and specific decisions in a human organization. The top management team has to make the firm profitable and, at the same time, create a good work environment, serve clients well, invest for the future, create sustainable relations with suppliers and be involved in broader societal activities. Good senior managers are those who are able to integrate those seemingly contradictory objectives. The transformational power of an institution like the modern firm and its leadership derives from the fact that, with its internal dynamism, it has the potential to set long-term integrative goals for itself and achieve them.

A more comprehensive, positive view of the firm and business leadership will help transform the firm into a more respected institution. A firm's reputation once depended on its products, brand or innovation. These attributes may be valuable, but respected firms embrace many of those dimensions and integrate them in a coherent way to serve customers better. In the automobile industry, for example, Audi may not have the best technology or the best product, but its management team does a great job of integrating those dimensions and developing a unique car company. Companies may become exemplary institutions in society by adopting this integrated perspective, which combines short-term and long-term goals, economic and social value, and economic efficiency with human development.

It seems clear that the growth of firms as respected institutions has implications for the kind of leadership that should be developed and exercised by the board of directors and the executive committee. These implications go beyond economic value creation to include other dimensions, such as customer satisfaction, people's development, long-term financial health, competitive positioning, investors' trust and impact on society – areas that are at the heart of a respected company.

6. SOME FINAL THOUGHTS

In this chapter we have analyzed some roots of the current corporate crisis and the erosion of corporate reputation. Specifically, the emergence of the charismatic CEO, the shorter tenure of senior executives, the stronger influence of capital markets and new executive compensation mechanisms have shaped business leadership in a powerful way and helped create most of the drivers of the current crisis.

Companies may employ different strategies to emerge from this crisis. The first is to wait, be patient and hope that when market conditions improve and growth resumes, business will go back to normal. It may be so, but the learning developed over the past two decades tells us that the model of the firm and the prevalent view of business leadership must change if we want to avoid a crisis-prone economic model.

The second option is to rely on government intervention. Big government is back in most Western countries, and regulation seems to be more accepted today than it was just a few years ago. Today, even the nationalization of some industries, such as banking, seems to be an option supported by reasonable people. Nevertheless, we have outlined how even some ambitious corporate government reforms designed over the past few years have failed in preventing the current crisis.

Regulation, while necessary, is insufficient to improve corporate governance. Adopting internationally recognized best practices for boards may help, but there are other dimensions to a company's governing bodies; board structure is only one. Trying to overhaul and improve corporate governance through piecemeal reform is like trying to patch a garment that really needs to be thrown away.

The third option is to rethink the nature and purpose of the firm and its role in society, and the tasks and responsibilities of business leaders and boards of directors. If companies are considered pure profit maximizers, and senior executives and board members take this goal and its achievement as their key reference for the firm's success, they will miss important dimensions that are necessary to make their companies respected social institutions. Economic efficiency and financial profitability are important drivers of economic welfare and reputation, but they are not the only ones. Moreover, profitability and economic efficiency should be put in a historical context that replaces short-term gains with long-term benefits. A longer time frame for corporate success requires special leadership that takes into account the fact that firms are made of people, that leaders find their mission in serving those people, that leaders lead by example, and that firms are delicate institutions that can work wonders for individuals and societies if they are properly understood and professionally led.

The impact of firms and business leadership in society is so important that we cannot avoid thinking about them, examining what has been wrong with them over the past decades, and redefining the purpose of companies and the notion of business leadership. The success of firms as well as the well-being of individuals and the progress of society are at stake should the dominant ideas not change. This is what we will try to do in this book.

KEY LEARNING POINTS

- The current economic and financial crisis has some macroeconomic roots, such as the very lax monetary policy that has prevailed for many years or the savings glut in Asia. Nevertheless, it also reflects a deep leadership and governance crisis in some large companies around the world.
- Macro policies can help solve the crisis, but there is a need to rethink the notion and purpose of the firm, the role of capital markets and the job of senior executives in tomorrow's society.
- Corporate governance reforms – in general, new regulation – may be necessary in some cases, but new laws will not help the world economy emerge from the crisis. Such reforms can prevent some new accidents, but they will not stimulate entrepreneurship, innovation or corporate growth, all of which are needed in a healthy and prosperous society. In the end, it is better for senior managers to think about innovative solutions to better serve clients rather than tinker with governance reforms whose practical value may be limited.
- Changes in boards of directors' structure and functions could be useful and necessary. Unfortunately, there is little evidence to show that corporate performance will improve as a result. The leadership provided by the senior management team has a more direct impact on corporate performance, although its quality also depends on the quality of the board of directors.

- The current fight between boards of directors and senior managers in some companies is a bad indicator of the quality of the organizational leadership. Different views of business problems are a source of innovation, but continuous confrontation between the board of directors and senior managers tends to degenerate into a defensive war that can paralyze a good company. Boards of directors and senior management teams are the twin wings that a good company must develop in order to lay solid foundations for a successful future. The leadership that both can provide is indispensible in a great company, and the two leadership drivers will complement one another.

Part II Rethinking the firm's purpose

2 The firm's mission and purpose

I. INTRODUCTION

In the field of health care, disease management has grown in importance. This new approach is key to both improving patients' quality of life and helping to contain ballooning health-care costs. In particular, patients suffering from chronic diseases stand to benefit greatly. Medtronic,[1] a US firm with headquarters in Minnesota, whose market value was approximately $35bn at the end of April 2009, is one of the world's leaders in developing this concept.

Medtronic was founded in April 1949 by Earl Bakken and Palmer Hermundslie. Initially, its focus was on the repair of electronic hospital equipment, especially delicate laboratory equipment. Eventually, the company started to manufacture and sell medical equipment in the Upper Midwest; it also produced some custom-made products. In 1957, Bakken invented the first wearable pacemaker.

From those beginnings, Medtronic began growing globally. By the end of 2008, it was operating manufacturing facilities, research centres, sales offices and education centres in more than 120 countries. Among its most important contributions to the health-care field was the idea of disease management, an innovative concept that started with Bill George, Medtronic's chairman and CEO from 1989 to 2001, and Art Collins, who replaced George in 2001. The purpose of disease management is to help develop long-term strategies for chronic diseases, which are growing more prevalent around the world and garnering ever-rising treatment costs. A key innovation linked to this concept is the Medtronic CareLink Network. Established in

---

[1] See A. Corrales and D. Melé, 'Medtronic Inc: From corporate mission to organizational culture', IESE case n. 0–305–066, 2005.

Table 2.1. *Medtronic's mission*

- To contribute to human welfare by applying biomedical engineering in the research, design, manufacture and sale of instruments or appliances that alleviate pain, restore health and extend life
- To direct our growth in the areas of biomedical engineering where we display maximum strength and ability; to gather people and facilities that will augment these areas; to continuously build on these areas through education and knowledge assimilation; and to avoid participating in areas where we cannot make unique and worthy contributions
- To strive without reserve for the greatest possible reliability and quality in our products; to be the unsurpassed standard of comparison; and to be recognized as a company of dedication, honesty, integrity and service
- To recognize the personal worth of employees by providing an employment framework that allows personal satisfaction, security, advancement / opportunity and a means to share in the company's success
- To maintain good citizenship as a company

Source: Medtronic.

2002, the network gives patients the opportunity to download information from their implanted devices and send it to experts over the Internet for examination. By the end of 2008, 250,000 patients at almost 2,400 clinics in twenty countries were using this service.

From an organizational viewpoint, Medtronic boasts more than just technological innovation. This firm has also been successful in framing its pioneering purpose and goals; its founders gave the firm a very strong sense of mission. Bakken believed that human benefit should be Medtronic's main purpose. More than sixty years later, that mission still helps the firm make decisions and guides its adoption of policies (see Table 2.1).

Medtronic's senior leaders believed that this mission was a guiding force for the company and its activities. It reminded employees that the firm's purpose was to contribute to human benefit and human welfare by helping people live fuller, healthier lives. The primary goal of the company's founders was not to make money but to improve the human condition. In tandem to the mission, George developed a very practical, deep philosophy of the firm's purpose and goals, and the nature of business leadership. He stressed the relevance of the firm's purpose by saying that 'without clarity of purpose, it is difficult if not impossible for your customers, your employees, and your shareholders to know what your company stands for and where it is going. ... Decision makers have no framework for making decisions' (2003, p. 110). Speaking on the firm's goals, George commented that: 'The real bottom line of the corporation is not earnings per share, but service to humankind. To achieve sustained success, a corporation who thinks about its long-term best interest must lead with its values – from top to bottom' (2003, p. 42).

Moreover, George believed that focusing on short-term profits was a terrible mistake, one that could potentially harm long-term decisions: 'By focusing solely on generating immediate returns from shareholders, many executives ... lost sight of the first premise of business: companies can only survive so long as they serve their customers better than their competitors do' (2003, p. 62). Furthermore, he also believed that service was an essential dimension of good leadership: 'The criteria for measuring the success of our leaders should be how they serve everyone who has a vested interest in the success of the enterprise' (2003, p. 102). Serving each stakeholder was a key element in George's management philosophy and, for him, stakeholders' importance went in this order: customers, employees, shareholders, suppliers and communities. He believed this was the only way to create sustained, long-term shareholder value.

This perspective of a firm's purpose, goals and priorities provides a new pathway in thinking about what a company is and what its objectives and goals should be. For the past three decades in the

Western world, short-term profits and short-term market value have dominated financial paradigms.[2] Today, we are in the middle of the deepest financial crisis since the Great Depression in the 1930s. It is worth examining what companies should aim to be, what role profits should play and what priorities different stakeholders should have when thinking about the firm. Medtronic's purpose provides a fresh starting point for this discussion.

2. THE NEED TO RETHINK THE FIRM'S PURPOSE

The economic system based on free enterprise – that is, on private ownership and the freedom to produce, invest, buy and sell – has proven superior to every alternative in terms of economic efficiency. Economic development in recent decades has shown that free enterprise produces better results for business and society than does any other option. Many countries that lived for decades under a socialist system, from Eastern Europe to China and India, have since transitioned to a free-market economy. Although the current financial crisis has taught us valuable lessons and led to changes in the regulatory oversight of some industries and firms, there is still no alternative to the free-enterprise system. Nevertheless, it would be naïve to think that this model of economic organization cannot be improved, in particular, when this model has recently experienced a number of setbacks.

One of the most controversial aspects of a free-market economy concerns the goal and purpose of the firm. Some authors are adamant that a company's goal is to maximize its profits or market value (depending on the formula chosen). Friedman (1970), for instance, argued that the primary responsibility of any firm is to increase its profits; any concern for other alleged responsibilities would mean neglecting what must be the company's core responsibility.

---

[2] Davis (2009) and Ghoshal (2005) offer a good discussion of the increasing dominance of economics and financial performance indicators in the corporate world over the past decades.

In practical terms, however, profit – or market value – maximization raises certain questions, as we shall see. As a goal, it is simple to define but complex to articulate and implement. To maximize is to obtain the best possible results under certain constraints. But must maximization be an absolute goal? Should the legitimate interests of parties other than the shareholders be taken into account? In a knowledge society, who ultimately owns the company: the owners of the capital or the professionals who accumulate, deploy and apply knowledge? Probing deeper, why do companies exist: to provide a return to their shareholders and nothing else? To satisfy their customers' needs?

These questions loom larger than ever today, in the wider context of the current corporate crisis, a spate of corporate scandals, breakdowns of trust, ballooning executive compensation and perceptions that some senior executives are more interested in personal power and material wealth than their company's long-term future. Serious infringements on basic ethical rules, the erosion of trust between shareholders and corporate officers, and a vague impression that CEOs wield absolute power have brought questions about the way the market economy works – and, in particular, about the mission and goals of the firm and its role in society – to the forefront of the debate.

Corporate reputation may improve if there is a previous reflection on the firm's goal and purpose. For decades, the logic of economics – as a social science – has dominated most discussions around the firm's goals (Ferraro *et al.* 2005; Ghoshal 2005; Gintis and Khurana 2006). Economics has a lot to contribute to this area, but does not have a monopoly in explaining the theory of the firm. Moreover, its assumptions are hypotheses that make models simple and workable, but do not necessarily explain the real world reasonably well. Some of those hypotheses – like market value maximization or how to link executive pay with performance – have only limited scope and need to be considered together with other firms' dimensions. If they are taken alone, as the only objective, they may be misleading for shareholders and senior managers. Moreover, some of those hypotheses may be the seed of terrible mistakes for companies and society at large, as the current financial crisis is highlighting.

Business experience highlights that management is not only a science that can be explained by economics models; it is also in many ways an art and a profession. So the possibility of explaining scientifically how companies work and improve their management in a formalized way is important, but limited. On the other hand, management is a relatively new profession, gaining popularity only in the twentieth century. In formulating their models and recommendations, management scholars have borrowed many notions and concepts from economics and, to a lesser extent, from psychology and sociology. But, as we will see, modelling management as if it were a science like physics is a big mistake.

In economics, the firm is presented and treated in a simple way. Some authors treat it as a black box, in which certain production mechanisms transform certain inputs into final products or services. The owner or entrepreneur has the ideas, organizes the work, coordinates the employees, raises funds and appropriates any profit or loss generated in this process. The hypothesis underlying many economic models is that the entrepreneur is interested exclusively in maximizing profits. Some authors accept that she may also pursue other goals; however, they believe that including these other goals would complicate their models, and so they generally ignore them.

Under the rising influence of modern financial theory on economics in general and management in particular, this hypothesis has gained even wider acceptance. As companies have grown more dependent on capital markets, financial analysts have become prophets in the business world; they act as sellers of business ideas and ventures, basing their opinions on the goal of maximizing the firm's value for shareholders (Jensen 2000). This is the modern equivalence of the goal of profit maximization. The main difference is that profits tend to reflect an economic reality as presented in financial statements, while market value is a signal of investors' expectations; they take into account those profits, but also other variables and ideas shared by market participants. Thus, companies are bought, sold, merged, taken over or split up, whatever the shifting ideas and fashions among financial analysts dictate. Media, investment banks and consultants spread these ideas to other, unlisted companies. This has led to truly absurd situations, where a company undoes what it did yesterday, only to redo it tomorrow. The valuation of Internet companies, 3G technology or CDOs provides clear examples of the foolish mistakes we make when we blindly follow fashion.

Institutional investors also are under extraordinary pressure to obtain high returns on their investment portfolios, which further complicates the situation. To achieve such returns, they drive companies to deliver better performance in less time. Companies are delicate institutions. Not many institutional investors or financial analysts have the patience to observe how a company develops in the long term. Often, they simply do not have the information they need to assess whether a company is doing what it needs to do in order to improve over the long haul. The pitfalls of company valuation are notorious.

The problem is that we are liable to confuse ends with means. For a company, making money and being efficient are necessary, but not sufficient, conditions for long-term survival. When a company makes short-term economic gain its sole purpose, it neglects other decisive factors that may put the firm at risk in the long term. And when society as a whole succumbs to this misunderstanding of means and ends, it makes a serious mistake. It jeopardizes the notion and functioning of the company, one of the twentieth century's most successful social institutions and one that has given many countries a level of material well-being unprecedented in the history of humankind. Perhaps unwittingly, it is killing the goose that lays the golden eggs.

In light of this situation, it is vital to stand up for a more complete view of the firm's mission and goals. The dominant paradigm, which advocates profit maximization, is a simplification borrowed from economics that is designed to make complex situations more manageable. Moreover, this vision of the company is inefficient in the long run because it gives exclusive importance to profit, which, while certainly important, is just one of several critical factors.

Before we delve into the reasons why profitability is not the only important criterion, in the next section we will describe the emergence of the profit maximization paradigm in economics and the shareholder value maximization paradigm in modern financial theory. After that, we will discuss the strengths and limitations of the maximization hypothesis. Lastly, we will expound on a somewhat broader view of the company's goals and purposes, one that includes efficiency as a necessary, but not sufficient, condition to ensure the company's long-term survival and the accomplishment of its societal mission.

3. RATIONALITY AND PROFIT MAXIMIZATION

Economics assumes that individuals and companies try to allocate scarce resources for various uses and that they try to do so efficiently. Since human beings are assumed to have perfect rationality, the hypothesis is that individuals and companies seek the highest efficiency. Maximum efficiency is achieved when individuals maximize their economic well-being (their utility) and companies maximize their profits or their market value. If financial markets are efficient – a very difficult condition today – this value will coincide with the company's maximum market value.[3]

Under strict economic logic, therefore, the firm's goal is to maximize its market value. Consequently, the firm's top management should direct every decision and action toward increasing the company's value.

If this hypothesis about company behaviour is widely accepted, it is not because it is supported by much empirical evidence as to

---

[3] Argandoña (2006) and Fox (2009) offer an excellent discussion of this argument.

how companies behave in the real world. This hypothesis is not an empirical conclusion; it assumes that what may be rational for an individual (maximizing his utility with scarce resources) will be equally rational for a company (maximizing its profit).[4] However, saying that this is the firm's purpose, or that maximizing economic efficiency is the firm's purpose, is an oversimplification. We all value economic efficiency, but we also value other dimensions that are unrelated to economic efficiency but tremendously important to us. Claiming that rationality or efficiency, or other criteria for deciding what to do, is the reason why a person or company does something is an audacious hypothesis that we shall question in the sections that follow.

More than just a theoretical issue, this issue is very relevant to corporate governance. Basically, we are talking about the purpose of the firm. Under the maximization hypothesis, management's goal is to drive the company's market value as high as possible. The main challenge is aligning shareholders' incentives with those of directors and management. Compensation systems that link executive pay to the value of the company's shares may have a place in corporate governance if they are designed and implemented in the right way. However, this hypothesis has important implications for other agents who invest in the company (individuals, for example) and for the social dimension of companies' actions.

The idea of profit maximization dates back to Adam Smith. In *The Wealth of Nations* (1776), Smith explained his famous hypothesis of the invisible hand. In conducting business transactions, entrepreneurs pursue their own interests; in doing so, they achieve an economic outcome that is efficient for society as a whole. Smith argued that 'every individual necessarily labors to render the annual revenue of the society as great as he can. He generally, indeed, neither intends to promote the public interest, nor knows how much he

---

[4] Fox (2009) provides a fascinating explanation on how the notion of perfectly efficient capital markets developed, and how the notion of rationality in those markets evolved.

is promoting it ... By pursuing his own interest he frequently promotes that of the society' (*The Wealth of Nations*, Book 4, Chapter 3). The invisible hand combines the selfish, individual interests of a group of decision makers and translates them into an efficient economic outcome for society. This hand operates through the market, which is the context buyers and sellers interact in pursuit of their private interests. Smith suggests that the market, operating freely, is efficient, independent of any ethical consideration.

The notion that an economy based on free agents and markets would lead to efficient outcomes gained academic credibility with Walras (1874) and, later on, with the general equilibrium theory of Arrow (1951) and Debreu (1959). These models assume that decision makers are rational and therefore maximize their personal utility, and that companies maximize profits or minimize costs. Both personal utility and profit are expressed through functions of certain variables that the decision makers are thought to maximize, subject to certain constraints.

An efficient market economy requires a large number of profit-maximizing firms operating in perfectly competitive markets. However, market efficiency, as described in the general equilibrium models, is limited for various reasons. First, a significant percentage of transactions takes place not in markets but within companies. This fact casts doubt on the hypothesis that competing companies doing business in a market may reach a Pareto-efficient equilibrium. Empirical evidence suggests that certain transactions are conducted more efficiently within a company than in an open market (Williamson 1975). If this is true, it limits the general validity of the hypothesis.

Second, the market economy, as presented in general equilibrium theory, raises problems concerning the existence of externalities and the value of information for different decision makers. In fact, when markets are imperfect and information is incomplete, individuals' actions affect other individuals (Greenwald and Stiglitz 1986; Stiglitz 1994). This concept is apparent in well-known problems such as moral hazard or adverse selection.

As we shall see later, managers do not always know how to maximize their company's value in practice, because value maximization is not a practical proposition. Unfortunately, it only offers some general advice, but does not provide a practical rule of conduct for managers. Even if we assume that profit maximization is an imperfect representation of the efficiency rule that should guide a company's actions (for example, offering goods and services and thereby creating added value), it cannot easily be translated into a workable criterion for decision making. Even economics and management experts have reservations about the profit maximization hypothesis, as we shall see in the next section.

4. THE PROFIT MAXIMIZATION HYPOTHESIS: LIMITATIONS AND ALTERNATIVES

4.1 An assessment of the profit maximization hypothesis

Economists generally accept the hypothesis that individuals seek to maximize their utility and companies their profits, or their market value. The hypothesis assumes that decision makers are rational agents who seek the most efficient way of deriving utility from scarce resources.

This hypothesis has an important benefit: it is easy to use in formal analysis. In mathematics, it is possible to maximize functions representing the behaviour of individuals and corporations. However, shareholder value maximization is strongly normative and has important limitations.

The first limitation is that positioning shareholder value maximization as the company's only goal puts managers in a bind. When managers are assessed on the firm's financial performance, the compensation system drives them to seek results that have an immediate impact in the company's value. They may tend to ignore other goals. In order to improve the company's short-term performance, managers may make decisions that are undesirable from a medium-term perspective. In the long term, markets are likely to recognize this error and punish the company and its managers accordingly. Nonetheless, the incentive system has distorted managers' behaviour and harmed the company, possibly even depressing its market value.

The second limitation is that senior managers are unlikely to know *a priori* whether a particular decision will increase the company's value. Their rationality is limited. In the particular case of listed companies, capital markets do not always discount all the necessary information about whether a decision will or will not have a certain effect on the company's future development. In some cases, the information simply does not exist, something that is often true of companies in high-tech industries. In other cases, the information exists, but the markets do not know how to discount it. Lastly, markets sometimes evaluate available information incorrectly. The shareholder value maximization rule assumes that markets are efficient, which is debatable.

Another limitation of the maximization hypothesis is its implementation. As a rule, the financial impact of business decisions is assessed in terms of net present value. This is a criterion for ordering alternatives according to financial priorities. It does not tell us any more than what it is intended to measure – that is, the present value of a decision (usually a decision about an investment project that is expected to generate certain cash flows). Using net present value to determine that the best decision for a company is the one with the highest present value entails making quite a leap in logic. The reason is obvious: some dimensions of business decisions cannot be expressed in financial terms. Corporate learning provides a useful reflection. If a company invests in a new production process, what experience will employees acquire that may prove useful for future projects? We have no way of measuring the value of what they might learn. However, they will definitely learn something, which may have a value that is far from negligible.

Economists and management scholars have criticized the maximization hypothesis for this very reason (Simon 1947; Arrow

1986; Rosanas 2008, 2009). Simon (1947) maintains that managers' bounded rationality makes maximizing behaviour impossible. He insists that managers' task is to achieve satisfactory, not maximum, results. In Simon's view, 'the theory of management is the theory of the behaviour of people who pursue satisfaction, as such people do not have a tendency to maximize' (1947, p. 27).

In a later work, Simon (1986) recommended that 'we stop debating whether a theory of substantive rationality and the assumption of utility maximization provide a sufficient base for explaining and predicting economic behaviour. The evidence is overwhelming that they do not. ... We already have in psychology a substantial body of empirically tested theory about the processes people actually use to make bounded rational, or "reasonable" decisions' (Simon 1986, p. S223).

Alchian (1950) likewise preferred to drop the profit maximization rule because managers do not know *a priori* which solutions will lead to maximum results *ex post*. Accordingly, he chose to talk about minimum goals that managers should deliver and that ensure a certain degree of efficiency, and contribute to the company's survival.

Within the decision-making process approach, March (1994) is another advocate of the satisficing hypothesis, preferring it to the maximization assumption. He explains that satisfaction is preferable from two complementary perspectives. First, from the point of view of knowledge, satisfaction is a simpler criterion, which is an advantage in a complex environment. Second, from a motivational point of view, satisfaction seems to be a more reliable assumption; people pursue a variety of goals, and they cannot achieve all their goals to a maximum degree simultaneously.

Sen (1987), Stiglitz (1994) and Ghoshal (2005) emphasize not only the limitations of the maximization assumption as it applies to the behaviour of individuals and firms but also the implicit reductionist conception of the nature of human beings that it assumes. Stiglitz (1994) criticizes the idea that a person who acts exclusively out of rational self-interest for being narrow. Sen (1987) highlights the limitations of an approach that omits such central human motivations as generosity or spirit of service. He concludes that a proper formulation of social choice theory must include a plurality of motivations.

Pérez López (1993) takes his criticism of the profit maximization hypothesis even further. After distinguishing between the purposes of a firm and its managers, he adds that profit maximization 'cannot in any way refer to the purposes of the firm as such; that is to say, the firm as a decision maker cannot possibly have the purpose of maximizing the profits obtained by any one member or group of members. The firm generates profits for all members whose collaboration is required for the firm to exist'.

A final consideration is that some respected entrepreneurs and business people have complementary goals. Experience supports this claim, and the opinions of certain contemporary business leaders reinforce the point. By stating this, we simply mean to show that profit maximization is not an empirically proven fact[5] but merely a hypothesis that fails to explain the actual behaviour of certain well-known companies.

In this respect, George Merck II, the founder of Merck, pointed out about his firm: 'I want to ... express the principles which we in our company have endeavoured to live up to ... We try to remember that medicine is for the patient. We try never to forget that medicine is for the people. It is not for the profits. The profits follow, and if we have remembered that, they have never failed to appear' (Merck 1950).

John Young, Hewlett-Packard's executive president from 1976 to 1992, expressed a similar point of view: 'Maximizing shareholder wealth has always been way down the list [of objectives]. Yes, profit is a cornerstone of what we do – it is a measure of our contribution and a means of self-financed growth – but it has never been the point in and of itself. The point, in fact, is to win, and winning is judged

---

[5] For a broad overview of the goals actually pursued by real companies, see Donaldson and Lorsch (1984) and Collins and Porras (1994).

in the eyes of the customer by doing something you can be proud of' (quoted by Collins and Porras 1994).

These and other testimonies underline a simple and obvious point: a company is a group of people who use financial and technological resources to offer goods and services to society, creating economic value in the process. The more value a company adds over time, the better. The maximization rule is not enough to generate value, nor is the rule that says a company must make a profit (that is, be efficient): this would be a tautology. Obviously, a company must make a profit and use resources efficiently; otherwise, it will soon cease to exist. More importantly, the fact that a company is able to make a profit today does not necessarily mean it will be able to make a profit tomorrow. In other words, the profit objective is necessary but not sufficient.

In summary, the free-market economy produces optimal results (in terms of efficiency) only under certain conditions. If these conditions are not met, the market economy becomes less than ideal. This is not to say that economic activity should not be based on markets. It should be, for two main reasons. First, the market economy, though imperfect, is more efficient than alternative systems, such as central planning. Second, the market economy respects certain basic human rights, such as the right to free enterprise and the right to private ownership. As mentioned, companies have an economic purpose, but that is not their only purpose. In Section 5 of this chapter, we will discuss this question in more detail. But first, let's consider some other limitations of maximization.

4.2 The profit maximization hypothesis, individual behaviour and trust

Smith's theory presupposes a concept of the person known as 'homo oeconomicus'. This person is driven by self-interest in both professional and personal life. Within economic theory, the idea of self-interest developed into the concept of the maximization of utility by decision makers, which, in the case of the firm, translated into profit maximization. This is where the notion of shareholder value maximization took root.

This view of the firm and business activity is the source of serious problems. First, it is assumed that people seek to maximize their own utility. Second, it is assumed that the market, as the best resource allocation mechanism, is uninfluenced by market partici-pants' value-based preferences. In this respect, markets are neutral. Because of these assumptions, ethical criteria are effectively excluded from the behaviour of people and decision makers and from the func-tioning of the market. Let us question these assumptions.

The first question is, how can the unconditional pursuit of self-interest be compatible with building trust between people? Trust, an intangible value, enables people to cooperate and achieve mutually compatible goals in society. For trust to grow, however, individuals must expect that others will act out of interest for others, not exclu-sively out of self-interest. Otherwise, trust is unlikely to materialize. Immediate experience shows that people mistrust those who appear to seek only their own personal advantage. Conversely, they tend to trust those who are seen to act unselfishly.[6]

An organizational context in which trust is particularly vital is the firm (Arrow 1974). When people within a firm trust one another, they learn faster and are more committed. A firm is unlikely to sur-vive unless the people in it learn and acquire new capabilities, hab-its and virtues. Without such learning – which is not the same as acquiring technical expertise – there can be no product or process innovation, and every error becomes a heavy burden rather than an opportunity to improve, as Nonaka and Takeuchi (1995) have shown.[7]

---

[6] In economic terms, people trust those who have acquired a reputation for not thinking exclusively of their own goals. Here, too, each person's track record counts, as Kreps (1984) points out with reference to a company's culture and valves.

[7] Pérez López (1993) discusses this subject at length and expands upon some of the points made by classic management authors such as Barnard (1938) and McGregor (1960).

The learning process is tremendously complex and difficult to dissect. Yet it appears that the acquisition of capabilities and virtues is related to trust. Trust, it seems, is the quality of the environment in which learning takes place and becomes possible. Trust between people requires that people consider not only their own self-interest but also the interest of others.

Self-interest is understood here in the strict sense: what is best for a person. In the broader sense, however, self-interest must necessarily include the effects of a person's actions, such as the risk of going to prison if one commits a crime. In such a case, self-interest must also take this risk into account.

In particular, managers learn when they make decisions. Pérez López (1993) offers useful insights on maximizing behaviour and learning:

> When formulating a company's purpose, it is not rational to simply say that the company must maximize profits. If by that one means that the firm must choose whatever action plan the decision maker considers most effective at the time of the decision (i.e. the most effective action plan 'a priori'), then that plan must obviously be the same as the plan that actually maximizes profits 'ex post', in which case the decision maker has nothing to learn from the decision. If, as is usually the case, the decision offers the decision maker a learning opportunity, what the decision maker learns is how to make a better decision than he could have made before. This implies that what the decision maker considered optimal 'a priori' was not in fact optimal.
>
> By contrast, if by maximizing profits one means that the firm must choose the action plan that is in fact optimal (i.e. the plan which, in the usual parlance, actually maximizes profits in the long term), then we are at the opposite pole and have to assume that, to make such a choice, the decision maker must have nothing to learn from any possible decision because his internal state is already perfect.
>
> *(Pérez López 1993, my translation)*

If we accept that self-interest, in the narrow sense, is insufficient or harmful for building trust, we face a serious problem. Self-interest, one of the hypotheses assumed by the efficient markets model, is insufficient and no longer valid since some participants will distrust others when it comes to the market's allocation of resources. They will think they are likely to be cheated by others who pursue only their own self-interest (in the narrow sense). Our conclusion, therefore, is that profit maximization is an excessively reductionist and limited goal.

4.3 Ethics and markets

When we consider the maximization hypothesis, it is helpful to distinguish between the plans and decisions of individuals (and decision makers in companies) and the plans and decisions of the market. It has been said that the goal of ethics is for decision makers to act justly, in accordance with certain moral criteria. The degree of validity of these criteria is decisive for the improvement of both the individual and the functioning of the market in the long run.

In any case, in order for the market to function satisfactorily, ethical behaviour is indispensable. In other words, to what extent does the market mechanism cease to function when decision makers fail to act in accordance with ethical criteria? The market may be understood as a meeting point where buyers and sellers of goods and services express their preferences with respect to these products through their price setting and buying and selling behaviour. The market may be a physical place (such as a shopping mall) or a virtual place (such as a computer network for trading financial products).

Smith contended that the self-interest motivating market participants is a necessary and sufficient condition for efficient market functioning. His proposition is something of a simplification. The market enables the transfer of information and the calculation of certain results in terms of prices and quantities, regardless of whether or not participants act in accordance with their own self-interest.

As we pointed out in the previous section, efficient market functioning seems to require that individuals do what is right from an ethical point of view. If individuals deceive one another about their intentions or the goods and services they offer, numerous imperfections emerge in the market, disrupting the exchange of information. Asymmetric information and moral hazard are two such well-known problems.

In addition, in order for markets to function effectively, certain basic rights of the person must be recognized: private property, free enterprise, freedom of contracting and compliance with the laws on business transactions. In other words, more than just the pure self-interest of participants is required to make the market work. If these conditions were not met consistently, the market would cease to exist.

Therefore, the proper functioning of the market, and of a market-based economy in general, presupposes certain institutions and cultural and social values (Argandoña 1991; Hausman and McPherson 1993). To put it another way, the market is not merely a gigantic computer that makes economic calculations. It is a social institution that cannot make economic calculations unless the conditions are right. As a set of institutions, rules and values, the market is a means, an instrument. It cannot perform its function efficiently without ethical criteria.

5. AN ALTERNATIVE VIEW OF THE FIRM

As the markets have grown more powerful, however, and as capitalism has evolved toward a capital market-based economy, another idea has taken hold: that top managers are mere agents, bound by a contractual obligation to shareholders, who delegate the task of running the business. The idea of CEOs and senior executives as agents has changed the notion of professionalism that dominated business for several decades (Khurana 2007). Furthermore, the acceptance of self-interest as the sole criterion of action threatens ethical values in the firm; indeed, it threatens the firm itself as an institution and makes clear that we need a different notion of the firm.

5.1 Mission and purpose of the firm: some business leaders' perspectives

Following from the profit maximization hypothesis is the idea that the firm can have no purpose other than to use its resources as efficiently as possible, within the limits of the law. Friedman and Friedman (1962) summarized this view in their classic statement: 'There is one and only one social responsibility of business – to use its resources and engage in activities designed to increase its profits so long as it stays within the rules of the game, which is to say, engages in open and free competition without deception or fraud' (p. 133) .

Some respected business leaders have voiced their disagreement with the simple hypothesis of profit maximization. Both social activists and CEOs of well-known companies share and propound a desire to define a mission for the firm and ascribe purposes to it beyond purely economic goals. A company's mission defines and specifies what the company aims to be as an organization, how it proposes to contribute to society, and what rules of conduct its members aspire to follow. The mission gives the firm a reason for existing, an object or a meaning that relates to how the firm proposes to serve its customers. In the previous section, we cited the testimony of entrepreneurs and CEOs regarding the purpose of the firm.

Bill George,[8] former chairman and CEO of Medtronic, argued that shareholders come third in a company, after customers and employees. A company's first duty is to its customers. Its mission in society is to produce and distribute goods and services to customers; to that end, it must hire, train, develop and properly reward its employees. In third place comes the concern for shareholders and shareholder return. The goal of shareholder value creation is insufficient for securing people's commitment to a firm.

Accordingly, George suggests that shareholders' interests should not have primacy. He offered two arguments to support this.

---

[8] For an account of his views, see George (2003).

The first argument is that without satisfied customers and commit-ted employees, a company is very unlikely to achieve satisfactory financial results. The second argument is more philosophical, pro-posing that the idea of maximizing shareholder value is insufficient for motivating employees and securing their commitment, or for attracting clients and developing long-term relationships with them. George pointed out that 'by focusing solely on generating immedi-ate returns from shareholders, many executives ... lost sight of the first premise of business: companies can only survive so long as they serve their customers better than their competitors do' (2003, p. 62). Therefore, shareholder value maximization cannot be the firm's pri-mary objective.

A second line of criticism concerning the firm's purposes in a market economy concerns the way companies report to shareholders. Traditionally, companies publish quarterly results, and their CEOs or CFOs make regular announcements regarding progress toward quarterly targets. Daniel Vasella, chairman of Novartis, made an important criticism of this system.[9]

Vasella's argument is simple. The usual practice among listed companies is to publish official results at the end of each quarter and give unofficial progress reports during each quarter. These reports are often treated as the only criterion for judging a company's per-formance. As a result, many CEOs and analysts have come to iden-tify company success with satisfactory quarterly indicators.

Needless to say, there is nothing intrinsically wrong with a company's setting itself quarterly targets and consistently meeting them. But if companies confuse long-term success with short-term profit, they may be tempted to massage the figures to persuade ana-lysts and investors that the company deserves their fullest confi-dence. As Vasella said, this is no more than a threat or temptation. But it is a type of temptation that can discourage innovation and customer service improvements and delay the introduction of new

---

[9] See D. Vasella, *Fortune*, 18 November 2002, 67–71.

products, on the grounds that they may not have the desired short-term effects.

Vasella also argued that an assessment of a company's or a CEO's performance based on meeting quarterly targets can have a poisoning effect. A CEO may begin to seem successful if analysts and the media say so, rather than if customers, employees and even shareholders consider him successful over the medium to long term. CEOs of listed companies cannot ignore financial markets, and, indeed, they must take investors' expectations very seriously. But they cannot put short-term investor satisfaction first. If they do, their companies may end up sacrificing the efforts required for long-term success merely to satisfy those who happen to have a financial interest in the companies in the short term.

Regarding shareholder value, Vasella did not question the importance of obtaining the greatest possible return for shareholders, but he does question whether a system of short-term profit announcements is the best way to achieve it. In fact, he believes that quarterly reporting can actually destroy trust between shareholders and management, as managers find themselves under intense pressure to deliver results each quarter – even though those results may not be optimal in the longer term. In conclusion, the profit maximization hypothesis may be useful, but only if we take a long-term view. This proviso adds an element of complexity to the criterion for deciding the firm's goals and how they are to be achieved.

On a somewhat different plane, Jeff Immelt, chairman and CEO of General Electric, drew attention to an additional dimension. He put virtue (the classical ethics notion that helps perfect or improve the human person by exercising his capabilities in free actions) on a par with profitability and growth.[10]

Immelt's argument is straightforward. For a company to be great, it also has to be good in a moral sense. The reason people will want to work for a good company is that 'they want to be about

[10] See the interview with Jeff Immelt, 'Money and morals at GE,' *Fortune,* 15 November 2004, 64–8.

something that is bigger than themselves. People want to work hard, they want to get promoted, they want stock options. But they also want to work for a company that makes a difference, a company that's doing great things in the world' (Immelt 2004 – see note 10).

This argument leads straight into a qualitative discussion of the role of ideas and values in business. In the past, embarking on such a discussion would have been equivalent to questioning the market economy system. Today, by contrast, it means considering how the market economy system can be improved and perfected so as to do justice to other, higher dimensions.

Immelt argued that the discussion about values is crucial to General Electric's future success. Values affect how a company is managed, how employees are treated, what companies it does business with and in which countries it operates. Immelt goes on to suggest that companies are obligated not only to make money and obey the law but also to help solve some of the problems of the world in which they live. Furthermore, good leaders help others and, ultimately, try to meet others' needs.

David Packard, one of Hewlett-Packard's founders, reflected on why a firm exists in this way:

> I want to discuss why a company exists in the first place. In other words, why are we here? I think many people assume, wrongly, that a company exists simply to make money. While this is an important result of a company's existence, we have to go deeper and find the real reasons for our being. ... We inevitably come to the conclusion that a group of people get together and exist as an institution that we call a company so they are able to accomplish something collectively that they could not accomplish separately. ... You can look around and still see people that are interested in money and nothing else, but the underlying drive comes largely from a desire to do something else – to make a product – to give a service – generally to do

something which is of value. ... The real reason for our
[Hewlett-Packard's] existence is that we provide something
which is unique, that makes a contribution to society.

(Packard 1960)

The previous reflections, made by distinguished business leaders, are a very clear signal that the hypothesis of profit or market
value maximization is not accepted among senior executives as the
primary or exclusive goal of companies. A company must be profitable, but it should also try to achieve other important goals.

5.2 An alternative notion of the firm

In contrast to Friedman's particular view of the firm's purposes,
we propose a different notion, one that tries to integrate economic,
social and ethical dimensions. A firm is a group of people who work
together to offer goods and services that are useful to its customers,
creating economic value in this process, fostering the development
of people who work in it, and respecting the laws and the environment in which it operates. In order to survive, the firm must make
a profit and be as efficient as possible. But this is just a necessary
condition; the firm's mission entails some additional dimensions
(Rosanas 2008). It includes serving customers and enabling employees to grow by helping accomplish the firm's mission and purpose.
The more fully the firm achieves this purpose, the better it will be
positioned to accomplish its long-term mission.

This notion of the firm recognizes the company as a group of
people whose efforts are directed to a purpose that unites them tem-
porarily. It recognizes that work in companies takes place in the
broader context of human society. As a group within human society,
the firm must contribute to the common good of the society to which
it belongs. Naturally, it achieves this in its own specific way: by producing goods and services efficiently and generating economic value
in the process. The purpose of the firm, thus understood, is not just
to make a profit but to grow and develop as a human group pursuing

a specific mission in society. The firm must be efficient; were economic efficiency not part of its mission in society, it would be not a firm but an NGO. Besides the firm, other types of organizations rely on people's work, meet certain needs and provide a service to society; the distinguishing feature of the firm is that it provides goods and services efficiently and creates economic value. But economic efficiency is only part of its mission – a necessary but insufficient condition for its long-term survival as a group of people with a specific societal mission.

A company whose sole purpose is to maximize its profits or market value will be unattractive to many managers and other professionals. Crisis lies in wait for any such company that fails to meet one of its goals (economic efficiency) in the short term. But failure may happen as well if the company neglects to make its products and services customer-friendly, or fails to develop a committed group of people, or cultivate good relations with the community in which it operates. The recent crises faced by global companies such as AIG or RBS are timely reminders of how structurally weak many organizations are. A company that aims to achieve all we have proposed here may be thought to have a more difficult task than one that aims merely to maximize profits. But there are companies that try to integrate those important dimensions and develop more respected institutions in society. Companies that do not nurture those other dimensions will not achieve sustained long-term profitability.

It is true that companies are economic organizations, yet they have not solely economic goals. The development of respected companies requires efficiency as well as a strong commitment toward people and society, which is indispensible to developing their trust. A better definition for companies would be institutions whose clearly economic purpose distinguishes them from other institutions, but which have other important dimensions as well. The social legitimacy of a company in the twenty-first century and the efficiency with which it fulfils its purpose largely depend on its process of institutionalization – that is, its transformation from an efficient economic

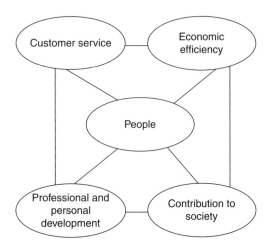

FIGURE 2.1 Reframing the notion of the firm

mechanism into a respected institution, based also on ethical values (Argandoña 2008; Melé 2008), that is rooted in and reaches out to society.

The model of the firm that we are proposing thus has the following core components: the firm as a group of people who collaborate freely; customer satisfaction and customer service; economic efficiency in business activities, including profitability; employee development through professional work; and lastly, certain contributions to society, centred around the elements but possibly going further, depending on the circumstances (see Figure 2.1).

This notion may be thought to rest on a blatantly naïve conception of human motives. True, it is rooted in a view of the person as having a unique dignity, certain rights and obligations, and a capacity for self-determination and commitment. It also attributes a role to intermediate institutions such as the firm in encouraging or providing opportunities for people to improve. This view was originally developed around the notion of the person in the Greek philosophy and the unique value of each individual in the Jewish and Christian tradition. Basically, this view affirms that each person is an end in himself, who has freedom to decide about his future, can freely cooperate with others to achieve certain goals and should never be a means to an end determined by some other person. It is clear that in the political arena, treating people as means is typical of totalitarian regimes. If this is unacceptable in political life, it clearly cannot be acceptable in companies.

After more than a century of experience of the firm as a mature organization, we know enough about what works and what does not. Admittedly, we do not have a complete theory of people-based management. But numerous scholarly works (Simon 1947; Drucker 1954; Pérez López 1993; March 1994; Ghoshal and Bartlett 1997) and the experiences of a good number of business leaders have taught us that the idea of the firm as a profit maximizer is limited and dangerous. None of these thinkers denies the importance of achieving very satisfactory financial results; but they all deny that financial success is the company's sole purpose.

For a firm to develop and survive in the long term, therefore, it must measure success by a different standard. A single-factor test such as that proposed by the maximizing hypothesis is not enough. A diverse set of indicators is required, covering economic, commercial, technological and human factors.

On the other hand, companies might find it difficult to act consistently in the face of such a diverse set of indicators. At least the economics approach had a clear answer on this point: aim to maximize profit. It is a simple definition, though in itself it is not very operational.

Our hypothesis is that a company's indicators must provide a more complete and comprehensive view of its situation, the risks and threats affecting its long-term survival and its potential for the future. We will discuss this in Chapter 3. The sustained ability to compete in the long run is a goal on which all of a company's stakeholders (shareholders, employees and so forth) can agree. And although this goal is more difficult to reduce to one specific indicator, it sets some targets that reinforce the company's sense of mission.

6. SOME FINAL THOUGHTS

In this chapter we have presented an overview of the mission and purpose of the firm. After reviewing the dominant paradigm (shareholder value or profit maximization), we discussed some of the limitations of this perspective. We then presented the thoughts of some reputed CEOs on the mission and purposes of the firm.

We found two basic questions underlying their views. The first question is, what should be the firm's goal? And if it has several goals, what should be the priority among them? The second question is: what should be the firm's mission in society? We attempted to answer these questions in Section 5.

Our intention here is not to question the fact that shareholders play an important role in firms but to question whether they are the only important players. Ghoshal (2005) claimed that some of the worst excesses of certain recent management practices are rooted in ideas that have emerged from business schools in the last decades. Ghoshal points out that one of the reasons why shareholder value maximization is such an attractive proposition is that it provides clear rules and standards by which a manager's performance may be judged. If managers pursue other goals, they may be distracted from that primary goal.

As Ghoshal observes, however, once the idea that managers must put shareholders' interests first was established, other theories objected, claiming that managers are incapable of doing this since they always put their own interests first. This gave rise to the notion of the agency problem, where shareholders delegate to directors or managers. The main challenge posed by the agency problem is how to bring the interests of managers in line with those of shareholders. To solve this problem, companies developed stock-based and performance-based compensation methods and contractual mechanisms for controlling management's behaviour. Unfortunately, such mechanisms proved notoriously unreliable, and other means of improving corporate governance were proposed, such as appointing independent, nonexecutive directors.

The claim that the problem is due to lack of supervision or lack of incentives remains unproven, however. On the other hand, maximizing shareholder value in the long term has a positive side in terms of efficient resource allocation. Some corporate abuses are due not to the company putting shareholders first, but to CEOs and top managers putting their own personal interests first. The underlying problem lies not only in determining the firm's goal, but also in defining its mission in society, what it is responsible for, and, within the mission of the firm, the mission of the CEO. These questions will be explored in Chapter 3.

KEY LEARNING POINTS

- Firms are complex organizations made up of people. The hypothesis that firms have to maximize shareholder value is an assumption of modern financial theory that satisfies theoretical purposes of clarity and simplicity in a very thorny area. Moreover, the current financial crisis has been created by individuals and corporations who were searching for maximum profit in the short run. Both theory and practical implications confirm that shareholder value maximization should not be the firm's only goal.
- Firms are made up of people who work together to serve clients with goods and services; firms create economic value in this process, as well as social value for the employees and society at large. All of these activities should be taken into account when thinking about the goals of the firm and the objectives of the senior management team.
- Indicators of corporate success should include not only profits and other indicators of economic efficiency, which are necessary for the firm's long-term health, but also how well the firm serves its customers, offers its employees opportunities for professional and personal growth, and engages with the communities in which it operates.
- A company's reputation will improve only if business leaders take seriously the notion of the firm as a human institution dedicated to serving people in an economically efficient way. The firm has to be

profitable, but profitability alone is not enough to ensure the firm's long-term survival or improve its reputation as an institution.

- This notion of the firm has clear implications in terms of the quality and content of corporate reporting. Such reporting should not be limited to mere financial information and should include indicators related to clients, employees, suppliers and communities.

3 The firm as a respected institution

I. INTRODUCTION

On 9 May 2008, Dr Narayana Murthy, founder and co-chairman of Infosys, gave the keynote lecture at the IESE MBA programme graduation ceremony. In the reflections he shared with the graduates, he emphasized that

> the founders of Infosys wanted to make it not the largest, but the most respected company. Infosys has to be very profitable, but this goal will be the outcome: it has to be a great company for employees and clients, and has to get involved in the community. In this way, people will respect it and would like to do more things with it.[1]

For an India-based company born as recently as 1981, such an aspiration was far from trivial. But Dr Murthy and the six other IT professionals who co-founded the firm were determined to make it happen. Since the beginning, they have all shared a common vision: building a world-class company and the most respected firm in India.[2]

As Dr Murthy explained, becoming a respected company requires a great team of excellent professionals who design and develop outstanding products and services, a business model that is profitable and sustainable, and a set of values that is really shared by employees. He added:

> We wanted to run the company legally and ethically, and show that, by putting the interest of the corporation above your own

---

[1] N. Murthy, Commencement address, MBA Class, IESE, Barcelona, 2008.
[2] For a broader description of Infosys, see Velamuri and Mitchell (2005).

interest, the company will be better off and shareholders also will benefit from it. We have always believed that the softest pillow is a clear conscience. We are also convinced about the importance of running the business using simple rules, because they are easy to communicate, easy to understand, and easy to practice.[3]

Values are at the heart of Infosys. Dr Murthy explained how relevant the firm's values are in making good decisions:

The value system at Infosys is like the British Constitution. It is unwritten but extremely well practiced. We also have unwritten rules, but we all know that we have to be as fact-based as possible. We start every transaction on a zero base. People are free to express their views and disagree with their superiors. We have two principles that summarize this: 1) you can disagree but without being disagreeable, and 2) in God we trust, everybody else brings data to the table. Only an argument that has merit wins. It is not about hierarchy, but merit.[4]

By the end of 2008, Infosys had become one of the most respected firms in the software industry, with remarkable economic success. The firm's revenues were above $4.1bn, with net profits of $1bn, and it had more than 91,000 employees working on five continents. Infosys is certainly a special case; not many successful international companies try to build respect in such an explicit way. Most companies' leaders think about business models and profitability, believing that respect will follow. This may be true when the economy grows, but in periods of flat growth or even decline, respect will not come from economic success. What are the foundations on which to build respected companies?

---

[3] N. Murthy, Commencement address, MBA Class, Barcelona, 2008.
[4] N. Murthy, Commencement address, MBA Class, Barcelona, 2008.

2. RESPECTED ORGANIZATIONS

Historically, companies have built their reputations on different pillars: excellent products, such as Mercedes or Nestlé; great services, such as IBM or Singapore Airlines; iconic brands, such as Apple or Nokia; unique experiences, such as Disney or Starbucks; or the quality of the organization and its management, such as General Electric or Toyota. In the 1990s, IT, the Internet and innovation became some of the new drivers of reputation. But the technology bubble burst and, afterward, many of the innovators went bust, corporate scandals exploded and corporate reputations hit new lows.

We are already seeing the negative impact of the current financial crisis on many companies, even those beyond real estate and financial services. In general, when a crisis hits, some companies will come under fire not only for their mediocre economic performance but also for their poor risk management and reckless behaviour. The reputation, good judgement and ethical behaviour of their leaders will be questioned. Certainly, business cycles cannot be avoided completely; but can corporate reputation be better preserved? Can employees, clients and shareholders feel proud of a company even when it faces an economic slowdown? Can business leaders work for the long term and build successful and respected companies?

During the hubris that followed the technology bubble in the 1990s, public opinion, employees and shareholders were extremely critical of some business leaders' behaviour. Governments reacted by enforcing stricter standards of corporate governance and financial reporting. Many companies launched new initiatives that would highlight their social responsibility; they considered better corporate governance and a stronger social commitment indispensable. But some sceptical business leaders remarked that this approach might be useless, pointing out that when profits recovered and the stock market climbed to new heights, social concerns would disappear.

Indeed, after the technology bubble in the late 1990s, many companies embraced better governance and social causes. Yet corporate reputation in many countries is still lower today than it was at the turn of the century. Moreover, different polls in Western countries report that companies do not rank very highly as respected institutions;[5] indeed, the polls indicate that companies face significant conflicts of interest and that there is uneasiness about their role in society beyond the effective provision of goods and services. How can we make sense of these changes in perceptions and attitudes toward companies and business leaders?

Society's expectations of a company have evolved over time. Corporate behaviour and the emergence of new social values have changed perceptions and expectations about firms. During the second half of the twentieth century, companies were seen as key instruments for promoting economic growth, investment and employment – they were essential for economic and social welfare. The fall of the communist regimes in Eastern Europe in the late 1980s confirmed not only the superior efficiency of the market economy as an economic model, but also the key role of private enterprise, with its ability to launch new companies, innovate, create jobs, raise capital and invest, all indispensable conditions for society's progress.

As organizations that are highly efficient at offering the goods and services that society demands or expects, companies fulfil a key economic and social mission. However, the corporate crisis and recent scandals have fanned the debate over the role of companies in society. New questions have emerged: What is the purpose of a company? Should companies pursue solely economic profits? Should

---

[5] A US survey conducted by Edelman, a public relations firm, in 2008 found that the trust of citizens in US firms had fallen from 58 per cent in 2007 to 38 per cent. Only 17 per cent of Americans said they trusted company chief executives. Moreover, less than 50 per cent of US citizens thought that free markets should work without government intervention. In Europe, things are not much better. An FT/Harris poll (April 2009) asked people about how their perceptions of managers had evolved during the current financial crisis. In the UK, 67 per cent said that their perceptions had worsened. In Germany, it was 75 per cent.

they also seek other benefits? What specific duties do companies have in the society in which they operate? Is efficiency the key factor in strengthening corporate legitimacy? Do firms also have some distinctive feature, beyond the economic dimension, that turns them into respected institutions? In Chapter 2 we offered a new notion of the firm that goes beyond the economic focus that has dominated the discussion on the firm's purpose for many years.

We argue that companies are first and foremost organizations made up of people who strive to efficiently fulfil certain economic needs. Thus, companies as institutions have a special identity that comes from their purpose: to provide their customers with goods and services by efficiently allocating limited resources and generating economic value in the process. Business leaders must take into account the fact that firms are made up of people working with other people to serve customers. Consequently, people's development and the social and ethical dimensions of companies are part of their essence. Companies also operate in a given social context: they are a reflection of this society, employ its citizens, work for this society and influence it in many ways. As a result, social realities permeate the company, and it cannot stand aloof from them.

The reason for viewing companies from this perspective is not pragmatism or enlightened self-interest, although some people believe that this way of operating may be more profitable. Nor is it a question of following the wave at a time when companies seem to be atoning for their guilt toward society by committing themselves to projects that seem to have a stronger social impact. Rather, the true reason lies in the very nature and identity of companies and the mission they should strive to fulfil.

Companies are economic organizations, but their goals go beyond economic performance. Respected companies need to be efficient, but also display a strong commitment toward people and society, which is indispensible to developing their trust. For this reason, companies are institutions whose clearly economic purpose distinguishes them from other institutions, but which have other important dimensions too. The reputation and legitimacy of a company and the efficiency with which it fulfils its purpose largely depend on its process of institutionalization – that is, its transformation from an efficient economic organization into a respected institution that is rooted in society.

In today's society, expectations about firms go beyond their short-term economic success. Besides being profitable, firms must serve clients, have competent and loyal employees, and be respected by these stakeholders and society at large. Hence, corporate reputation has different drivers: economic efficiency, people's competence, customer loyalty and social impact. Unless companies try to develop a coherent and balanced framework to deal with these drivers in an integrated way, they will get lost in a world of competing and increasingly demanding stakeholders.

In this chapter, we introduce the idea of a respected company. This is a firm that is remarkable for its success in a variety of areas, not only for its short-term financial performance. Its reputation is also strong among different groups of people: customers, employees, shareholders and society. We also introduce and discuss the areas that help develop a respected company: its economic performance, the way it attracts people, its customers' loyalty, and its social impact. These areas are based on four pillars: business idea, mission, people, and governance and management (Figure 3.1).

Companies must be successful in a variety of dimensions, and these dimensions tend to reinforce one another. In the long term, it is not possible to be successful in just one of these dimensions, whether that is economic profitability or social impact. A company needs them all in order to build a reputation as a respected company and to be respected. Decision making means choice – but choice does not mean exclusion. It means good judgement in the way business leaders define their diverse objectives. CEOs must integrate them, one way or another. In this new world of growing expectations for companies, the name of the game is smart integration, not exclusion. The CEO's job is to fulfil what seem to be incompatible objectives in the short term.

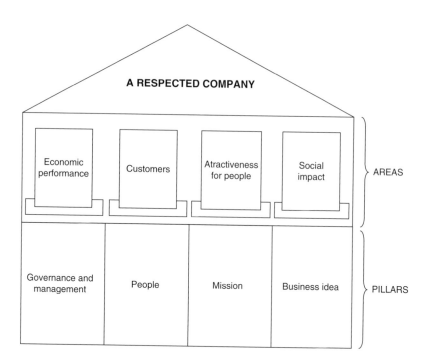

FIGURE 3.1 A respected company: some pillars

It may seem that by widening the senior executives' focus, firms will be less efficient. Nevertheless, the integration of object- ives may be the only way in which senior leaders can gain the respect of a wider range of stakeholders, whose commitment to the firm is indispensable to its long-term survival.

The case of Nestlé, one of the world's most successful and admired food companies, illustrates how this combination of goals can work and how this wider range of goals is compatible with great financial performance. Over the years, Nestlé has developed a set of management principles and values that permeate the entire organization, from product research and design to people develop- ment. 'The Nestlé Corporate Business Principles' is a brief booklet that was approved by the firm's board of management in 1998 after many years of global business experience. It clearly describes what Nestlé stands for, what it is trying to achieve, and how these values are put into practice – in particular, how these principles shape the company's managerial style. It is worthwhile to consider how the booklet describes the company's main goal: 'Nestlé's business objective, and that of management and employees at all levels, is to manufacture and market the company's products in such a way as to create value that can be sustained over the long term for sharehold-ers, employees, consumers, business partners and the large number of national economies in which Nestlé operates' (Nestlé 1998).[6]

Today, Nestlé is not an isolated case. More and more companies that are admired for their excellent performance across industries and countries are trying to redefine their values and managerial principles in order to improve their efficiency and increase the respect they receive from society for reasons beyond their economic contributions.

In the following section, we discuss the notion of the firm as an institution and reflect on what makes a firm a respected institution.

3. THE FIRM AS AN INSTITUTION

The view of companies as institutions means that good leadership and governance should promote economic efficiency, but attention cannot be focused exclusively on the firm's economic dimension. Business leaders must also take into account other aspects that make firms respected institutions in society.

An institution is an organization structure (Scott 1995) with a set of norms and values and a body of knowledge that guides its behav-iour and influences the way society perceives it. Institutions develop activities according to certain expected patterns and offer society some stability. If institutions work efficiently and properly, they become respected and earn trust from external parties. The company as an institution also goes beyond basic and very noble notions of corporate social responsibility (Benioff 2004), social entrepreneurship (Elkington and Hartigan 2008) and philanthropy (Bishop and Green 2008).

More specifically, the firm is an institution that has some attributes related to its culture and values that guide its operations,

---

[6] 'The Nestlé Corporate Business Principles', Nestlé 1998.

its economic efficiency, the way it develop its people and deals with clients, relates with shareholders and the quality of knowledge it generates (Table 3.1). Firms that do a better job in developing those attributes in a holistic way will also grow as respected institutions.

Respected institutions enjoy legitimacy. This quality is developed by adhering to standards of behaviour and efficiency over time, according to the specific nature of each institution. A company's legitimacy in society comes from the efficiency with which it fulfils its economic purpose as well as from the way it treats and helps develop its employees; the values that shape its culture; its relationships with customers and other interested parties; the capacity to create and apply practical knowledge; and, ultimately, its behaviour as a citizen in the society in which it operates and from which it benefits in so many ways.

The underlying goal of treating the firm as an institution is not to improve the firm's corporate reputation in the short term. A short-term improvement in reputation may indeed result from a company's policies and actions, but it is not its direct purpose. On the contrary, a company's institutionalization involves its transformation from a mere economic entity into an organization rooted in society that reaches out to that society, and where the people participating in the project have opportunities for development and improvement.

As a result, a company's management team must keep watch over its economic dimension, yet it should also bear in mind that although a company's purpose is economic, neither its foundation, its knowledge (which resides in people), nor the context in which it operates are exclusively economic.

This perspective may yield some unexpected effects, such as a lack of focus on economic goals or an inefficient allocation of resources. However, the senior managers' job consists precisely of making apparently different and at times contradictory goals compatible. And just as in other realms of business activity, the difficulty of achieving this objective should never serve as an excuse for not tackling it responsibly.

Table 3.1. *The firm as an institution: some assets*

– Corporate culture and values
– Economic efficiency
– People development
– Customer relationships
– Shareholder relationships
– Knowledge development and application

Daniel Vasella, the CEO of Novartis, was even more explicit in this respect.[7] He presents reasons why a company's success cannot be evaluated by using strictly economic criteria. The first is that the quarterly results, which is one of the economic indicators used mainly in listed companies, do not show a broad enough perspective of the company's long-term strength. The second is that using these or similar indicators as the yardstick of an executive's success can be dangerous for senior executives, because they only consider one dimension. The third is that a company should think in broader terms: its people, culture, values and the way it helps to solve the problems of the society to which it belongs.

In this way, Vasella underscored the need to envision a company as more than a purely economic entity with economic purposes. Senior executives cannot ignore the obviously unavoidable economic reality, yet they must also include sociological and ethical variables in order to rise to the company's main challenges and build a more solid social legitimacy for their institution.

Bill George, the former CEO of Medtronic, mobilized efforts and managed to achieve outstanding performance for his company. When reflecting on his experience, George (2003) pointed out that companies need real leadership, not just effective leaders. That is, they need business leaders with integrity who are committed to their organization and concerned about its long-term development and survival; they need leaders with a sense of corporate purpose,

---

[7] See interview with D. Vasella, *Fortune*, 18 November 2002.

people who embody the company's values; and, finally, leaders who aim to meet shareholders' needs yet are, at the same time, concerned about how they can better serve society.

In other words, George did not downplay the importance of generating economic value, but he stressed the key importance of taking the interests of third parties and society at large into account for the company's day-to-day operations.

These business leaders' reflections highlight the wisdom of viewing the company as an organization that is not strictly economic in nature, even though from an economic standpoint it must be very efficient. Companies must be involved in the society in which they operate while bearing in mind other purposes, especially serving their customers and the development of their employees. This is a vital condition for transforming a company into an institution whose purposes go beyond the strictly economic.

4. THE FIRM AS A RESPECTED INSTITUTION

A respected company is an organization that is remarkable for its success along several dimensions over a long period of time. It goes beyond the notions of corporate social responsibility and philanthropy. It must show excellent economic performance as well as relevant achievements in areas that are at the core of what a company is. The development of a respected company is built upon economic success, its efficiency as an organization, its people, its clients and its policy toward society (see Figure 3.1). It considers these dimensions not only for economic reasons, or because being ethical or responsible pays, but because it has a sense of mission and purpose that includes factors that go beyond profits. As we discussed in Chapter 2, a company whose only mission is to make money has a poor understanding of its potential. A company's mission clarifies what makes it different from other companies. It helps engage people, attract new talent and make clients feel that the company is special. In a nutshell, the sense of mission acts as a pillar upon which a respected company is built. We will briefly review these dimensions.

Jeff Swartz, chairman of Timberland, an entrepreneurial US firm that has been chosen several times as one of the most successful in its industry, has a special view of what a firm is:

> I believe that business is an institution of civic society; I believe that business is connected to other institutions of civic society; I think business has a power and a responsibility that is broader than just earning the maximum profits it can for its shareholders every quarter ... I believe that, as CEOs, we must deploy our creative and productive power to strengthen both our balance sheet and civic society at the very same time. This is a different kind of vision and it's the vision that guides what we do at Timberland ... Who we are is 6,000 passionate, eclectic men and women who believe in a model of commerce and justice; who believe that it's possible to deliver superior returns consistently for our shareholders – we are a publicly traded company. We believe that we can deliver superior returns consistently over time for our shareholders, while at the same time our business mission includes an awareness of an accounting for the assets of our business.[8]

A company cannot exist without clients. As a general rule, the more loyal these clients are, the more successful the company will be, in terms of both profits and reputation. To win loyal clients, the company must do a very good job not only at manufacturing goods or providing services of reasonable quality at reasonable prices, but also at understanding clients' needs and constantly thinking about how to make clients happier with the firm's offerings. Interestingly, some of the best brands in the world do not belong to the largest companies in an industry, not even to the most profitable ones. For instance, in the automobile industry, General Motors and Ford were the largest firms in the world for many years, but smaller companies, such as Audi and BMW, had a stronger reputation and more solid financial

---

[8] See Swartz (2005).

performance. In the personal computing industry, Apple is the most admired brand in the world, even if its market share is small.

A firm can be financially successful in the short term without having a strong reputation among its clients, but this paradox survives only for a brief period. The rise and fall of some large airlines in Europe and the United States in the late 1990s and 2000s provides a useful reference. Some of these companies were buoyed by a strong demand for air travel and cheap oil prices; they paid little attention to customer service. For some companies, customers were just a burden they had to deal with. When the economy started to decline and air travel suffered, their ability to attract and retain customers was extremely weak. In the long term, customer loyalty is one of the most accurate indicators of a successful company.

People and people's development are also important attributes of respected companies. An efficient, financially successful company with a good management team is a magnet for talent. It can attract people not only by providing economic incentives but also by offering opportunities to learn, grow and participate in a very interesting and challenging venture, one whose mission includes economic performance but goes beyond profit.

If a company's differential purpose is its economic objective, a respected company must do a great job along this dimension. Profitability and value creation must be as good as possible. Shareholders and investors have placed their trust in a firm, and they fairly expect to receive a good return on their investment. Excellent financial performance in the long term also speaks very highly about the quality of business leadership. Financial performance can be expressed and encapsulated in a variety of indicators. Some may be more relevant than others, depending on investors' expectations. Nevertheless, a respected company does not disappoint investors; when there is bad news, the company comes out to explain it to the financial community.

A respected company also must be a very efficient organization. This dimension has a very clear impact on performance beyond the financial realm. Even an inefficient organization may generate good financial performance in the short term, but this will not be sustained in the long term. A good organization includes several ingredients: first, a clear definition of goals, functions and processes; second, an efficient way of serving customers; and third, good management. In a nutshell, a good organization is not only an efficient one, led only by rules and processes, but one in which management has a very clear and positive impact in highlighting challenges and goals, establishing priorities, motivating people and executing efficiently.

Finally, a respected company has a positive impact on society by doing what it is supposed to do: serve clients well, be efficient, be profitable, create jobs and attract talent. But society's expectations for companies go beyond those dimensions. These expectations change from country to country and evolve over time. They concern the basic challenges that society faces, such as education, research, health care, housing, global warming and immigration, among many others. In general, a single company cannot tackle all of these challenges, but since these dimensions directly impact the firm and its operations, business leaders must consider how a firm's goals and strategy can encompass some of these challenges efficiently. It is worth mentioning that we are referring here not to a company's legal obligations but to the challenges and opportunities within the societies in which companies operate. A respected company may have neither the resources nor the duty to solve every challenge, but it has a duty to think about them and try new solutions that may contribute to bettering society.

This is not just a theoretical discussion. Jeff Immelt,[9] CEO of General Electric, argued that if a firm wants to attract top-notch professionals, it must be viewed as a company that does things differently and positively impacts society. GE strives to achieve this by considering a number of factors, such as the way the company

---

[9] See 'Money and morals at GE', *Fortune*, 15 November 2004.

treats its employees, which countries it decides to operate in, the partners it works with, the technologies it invests in, and the responsibilities it takes on in the communities where it operates. Immelt added that in the early twenty-first century the gulf that separates the richest and poorest people in the world is still very wide, and that companies can help to close this gap by investing, developing new and cheaper technologies and renewable energies, taking care of the environment and supporting education. In short, the challenge facing General Electric is twofold: to be not only one of the world's most widely admired businesses but also an institution that, besides fulfilling its economic purpose efficiently, also contributes to society in a host of ways that extend beyond mere economic efficiency.

How can respected companies move beyond economic performance? Designing a balanced scorecard that can make strategy more actionable or help monitor different performance drivers is useful, but not enough. Companies must define a broader frame of dimensions and goals that are at the core of a respected company, and develop a more holistic view of how well a firm performs.

Table 3.2 shows some dimensions of performance according to two basic criteria.[10] The first is the external or internal perspective of performance. The second is the quantitative or qualitative nature of performance. Some areas of firms' performance are identified, each one referring to the previous pillars of a company as a respected institution. Those areas are split up into external and internal.

The external areas include customers, investors and capital markets, attractiveness for talent and society at large. We consider for them both quantitative and qualitative indicators. Among the quantitative indicators, we include some traditional ones, like

---

[10] Kaplan and Norton (1996) introduced the notion of the balanced scorecard, with four perspectives around corporate performance: financial, customer, internal and learning. Taking into account nonfinancial dimensions in assessing a firm's performance was a very important step forward. The purpose of the model presented here is not so much to illustrate a new portfolio of indicators, but to consider the driving factors that help build respected companies and some of the indicators that should be used for this purpose.

return on equity (ROE) or stock market performance, but also others like customers' satisfaction and retention or research and development efficiency. The qualitative indicators include areas like accountability, transparency, reputation, innovation or social commitment.

The internal areas help consider how the firm performs regarding its people, the effectiveness of its organizational structure and the quality of management and governance. The main quantitative indicators reflect people's development, productivity or return on investment, while qualitative indicators focus on leadership development, people's diversity, governance processes and the quality of the managerial processes.

As a way of summarizing those indicators, we introduce some overall categories of performance (Table 3.2, 'Overall concept' column): loyalty indicators for customers, economic performance for investors, organisational attractiveness, citizenship indicators for society, talent development, organisational efficiency, and the quality of the managerial processes and governance.

These categories make explicit the idea that corporate performance should take a multidimensional approach. Boards of directors, senior executives, rating agencies, investment funds, investment banks and investors should stop pondering the firm's potential only in terms of its economic performance. The financial focus is important, but is not enough to develop respected firms in the long term. Other dimensions, such as customer satisfaction, customer retention, R&D, productivity, people's development and quality of governance, should be key for assessing how well a company is doing. It is true that each party would like to focus on some of those indicators, but a key challenge for good governance and leadership is to make those objectives compatible with one another. The firm is a unity and a holistic perspective should have pre-eminence over partial views of the firm. Those indicators described aspire to be more holistic and better reflect how respected a company is by different parties.

Table 3.2. *A respected company: performance indicators*

Areas		Quantitative indicators	Qualitative indicators	Overall concept
External	Customers	– Customer satisfaction – Customer retention	– Reputation – Innovation	Loyalty
	Investors & capital markets	– ROE – Stock market performance	– Accountability – Transparency	Economic performance
	Attractiveness for talent	– Turnover – Human capital's value	– Retention – Attractiveness/ Unity	Organizational attractiveness
	Society	– R&D – Taxes	– Social commitment – Education	Citizenship

Table 3.2. (cont.)

Areas		Quantitative indicators	Qualitative indicators	Overall concept
Internal	People	– Development activities – Productivity – Efficiency – Internal promotion	– Leadership development – Diversity – Learning	Talent development
	Organization	– Productivity – R&D – ROI – Product development	– Quality of management – Innovation – Learning	Organizational efficiency
	Management and governance	– Board members – Board performance – Management performance – Diversity – Backgrounds – Executive turnover	– Governance processes – Strategy making – Leadership development – Control systems – Compensation	Management and governance effectiveness

5. INSTITUTIONAL STRUCTURE: KEY FOUNDATIONS

A respected company needs an institutional structure that provides its basic underlying architecture and becomes the engine that helps its people fly higher. The institutional configuration goes beyond a simple business model. It enables the firm and its leaders to undertake new projects, think about growth and project themselves into the future, beyond the vagaries of the business cycle. It requires certain key elements (see Figure 3.2): an idea promoted by an entrepreneur; a mission to fulfil through the idea and values that support the firm; talented, committed people; a customer-service orientation; a board of directors and executive team that organize the company's power and decision making; capital and a financial structure provided by shareholders and investors who will fund the idea; and a governance structure.

5.1 The idea

Behind any company there is an entrepreneur, with a business idea. This idea involves a way of serving customers and providing goods or services efficiently; if the idea is truly good, it will be somehow different from what other companies do or will aim at different customers or markets. Apple's 'Think different' is a summary of a business idea on how to make the experience of Mac users unique, easier and more rewarding, making the firm different from their competitors; and it also helps commit its employees to outstanding technology excellence for the new generation of Apple's products.

A business idea is not enough. It may be turned into a company depending on the entrepreneur's operational or managerial capability, his strategic ability to position the product or service in a unique way in customers' eyes, and his ability to get others – shareholders, investors, employees – to sign on to the project.

There is a business idea behind any company, but an idea alone does not make a company. An idea must be made reality, and it must also be updated over time. An idea may be excellent when conceived but poorly executed. Or, conversely, it may be poor when conceived

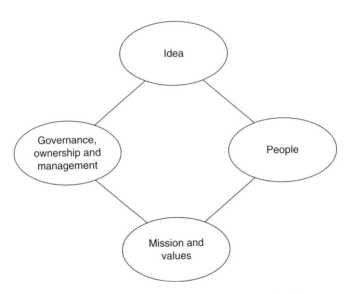

FIGURE 3.2 The firm's institutional structure: key foundations

and improved upon execution. However, generally speaking, no ideas withstand the test of time forever. Ideas usually change because the entrepreneur improves on them, other companies come up with better ideas and rivalry spurs change, or customers demand better products or services. Over time, the original idea must be adapted to fit new circumstances.

A business idea's survival depends on the scope of the need it is designed to satisfy. However, it also depends on how it is communicated to customers and implemented, the type of advantages it provides compared with alternative products and services, and how it combines with complementary goods and services, if applicable. A good business idea also must connect with a need perceived by society. The recent explosion of netbooks in the personal computer industry provides an interesting example. As a product, the netbook was neglected by many PC makers, who thought that their capabilities were not strong enough for sophisticated users. Nevertheless, average users did not think so and when better products were offered, the demand exploded. In this way, a good business idea should bring not only profits for shareholders but also tangible benefits for clients and society. A company's strategy must define how the company plans to fulfil its mission, what goals it wants to achieve and how specifically it plans to achieve them.

Finally, while an initial idea or project is behind every company, the continuity of the company demands many business ideas over its lifetime. Once up and running, a company needs new business ideas that help keep it up to date and committed to serving its customers better.

5.2 Mission and values

A company's mission is its *raison d'être*, a purpose that is related to the service the company wants to offer its customers beyond the quest for economic profit. It helps explain why the company exists and what it tries to do (Selznick 1957).

The strength of this mission depends on its authenticity and the senior management's ability to get employees on board to develop a project that goes beyond each one's job, as we will discuss in detail in Chapters 6 and 7. It is crucial for the entrepreneur or the board of directors to formally define this mission. The executive team should embody the mission; making it come alive in all the company's activities, divisions and initiatives; and constantly updating it.

A good company's mission should be a living guide for clients and employees. This is the case with companies such as Danone, Bertelsmann and Johnson & Johnson, for which the mission explains why the company exists and even defines what the company can or cannot do. Alternatively, a mission can be just words on a piece of paper. What distinguishes a living from a dead text is neither its literary quality nor its content. The real difference lies in whether a group of professionals strives every day to make the mission a point of reference for the company, or whether the text is nothing more than a declaration of intent.

Bertelsmann is a clear example of a company that sticks to its mission and basic values in all activities that it tries to develop. Its mission statement also defines some aspirations that the firm has:

We provide information, entertainment and media services to inspire people's daily lives. We aspire to make a valuable contribution to society. We strive to be leaders in our markets and achieve returns on capital that guarantee the growth and continuity of our corporation. Our joint efforts focus on creative content and customer relations. We seek to provide working conditions that are equitable and motivating for our employees. We commit ourselves to the continuity and ongoing progress of our corporation.

(www.bertelsmann.com)

Bertelsmann's mission is reflected in the way the company thinks about corporate growth, deals with people's development, considers restructuring businesses and relates to the societies in which it operates. Bertelsmann's values are present in its operations. This does not mean that a company with a strong sense of mission cannot fail. It simply means that the whole company strives to achieve success for every party by pulling all of them together and working for the same objectives with the same aspirations.

The mission is reinforced when the company's entire range of initiatives and actions refers to it naturally, when the mission is actually put to use from time to time rather than just serving as decoration. The mission should help stakeholders determine whether a decision strengthens or weakens the company's project. Furthermore, the mission can often provide guidance as to what should or should not be done.

A respected company is an organization that, together with its sense of mission, has some values and ways of doing things. These values help employees – and other people who interact with the firm – develop and grow. A firm with values and no profit will not survive, but an efficient firm without values will not be respected.

An integral part of a firm's values is its approach to management and decision making. A company's management philosophy shapes its identity as an institution. It enhances the decision-making process by helping to take certain critical discussions into account, and it also provides guidelines for how to lead and govern the company and how to treat the people working in it. In short, it contributes to ensuring that everyday problems and solutions are dealt with using criteria and experiences that have proven to be effective over the years.

The efforts of the board and the management committee, however they may be organized, must be permeated with certain core management principles that reflect that philosophy, without which the executive team would find it difficult to create value. These principles help define the management style and shape the way many people work. We will now discuss some of them.

Efficiency

Setting a clear agenda of goals and priorities and executing it efficiently is a hallmark of distinction in any organization. The agenda includes both the tasks to be performed and the goal set for each relevant item.

One of the most vital jobs is evaluating the work of the board of directors and management committee and the way each member contributes to the firm's effort and goals. Without this assessment, there is no real chance of improvement. The governing bodies must establish simple, systematic mechanisms for addressing this challenge, and they must disclose the results of this process to shareholders and employees. There is no doubt that a process like this means a huge commitment for both the chair and the executives, but it is crucial for improving the company and transforming it into an institution.

Transparency

A company's institutionalization requires that it shares information with all its stakeholders. Transparency is an attribute related to the quality of a company's information, which investors can use to assess the company's financial health and the behaviour of those variables that are key for the firm, as well as any direct or indirect circumstances that reveal the existence of conflicts of interest. It is difficult for a board of directors to list all the possible circumstances *a priori*. However, the principle of transparency requires a company to disclose those aspects that investors reasonably require, beyond the reason of curiosity, and that are necessary for respected firms and the sound functioning of boards.

Collegiality

It is useful for governing bodies to be collegial since governing is teamwork rather than an individual effort. The board should have a chair with clear leadership skills; however, it must also have members who are solid professionals and effectively involved in the board work. The chair must conduct the orchestra, but there is no reason for him to play all the instruments. Likewise, the chief executive, with his executive team, spearheads the management board's work, leads its efforts, and, at the same time, gets all the members involved as well. A good board must deliberate on the main issues in an orderly, systematic fashion; it must be able to open its doors to opinions that are contrary to ideas that have historically held pride of place in the company; and it must be able to assess all the alternatives to find a solution to adopt. It is logical for the chair to want to influence the decisions, but he must ensure that the debate process is orderly and open so that the board members are committed to the decisions they adopt and are ready and able to assess whether a given option or its alternatives are suitable for ensuring the company's long-term survival.

Long-term orientation

The governing bodies, namely the board of directors and the board of management, must be decision-making teams, not a mere aggregation of professionals. Both boards must be a benchmark of standards and sound management for employees, not a soapbox for the individual opinions held by the various members. They must work with a long-term orientation and act like a real team, not merely as a group of individuals, and to do so it helps if they have a purposeful sense of their mission in the company.

Board of directors and boards of management must pursue the company's long-term success and survival. It is rational for large shareholders to try to defend their own interests. However, the sound practice of a board of directors requires that any disputes among shareholders not be settled at board meetings. Otherwise, the efficacy of the board would be impaired.

Of course, the existence of these principles does not ensure that the company's purposes will be fulfilled; they can, at times, be affected by other intrinsic or extrinsic variables. However, bearing these principles in mind can help to improve the board's endeavours. What is more, these principles are important because as the company takes them into account, it clearly conveys concern for good governance internally and externally. This not only impacts certain financial variables but also inspires trust in the employees, investors and creditors. In short, these principles contribute to improving the corporate reputation and highlighting the company's identity as more than just an efficient organization.

5.3 People

A company is a group of people who work in a coordinated way to serve customers and generate economic value. People are the central pillar of what any company is and should be at the heart of what any firm does. Employees must work in order to make customers pleased with the firm, and they must work in a profitable way for shareholders. Respected companies like Danone, Henkel or Nestlé have a simple starting belief: to hire and develop great people committed to their firm and proud of it. They really make a difference, as we discussed in Chapter 2. We would like to highlight that companies should be respected first by their own people.

People's professional development within an organization is a complex, multilayered social process. In addition to implementing specific policies, respected companies promote their people and dignity, trust people and commit to their development. Respected companies display a great sensitivity toward their people and people's policies reinforce this orientation.

Respected companies are not soft organizations. They are demanding and expect a lot from their people. Learning is a top priority, supported across the organization. Assessment is organized not only around performance and capabilities but also learning and improvement. Respected firms know that in order to be successful they must develop and promote their people. They see them not as resources but as the players who help grow the firm and make it great.

5.4 Governance, ownership and management

A company's institutional context is partly defined by the relationships among ownership, control and management; these relationships are expressed in values and processes that organize the company's distribution of power and decision making. The right structure and a prudent use of power help a company to achieve its goals and turn it into a respected institution.

To a certain extent, a company's institutional structure dovetails with the contents of its governance in the usual sense of the term – that is, as a set of criteria and principles that regulate the company's decision-making power. However, the set-up of the institutional structure we are proposing here is much broader. A solid institutional structure reinforces the company's mission by providing it with a frame for the decision-making process. It enables the firm to achieve its mission and reach its strategic goals in a more streamlined fashion. Its institutional structure should therefore reinforce it and empower it to reach its long-term goal, namely the survival of the firm, albeit not necessarily the continuity of each of the businesses in which the company operates.

A company is a group of people, led by a chief executive, who set out to offer goods and services that are useful for customers, creating economic value and helping develop people in the process. In any company, there must be an idea – that is, a way of serving customers with useful goods and services. In any company, there are people working on an idea or project who will work together for as long as the project lasts. Their collective efforts exceed the contributions that each of them could make on an individual basis. Any company must have an executive team that guides and drives this process and helps coordinate each individual's work. And in any company, financial resources are used to make the required investments.

Consequently, in any company there is an idea, or several ideas, designed to serve customers, envisioned by an entrepreneur and pursued by a group of executives who coordinate other people's work. In the company's operation, the entrepreneur's own resources are used, along with resources provided by other investors. The resources' contribution to the firm generates rights for the different investors: shareholders, bondholders and other investors, as well as the power that each one has related to decision making. Shareholders delegate the management and its supervision on the chief executive and the board of directors.

The relationships that form among this group of key stakeholders – entrepreneurs, shareholders, other investors, chief executive, board members – are complex. Certain elements of these relationships define a business project from an institutional standpoint: the entrepreneur, investors, the top management team and shareholders' oversight of executives' actions.

The relationships among ownership, governance and management are classic in the study of how organizations are structured. The experiences of numerous companies show that there must be a balance between shareholders' real ability to exert an influence, as the owners of the company, and the executive team's decision-making authority. Sound institutional structures create an appropriate balance between those parties. If the company's management has too much influence in the decision-making process, and if shareholders or the board of directors have too little real power to influence truly important long-term decisions, the power will be left in the hands of management or the chief executive, with the concomitant risk of abuses in the exercise of this power. This scenario was seen in the United States in the 1990s: as chief executives' power increased, they exerted excessive external influence and developed new initiatives, not always with the backing of the board of directors.

On the other hand, if owners have excessive influence and control, they can paralyze the firm's management and decision-making capacity, rendering it incapable of reacting swiftly to changes. In such a situation, the owners would leave the executive team too little leeway, thus introducing distortions, slowing the process and possibly even sparking a disinclination for further commitment. This is the case with some companies in Continental Europe, in which the supervisory board system with sweeping authority can slow down matters and lead to excessive bureaucratic complexity in a world where quick decision making is imperative.

A clear definition of the structure of relationships among a company's shareholders, the entrepreneur who has the idea and the top management team is one of the essential challenges facing a company that seeks to be respected. A sound institutional structure allows it to fulfil its mission and ensure its continuity over time. Conversely, a flawed, unstable institutional structure is one in which capital is not stable, the shareholders exert a feeble influence, or executives chafe under excessive bureaucratic control over their decisions.

These ideas point to one of the reasons why governance structure is important. A company may have a crystal-clear mission, a well-founded strategy, a sound capacity to execute this strategy and an excellent human team – but if it does not have the appropriate governance structure, it is bound to fail. It will be like a car without the right chassis or a boat without a solid hull. Institutional structure is not the most important feature of a company, just as the chassis is not the most important part of a car; yet without the right one, the other elements will not fit well. With a good institutional context, a firm can be more efficient and more respected.

A central contributor to governance structure design is the entrepreneur, who has the idea and takes on part or all of the risk. At times, entrepreneurs may be so close to the project that it is impossible for them to separate what is good for them from what is good for the company. As a result, the process of institutionalization is sometimes driven by the chief executive, whose emotional distance from the project may be greater than the entrepreneur's but less than that of a shareholder who is merely an investor; the chief executive is thus able to see the challenge in a broader perspective.

5.5 Financial resources

Any business idea requires funding. An idea's potential and the team driving it determine how attractive the idea will be to investors. Finding investors to fund an idea is key to building a sound institutional structure, but raising capital is not enough. Firms need a financial structure that offers stability and enables them to take on new projects. Moreover, shareholders should fit in the business project, both personally and financially.

Investors who are committed to and enthusiastic about the company are a source of both current and future financing; they also serve as an excellent calling card for other potential investors. On the other hand, dissatisfied investors, like unhappy customers, are the worst publicity a company can have. Ultimately, a certain financial structure and investors who fit a certain profile can provide stability for a business project and contribute to its long-term continuity. Conversely, inappropriate investors can destabilize a project and become a source of conflict beyond the human, commercial and technological problems an organization might face.

This idea is valid for both public companies and companies whose shares are not publicly traded. In both cases, the entrepreneur must choose the investors who will be his travelling companions, ideally those who bring funding without added work and who are legitimate owners of the company.

In family-owned companies, these issues become even more complicated. It is vital to separate shareholders' decision making within the company from the decisions they make with regard to their personal assets and family relationships. The institutional structure of a family-owned company demands even clearer criteria about access to company management and the framework of relationships with the owners.

Nonetheless, from a financial standpoint, a public company has no fewer challenges. At times, analysts highlight the advantages of publicly owned companies, beyond the vagaries of financial markets, over family-owned companies in terms of their financing structure and ability to raise funds. However, companies that go public are exposed to new challenges, such as what type of shareholders the company will have, whether or not they will identify with the company's mission, whether they intend to stick with the project in the long term and whether they will seek to be involved in managing the company.

A company's institutional set-up also requires clear criteria on how to compensate investors and how these criteria can be modified over time in a predictable way. As soon as entrepreneurs sell their idea to a potential investor, the idea ceases to be solely theirs; they must share part of the profits with others, and they become party to how these profits are split within the company. A respected company must be efficient and offer investors a reasonable profitability. Without pleased investors the firm's reputation may also be in jeopardy.

6. SOME FINAL THOUGHTS

In this chapter, we have discussed what makes a firm not only an efficient economic organization, but a respected institution within society. A respected institution achieves more than just isolated or occasional recognition for its contribution; it generates respect on a more sustainable basis. This is what it takes to turn firms into respected institutions, organizations toward which people feel goodwill and that may even become legends.

In today's society, short-term economic success is not enough to build a strong corporate reputation. Firms need to make money and, simultaneously, serve clients, have competent and loyal employees, and be respected by all of them and society at large. Hence, corporate reputation has different drivers: economic performance, customer loyalty, attractiveness, organizational performance and social impact. Unless companies develop a coherent, balanced framework to deal with these drivers in an integrated way, they will get lost in a world of competing and increasingly demanding stakeholders.

Companies must be successful in a variety of dimensions, which tend to reinforce one another. In the long term, it is impossible to be successful in only one dimension, such as either economic profitability or social impact. Decision making means choice, but choice does not mean exclusion. It means good judgement in the way business leaders define their different objectives. CEOs need to integrate those objectives, one way or another. Now that expectations for companies are growing, the name of the game is smart integration, not exclusion. The CEO's job is to make possible what seem to be incompatible objectives in the short term.

Achieving success along these dimensions brings respect from different stakeholders. Shareholders are pleased with reliable economic performance; clients are pleased with the quality of goods and services; and employees are pleased with the professional opportunities the company offers them. Achievements in key areas generate respect across the board. A firm respected by shareholders or clients also generates respect from employees and gives them pride in their company. Shareholders who realize that clients and employees are pleased with their firm will be more inclined to reinforce their long-term commitment. The legitimate pride of working for or interacting with a company goes beyond the company's efficacy or scale; pride comes from knowing that the company is an institution that has people at its core.

This is an ongoing process that a company's executives must constantly pursue, not a goal or a destination to be reached. In fact, this process generates an aspiration to do better, a healthy dissatisfaction, by revealing that what has been achieved can always be improved upon. Likewise, an institutionalized company is an organization in which the system of corporate governance is reinforced by a level of aspiration that helps turn the company into a reference for society.

KEY LEARNING POINTS

- A respected company is an organization that is remarkable for its success along several dimensions over a long period of time.
- The pillars upon which a respected company is built are its mission, its people, its economic model, and its management organizational effectiveness.
- Those pillars help a company establish and develop key relationships with its stakeholders, which contribute to its social legitimacy and pave the way for increasing respect. Those relationships encompass clients' loyalty, people's performance, economic performance, organization efficiency and social-based initiatives. By focusing on these pillars, senior managers can help build a respected organization.
- Performance indicators are needed to assess how much progress a company makes along those dimensions. Some of these indicators are quantitative, and others are more qualitative. The indicators presented in this chapter (Table 3.2) focus on external areas, including customers, capital markets and society; as well as internal stakeholders, including people and organizational effectiveness.
- A respected company also needs an institutional framework, an internal structure that explains what inspires the company, how major decisions are made and by whom. The key foundations of a solid institutional structure are the business idea, mission and values, governance and ownership and financial structure, and people's development.

Part III The role of corporate governance in developing a respected company

4 Nature, goals and models of corporate governance

I. INTRODUCTION

Over the past few years, the business world has shown an increasing interest in the mechanisms that make corporate governance work. At the same time, good governance practices have been adopted by many companies and some governments have even passed guidelines to regulate basic issues in this area. Nevertheless, the challenge of corporate governance, both for companies and governments, is far from being efficiently tackled. In the cases that we present in this section, some basic problems of corporate governance are highlighted. They are related to executive compensation, the importance of large shareholders, mergers and acquisitions or the role of governments as shareholders in some companies. These and other dimensions make corporate governance an extremely complex issue, for which universal recipes do not exist.

1.1 The rage about executive compensation

On 10 July 2006, in the middle of a booming economy, *Fortune* magazine published 'The real CEO problem', an article that described in a lively way why some US companies' shareholders were outraged at the ballooning of executive compensation and why boards of directors and shareholders could not do more to stop the rot in a compensation system that seemed to be broken. The rage became furious in 2008 and 2009, when the financial crisis exploded, investment banks went bust and some CEOs were still making a lot of money while their firms were underperforming. The questions were: Is executive compensation efficient? Is it fair? Can boards of directors do something to tame the compensation monster? Should governments regulate executive compensation?

In May 2009, when some US and European companies seemed
to be reacting to the public mood in this area, amid a deep economic
crisis that was hitting many people around the world, Shell held its
annual shareholders' meeting. In a totally unexpected way, 59 per
cent of Shell's shareholders – following an activist investor – voted
against the firm's compensation report. The main reason was the
board of directors' decision to pay €4.2m in bonuses to five senior
directors even though the group had not met some targets. The vote
was not binding, but sent a clear signal about how Shell's shareholders felt about the board of directors and certainly defined a high-
water mark for other companies.

The debate about executive compensation is not only important
in terms of efficiency, performance, reputation or fairness, but also
points out the different perspectives that shareholders and boards of
directors have on this critical issue. Some proposals to smooth the
conflicts are urgent and necessary, since compensation not only serves
the purpose of paying people, but also points out the need to find a fair
and efficient distribution of decision-making power between boards of
directors and shareholders, and board members and CEOs. This is one
of the most important factors in corporate governance.

1.2 Large shareholders and family-controlled firms

On 23 July 2009, Volkswagen and Porsche's board of directors
announced a plan to merge both companies before 2011. While US
car makers were in the midst of a huge crisis, Volkswagen was doing
well. Under the leadership of Volkswagen, this merger would transform this firm, already the largest European car maker, into a bigger,
family-controlled company. The new, integrated car-manufacturing
group would have ten car brands under the same umbrella, including
Audi, Bentley, Porsche and Volkswagen. Porsche was 100 per cent
controlled by the Porsche and Piëch families. Ferdinand Piëch and
Wolfgang Porsche, chairmen of Volkswagen and Porsche, respectively, were cousins. Their grandfather was Ferdinand Porsche, founder of Porsche and designer of the Beetle.

This merger seemed to be the final step of a long conflict that started in September 2005, when Porsche acquired 20 per cent of Volkswagen. For almost four years, disagreements between the Piëch and Porsche families about how to combine the strengths of both companies – and about which company should take the lead – had led Porsche to build a controlling stake in Volkswagen of about 51 per cent. Its aim was to control Volkswagen and eventually merge both companies. Since it was much smaller than its target, Porsche used a risky financial strategy and spent about €23bn to gain a controlling stake. The cost for Porsche was huge: a mounting financial debt of €9bn. Eventually, Porsche needed a deal that would help save it from an extremely difficult financial situation. Volkswagen used Porsche's financial weakness to take the lead in the merger.

Since the beginning, this clash of shareholders sparked different reactions. Potential conflicts of interest between majority shareholders and other shareholders started to emerge when Porsche began building a large stake in Volkswagen. Two of Volkswagen's institutional investors, Tweedy Brown (British) and Union Investment (German), reacted fiercely to what they considered a conflict of interest that could adversely affect the position of other minority shareholders. The government of Lower Saxony owned 18.2 per cent of Volkswagen's shares and spoke out against the increase in Porsche's stake, wishing to protect its position as Volkswagen's largest shareholder. It used the legal tools to support the interests of Volkswagen in an eventual merger.

The case of Volkswagen and Porsche illustrates other complexities of corporate governance: the role of shareholders in a family business, the influence of large shareholders in strategic decisions, the perspective of institutional investors and minority shareholders, the effects of the institutional context of governance in a country like Germany and the weight of the public sector as a large shareholder. This episode also highlights the important role of trade unions in some boards of directors, as unions were strongly represented on Volkswagen's board.

In countries like Germany, corporate governance mechanisms are more complex because of the different types of shareholders represented on corporate boards (private investors, families, unions, public sector, and, in some cases, financial institutions). A unique system of cross-relationships prevails. What is more, until recently banks were major shareholders of large German companies; this situation has been slowly changing. Clearly, one cannot possibly understand, much less reform, corporate governance in countries like Germany unless its particular institutional context is taken into account.

This case highlights the fact that in Continental Europe, institutional investors play a much less prominent role than in the United States or the United Kingdom. This is not only because the volume of funds under management is smaller, but above all because in many European companies there is a hard core of shareholders (often organized around a family) that controls the board of directors and the appointment or removal of CEOs.

1.3 Governments' intervention in mergers and acquisitions: the defence of national champions

In corporate mergers and acquisitions, France and Italy have a particular reputation, based on their governments' determination to intervene in some companies' decisions to protect national champions and fend off foreign buyers. The €46bn takeover bid by Sanofi (a French pharmaceutical company) for Aventis (a German–French pharmaceutical company) in January 2004 was a clear case of how governments can influence business decisions. Aventis had been a takeover target for several non-French pharmaceutical firms. And in 2003, Alcan, a Canadian aluminium company, had absorbed Pechiney, a French company, through a hostile takeover. These developments had not gone unnoticed by public opinion and the French government, which did not like the idea of Aventis being controlled by a non-French company, even though it was already half German.

The French government intervened decisively to ensure that the Sanofi board would launch a takeover bid for Aventis, so that

French shareholders could control the new group. The French government's intervention in this incident was unofficial: the government had no mechanism to legally block a takeover of Aventis, and it held no shares in the company. However, once the government decided that it was not in France's interest for a non-French group to gain control of Aventis, it exercised its influence through informal channels. Governments' informal influence is enormous, and so it came about that Sanofi's shareholders found themselves involved in a merger that, in strictly business terms, was quite unexpected.

European governments' willingness to intervene in industry consolidation was quite understandable in the 1960s and 1970s, when the public sector had large industrial shareholdings, capital markets were underdeveloped and a critical mass of shareholders was needed in order to restructure companies and industries. In the twenty-first century, however, and in the context of the EU and its pillar of free capital movements, such intervention is unjustified.

Intervention on this scale is not confined to the pharmaceutical industry. For many years, France and Italy have protected other industries they consider critical to their economies, such as banking and energy, preventing foreign-driven concentration that might be harmful to what they regard as national interest. As a result, France and Italy now have inefficient financial systems and disproportionately few global financial institutions given the size of their economies.

The Shell, Volkswagen–Porsche and Sanofi–Aventis cases highlight some of the key issues around corporate governance and its role in improving corporate performance and reputation. The firm's governance embraces issues such as the role of the board of directors, shareholders and managers in governing a firm; the protection of minority shareholders; the duties of accountability and transparency in financial and strategic information for shareholders and other investors; or the role of independent and lead directors in the board. Those deals also point out that the economic and legal context of a country could be decisive in shaping governance.

Nevertheless, what is intriguing about those deals is that most of the discussions around them were related only to the role of governments in the strategic decisions involved, not to the quality of the decisions to be made or the strategic logic behind those deals and their impact on the companies themselves. This is an approach to corporate governance that still dominates the debate. Most of the discussions on corporate governance seem to be focused on its legal and institutional dimensions. Very little attention is given to governance as a framework for improving corporate performance and increasing corporate reputation. As we will see in the next sections, we need to develop a broader perspective of corporate governance, one that includes the quality of the decision-making process and the implementation of those strategic decisions. Success in those areas requires some intangible attributes, such as a sense of mission, corporate values and a focus on people development and customer service, among other factors. It is clear that these dimensions go beyond the legal perspective of corporate governance.

2. CHIEF EXECUTIVES AND BOARDS OF DIRECTORS: A CHANGING BALANCE

Recent corporate crises highlight the importance of sound corporate governance. The focus on maximizing shareholder value has failed to align senior managers reasonably well with the long-term development of the firm. Rather, at times it served only those shareholders who had a strong influence on the company's board of directors.

Over the past decade, many chief executives have taken on an enormous degree of power in their organizations, far beyond that awarded in the legal provisions or the company's by-laws. The underlying reason for this phenomenon was not only CEOs' zealous quest for power and fame, but also the neglect of duties by many boards of directors, who allowed these top executives to act freely and offer the board a *fait accompli*.

Recent corporate scandals, as well as what some regard as the excessively high compensation packages earned by some top US

executives, have unleashed a crisis in the model of corporate governance and paved the way for a revolution in how some investment funds
and other institutional shareholders manage their investments.

It was not always like this.[1] The 1990s brought new investment opportunities with the global surge in savings and the
increasing sophistication in financial markets that allowed access
to cheap, easily available financing. Investment banks spread the
word about the advantages of the new economy, and they encouraged their clients to go public or acquire other companies. Share
prices began to rise. Boards of directors of public companies grad-
ually began to approve compensation packages associated with
stock options, which replaced the more conventional plans, such
as compensation based on profits. Some experts argued that these
plans were necessary for aligning the interests of executives and
shareholders, as well as for attracting, motivating and retaining
pivotal executives. Ultimately, chief executives felt driven to
achieve significant growth in share value, and they wanted their
stake in this growth.

The advent of these incentives resulted in a lethal combination. Shareholders' interests in results, especially short-term results
expressed in quarterly profits and share price, dovetailed with the
chief executives' interests as they, too, sought to optimize their
compensation.

The combination of these goals is not inherently bad. However,
it can become a deleterious force when compensation becomes top
executives' goal or when shareholders do not accept decisions that
might jeopardize their desires in the short term, such as earmark-
ing more resources to innovation or investment. There is a very fine
line between a sound use of resources in areas needed to ensure the
company's future, such as investment and innovation, and a poor use
of these resources as a result of inefficient management. Frequently,

---

[1] See the historical description that Davis (2009) presents on the importance of
financial markets in firms' management.

neither investors nor financial analysts can grasp all these details, which remain in the hands of the chief executives and their teams. If these executives are guided by sound judgement and an interest in the long term, the company will continue to work smoothly. However, a problem may emerge when they act in their own interests first, without taking into account the interests of the majority of shareholders.

In view of this situation, many boards of directors chose to reclaim certain basic functions in the company, which they should never have given up in the first place. Indeed, the firings of prominent top executives in the past few years, such as Carly Fiorina at Hewlett-Packard, Jean M. Messier at Vivendi, Maurice R. 'Hank' Greenberg at AIG, Franklin D. Raines at Fannie Mae, Harry C. Stonecipher at Boeing, Michael Eisner at Walt Disney, Chuck Prince at Citigroup or Stan O'Neal at Merrill Lynch, were simply the manifestation of a deeper phenomenon. These firings represented boards' reactions to chief executives' seizure of power in their organizations. Most of these executives did not personally profit from business operations engineered in their own interests. However, many of them staked their claim to power in the company at the expense of the functions and responsibilities of the boards of directors, which alternated between internal disagreement and uncertainty as to how to proceed.

The pressure exerted by many institutional investors and the public impact of those corporate conflicts forced boards to reconsider their role in managing the company and supervising the chief executives. As a first step, boards seized upon a moment of weakness in these executives as an excuse to fire them and appoint new CEOs. In many cases, this was probably the best decision in the given circumstances. However, replacing one executive with another is not a guarantee that the new one will behave any better. In other words, is it really fair for a board to expect a change in management and the chief executive's performance unless it also changes its long-term way of thinking, the company's goals, the compensation packages, and its supervision and monitoring mechanisms?

Some people believe that shareholder activism is big news for the business world. It was about time, some of them assert, that shareholders, especially institutional investors, rolled up their sleeves and got involved in companies' problems, shouldered their responsibilities and did more than just bide their time while others managed their companies for them and rewarded them with solid dividends. However, this argument has two weaknesses.

First, institutional shareholders are neither necessarily good managers nor good board members. They may know how to manage funds. However, we can neither assume nor demand that they have expertise in managing companies. In fact, many of them would prefer not to get involved in those firms in order to avoid possible conflicts of interest or having to save face with their customers should an investment in a specific company not perform as expected. In this case, part of the responsibility falls on the company's directors or managers; but if the institutional investors became directors, the clarity of their role as investment advisors and portfolio managers would be blurred.

The second weakness is the belief that resolving the problem of overly powerful executives involves stripping them of this power and shifting it to the board.[2] A company, however, needs the initiative, leadership and drive of the chief executive. Having a company with a very good chief executive but a mediocre board would probably be preferable to having a mediocre executive with an excellent board. This dilemma is in no way easy to solve when looking at it only in terms of power. The underlying question is, what is power for? The answer is related to the company's mission and the specific function of the various governing bodies in achieving it. Chief executives and board members should be professionals at the service of the company's mission, and their pursuit of personal interests should not take precedence over the general interest. When chief executives

---

[2] Shivdasani (2004) offers an empirical evaluation of the efficacy of some mechanisms of corporate governance required by some institutional investors and shows that their effectiveness is not always clear.

act otherwise, they tend to err, even though in the short term this tactic may yield them some profit.

In view of recent corporate crises, governments all over the world have attempted to regulate certain areas of corporate governance more explicitly and broadly. In some cases, these regulations have shifted toward clear interventionism in certain areas, such as the Sarbanes-Oxley Act approved in the United States in 2002. In other cases, action has remained at the level of clear-cut prescriptions related to the obligations of public companies regarding disclosure to investors, or the implementation of mechanisms aimed at defending the interests of minority shareholders against possible abuses by large ones. Finally, some countries have adopted codes of good governance that are legally binding for public companies.

Regulating some aspects of corporate governance may be necessary, in particular the aspects related to the obligations of transparency, information, respect for minority shareholders' interests and functioning of the governing bodies. Just as stable business laws offer a framework for business transactions, an equally balanced and stable corporate governance framework ensures that all companies meet some basic standards. But, as we will discuss in this chapter, regulation is not enough to promote respected companies.

In this context, it is sensible to reflect on the nature and goals of corporate governance, which should help a company achieve its mission. Without a clear notion of a company's mission or an explicit definition of corporate governance in that direction, the dialogue between boards of directors and chief executives can become frustrating, and the balance will tip in favour of whoever has more power at any given time. In the long term, this situation makes the firm unstable.

Our notion of corporate governance goes beyond regulation and rules. We understand corporate governance as the set of institutions, organisations systems, policies, processes and decision criteria that a firm has defined, aimed at ensuring the company's long-term development, success and survival. Corporate governance includes the company's internal mechanisms, the work of the board of directors and the functions, tasks and responsibilities of the CEO. It also includes the legal regulatory framework in each country, but good governance certainly goes beyond that set of rules. In the next sections, we discuss different notions of corporate governance and the various perspectives from which it can be addressed. We then propose a more integrative vision of corporate governance, based on our own view of governance.

3. OWNERS AND MANAGERS: WHO CONTROLS WHAT?

The content and objectives of corporate governance tend to be country-specific. Generally speaking, most definitions of governance underscore the fact that companies and their governing bodies must operate within a set of legal norms, and within systems and processes that are voluntarily adopted by each company through its governing bodies.

One of the characteristics of free-market economies is the distinction among ownership, control and management. This separation and specialization of roles has helped companies improve the effectiveness of resource allocation and has ushered in a new group of top executives who are in charge of managing, coordinating and executing corporate strategy. Market economies would have been unable to develop without a group of professional executives to manage shareholders' investments.

Nevertheless, the separation of ownership, control and management has also generated certain significant dysfunctions. In their classic work *The Modern Corporation and Private Property* (1932), Berle and Means pointed out several risks inherent in splitting ownership and management, risks that are directly related to corporate governance. The first risk is that shareholders, who have delegated the managerial job to a board of directors or to a CEO, may be confronted with situations in which they are unable to effectively exercise control or supervision over decisions that could substantially affect the company.

The second risk is that the process by which companies issue shares leads to a fragmentation of the firm's ownership. This phenomenon is essentially positive in terms of the distribution of wealth and a society's prosperity. However, from the standpoint of corporate governance, this model poses the challenge of how a dispersed, fragmented group of shareholders can supervise a company properly and make the right strategic decisions.

On the other hand, the increasing complexity of companies and executive decisions leads not just to a separation of ownership and management, but also to the increasing difficulty that their shareholders have in knowing the company and its business well and fully understanding the issues involved in the major decisions to be taken. In most cases, shareholders neither have the time nor the capabilities to understand the firm's major challenges. In most advanced countries, for many decades boards of directors were often mere puppets who rubber-stamped the decisions already made by the CEO or executive team. Board members traditionally spent little time on their specific responsibilities, namely studying the matters at hand and questioning decisions with professionalism and attention. When they tried to do so, they came up against their ignorance of the firm's specificities, the way it operated, or certain technological or financial factors that, to be understood, required an investment of time and major effort.

Additionally, in many countries, concentrating the responsibilities of chairperson and chief executive in the same person has complicated efforts to design a sound system of corporate governance. In short, the separation of these responsibilities has both advantages and disadvantages. In theory, in a company whose capital is concentrated in just a handful of shareholders, concurrent ownership and management can be a highly positive formula for ensuring the company's long-term success. The interests of both shareholders and managers are aligned. This is the case with many successful family-owned enterprises.

However, in companies with a dispersed ownership structure that lacks important, prominent shareholders, the concentration of responsibilities can lead to unwanted problems resulting from the lack of harmony between the owners' and chief executive's interests. It would be unwise to reject this formula outright; in some cases, the concentration of functions has yielded positive results. Yet it is also clear that should conflicts of interest arise, or should the company begin to decline, the governing mechanisms are more effective when the chair of the board and the chief executive are not one and the same.

Against the backdrop of the problems derived from the separation of ownership and control, a movement arose in the United Kingdom in the early 1990s that aimed to strengthen the mechanisms of corporate governance. In 1991, three British institutions – the Financial Reporting Council, the London Stock Exchange and the Institute of Chartered Accountants – established the 'Committee on the Financial Aspects of Corporate Governance' (widely known as the Cadbury Committee), presided over by Sir Adrian Cadbury. The committee's goals included defining the responsibilities of CEOs and nonexecutive board members; determining companies' accountability to shareholders and third parties in terms of content, format and frequency; organizing the audit committee within the board; and, finally, delimiting the responsibilities of auditors and internal control systems.

A 1992 report drafted by the Cadbury Committee was warmly welcomed by both investors and the business community. This was the first attempt to respond somewhat systematically to the challenges of corporate governance in the late twentieth century, and it served as a preamble to subsequent contributions to this key business field in later years.

In the sections that follow, we analyze different models of corporate governance, their nature, their expression in certain key countries and the prospects for a convergence in the diverse models of corporate governance that can be observed today.

4. CORPORATE GOVERNANCE MODELS: AN
INTERNATIONAL PERSPECTIVE

Corporate governance operates not only within a particular regulatory framework, but also in an economic, financial and political space defined by the relations among economic agents (companies, public sector, investors and so forth). This context shapes the way in which companies are managed and how the challenges of corporate governance are understood and tackled.

Financial models and ownership concentration are two key drivers that shape a country's corporate governance model. The financial model is defined by institutions (banks, savings banks, capital markets, public sector, or private investors) that provide funding for nonfinancial companies, as well as the rules that regulate the relationships among those institutions, between those institutions and the regulators, and between financial institutions and nonfinancial companies.

A study of ownership concentration in various European countries and the United States reveals the diversity of financial models in which corporate governance operates. In the United States, listed companies have a large diversity of shareholders, none of which has a controlling stake. Family firms – that is, firms controlled by shareholders related to the same family – hardly exist. In other words, most family businesses that go public cease to exist as family businesses, as the family no longer plays any significant role as shareholder, let alone as controlling shareholder.

In Continental Europe the landscape is different. There is a larger proportion of privately owned firms, many of them family businesses. In many large family firms in Germany, France, Spain and Italy that have been transformed into public companies (such as Carrefour, Peugeot, Ferrovial and Fiat), a significant percentage of the shares remains in the hands of the founding family, which thus retains a degree of control. Therefore, US and European rules regarding ownership concentration have a different impact on the way boards of directors operate and companies are governed.

In the United States, with widely held corporations, it is more complex to build a hard core of shareholders. Institutional investors – that is, collective investment firms that manage the savings of thousands of citizens and invest in financial assets – dominate the financial landscape. Ownership fragmentation has helped institutional investors gain prominence as the large minority shareholders. However, institutional investors' performance in their dual role as asset managers and shareholders is clearly biased toward their first and original role as asset managers. Only recently have some of them started to use their voting power to support certain decisions and block others. For institutional investors, as we said in the previous chapter, involvement in corporate governance carries a heavy cost: it can lead to conflicts of interest and it requires management capabilities beyond their core competencies.

In Continental Europe, institutional investors play a much less prominent role. This is not only because the volume of funds under management is smaller, but because in many companies there is a hard core of shareholders (often organized around a family) that controls the board of directors and the appointment or removal of CEOs. As mentioned in this chapter's opening case, Porsche was 100 per cent controlled by the Porsche and Piëch families.

A country's choice of corporate governance model is directly influenced by the financial model that the country has developed, with its particular combination of capital markets and bank financing and its pattern of shareholder concentration. In this section we shall explore two issues. First, we will discuss the nature of financial models in today's more advanced economies and how they influence company ownership, governance and financial structure. Second, we will examine the different corporate governance models that we find in Europe and the United States, which are partly influenced by each country's financial model. Together, the financial model and the corporate governance model create a context that greatly influences the corporate governance issues that companies and individuals must deal with.

4.1 The notion of a financial model

A country's financial model defines the role that banks and capital markets play in financing and controlling companies. It largely determines the financial context of corporate governance. The financial model is defined by the institutions (banks, savings banks, capital markets, public sector and private investors) that provide funding for nonfinancial companies, as well as the nature of the relationships among themselves, between those institutions and the regulator, and between financial institutions and nonfinancial companies. Among other things, these relationships define the role that markets and banks play in channelling funds toward business investment, and the role of banks and capital markets in corporate governance.

Broadly speaking, we can distinguish between two types of financial systems: those based on capital markets and those based on banks. Each has different implications for corporate governance. Table 4.1 shows the main features of both models. In the capital markets-based model, the various financial markets are highly developed. Due to historical and regulatory reasons, banks play a smaller role in financing nonbank businesses. The paradigm of this model is the US financial system. At the opposite extreme is the model where financial intermediaries, mainly banks, exercise considerable influence. This is the case in Germany, Spain and Japan.

Market-based financial models
The characteristics of this model are as follows. Company financing comes mainly from capital markets. There is an almost total separation between investors operating in capital markets and companies. Investors do not have an influence either on companies' day-to-day management or in determining their long-term strategy, although they can block some decisions through the board of directors or the shareholders' general assembly. Their only influence comes through the markets' valuation (which may be more or less accurate) of companies' decisions and performance. Only in recent years have

Table 4.1. *Financial models*

System	Country	Banks as financial intermediaries	Banks as lenders	Banks as shareholders
1. Market-based system	USA, UK	Yes	No	No
2. Bank-based system				
– Universal banks	Germany, Spain, France, Italy, Japan	Yes	Yes	Yes
– Bank-industry groups	Germany, Japan	Yes	Yes	Yes

Source: Canals (1997).

institutional investors shown any real interest in supervising the companies they invest in.

Market-based financial models provide constantly updated prices for most financial assets and allocate financial resources among alternative projects competing for the same funds. At the same time, capital markets allow investors to diversify risk, so that the individual investor is ultimately responsible for his or her own investment decisions.

Besides these advantages, the capital markets-based system also has certain limitations. The first is the problem of corporate control and supervision that springs from ownership fragmentation. As we discussed earlier, when there are no shareholders large enough to take an active interest in the company, corporate governance will suffer. The second is the absence of committed or long-term funding, that large shareholders – including banks – can sometimes offer when they have invested in a firm for the long term. In capital markets models, entry and exit of investors is considered a key attribute, which has some advantages, but also disadvantages.

The bank-based financial models
This model relies mainly on financial intermediation by banks. Bank intermediation is the primary mechanism for channelling financial resources from household savings to firms. In this model, capital markets play a minor role.

The classic idea of banks is that they attract savings by issuing deposits or other financial instruments and channel them toward companies which need resources to finance their investments. They also diversify savers' risks.

However, this classical view of financial intermediation has been expanded to explain the purpose and function of modern financial intermediaries. Some authors (e.g. Diamond 1984) argue that banks exist in order to overcome the problems of asymmetric information and moral hazard that arise between savers and the companies that take savers' funds. The fact that savers generally have incomplete information about companies' situations could make it difficult for companies to raise the financing they need.

Bank intermediation may therefore have significant benefits for companies, since banks alleviate the agency problem. When acquiring information about companies is costly for finance providers, company financing will be more efficient if potential investors delegate the information-gathering task to specialized organizations. In other words, banks' role in company finance may be justified by their information acquisition and company supervision functions.

The delegation of these functions to banks results in substantial economies of scale: significant fixed costs can be absorbed through higher transaction volume. For example, banks can hold a portfolio of loans whose returns are uncorrelated. For this to occur, there has to be real competition between financial institutions so that the cost of financing does not include monopoly rents. Indeed, having banks as intermediaries can solve agency problems, but this argument cannot be pushed too far. If it were valid always and everywhere, companies would work with only one bank, which in real life never happens (Hellwig 1991). In any case, an important fact of financial intermediation is that banks can achieve significant economies of scale in information collection and processing.

This model also has certain limitations. The first and most important is the excessive risk banks incur by lending to and investing in companies. Banks' investment as shareholders in nonfinancial firms has been responsible for numerous banking crises – for example, France and Spain in the 1970s, 1980s and 1990s, Japan in the 1990s and the financial crisis in the United States and Europe in 2008 and 2009.

Another limitation of bank-based financial models is that control mechanisms are no longer based on the market prices of certain financial assets, but on each bank's ability to control the companies in which it has an interest. Naturally, this demands a much greater effort on the part of the controlling shareholder. The experience also shows that the bank-based model drives the economy to overinvest, leading to excess production capacity in industries dominated by bank-financed companies. Japan in the 1980s and 1990s was a case in point. The reason for this is that being backed by a bank can make a company complacent and prolong mediocre management indefinitely.

4.2 Some corporate governance models

Once we have discussed different countries' financial models, it is easier to analyze why countries have different corporate governance systems and why banks or investors play the role they do.

The US model

The distinctive features of corporate governance in US companies in recent decades are as follows. One feature is that firms' ownership is fragmented: companies are widely held, with no shareholder owning a significant stake. Shareholders act through investment funds or similar entities, or else invest directly in the stock market. US companies (unlike companies in Germany or France, for example) do not have majority or controlling shareholders. This has had some important consequences. First, there are no majority shareholders on companies' boards of directors. Instead, board members tend to be recruited from business or academia at the proposal of the nominations committee and appointed at the general shareholders' meeting; they do not usually have a significant equity interest in the company. They tend to be described as independent directors to indicate that they do not represent any shareholder in particular. Until very recently, however, their independence was relative. In some cases, they were former CEOs of the same company, or of related companies, such as customers or suppliers. In others, their independence was questionable because they provided other professional services to the company, such as consulting, legal services or even auditing.

The Sarbanes-Oxley Act of 2002 was an attempt to reform these practices and reinforce board members' independence. However, even when directors' circumstances suggest they are genuinely unrelated to the company, we must not fall into the trap of assuming they are completely independent merely because certain formal requirements are met. True independence is a state of mind in which the director's opinion is not called into question by material or affective ties to the company or its chairperson.

The second consequence of ownership dispersion and the absence of controlling shareholders is that the CEO, who in many cases is also the chairperson (a distinctive feature of the US system), plays a more prominent role.

The fragmentation of voting power in US companies has resulted in a concentration of power in the hands of the CEO. Many authors have blamed the corporate governance problems in the United States on the fact that the roles of chairperson and CEO are combined in one person. Hence the calls to separate the two roles (Cadbury 2002). In recent years, experience has shown that the CEOs of US companies have enormous power to make critical strategic decisions. In some cases, this has made companies more responsive and adaptable. Yet it has also opened the way to abuses, with CEOs making strategic decisions without consulting the board or they have misinformed the board about the consequences of certain decisions and the reasons behind them. However, it would be a mistake to think that the combination of roles fully explains the limitations of the US system and its recent failures.

We could also point to the dishonest behaviour of top managers in companies such as Enron, whose board kept the roles of chairperson and CEO scrupulously separate and complied with numerous, important corporate governance formalities. So we cannot generalize and attribute greater benefits to the separation of roles than it has in practice. Although splitting the roles of CEO and chairperson may help improve corporate governance, ignoring the importance of other mechanisms is foolish. We must continue to insist on the importance of ethics in the conduct of corporate officers.

In any case, in response to recent experience, boards of directors have largely retaken the initiative in strategic decision making and set clearer limits on the CEO's power. The departures of CEOs like Carly Fiorina from Hewlett-Packard, Michael Eisner from Disney and Stan O'Neal from Merrill Lynch, reinforced by the effects of the current financial crisis, seem to usher in a new era, one in which the board of directors reasserts its rightful responsibilities and works with the CEO without being his puppet.

Another distinctive feature of the corporate governance of US companies is the way they are financed. Banks play a less prominent role in financing business investment and have next to no shareholdings in nonfinancial companies. Although banks play a crucial role as underwriters of share and debt issues, companies raise capital mainly on the financial markets. Evidence of this is the large number of hostile takeover bids and the existence of the so-called market for corporate control; the constant monitoring of companies by legions of analysts; and the decisive role of mutual funds, which avoid becoming explicitly involved in corporate governance but nevertheless are important shareholders and so have significant (and increasing) informal influence.

A country's financial system thus influences the country's corporate governance system and the efficiency of corporate management, although it is worth bearing in mind that this is a multidimensional phenomenon. Similarly, in assessing the advantages and disadvantages of the US governance model compared to those of other countries, we must not lose sight of the fact that a corporate governance system must include more than just a financing model and a legal framework that protects investors. These help create a level playing field, but the differential impact of corporate governance comes from the specific design of each company's corporate governance mechanisms within its national framework.

The British model

The United Kingdom has a rich tradition of corporate governance founded on common law, which has influenced corporate life in that country since the modern company first came into existence in the seventeenth century (Micklethwait and Wooldridge 2003). The Royal Charter granted on 31 December 1600 to The Company of Merchants of London Trading into the East Indies, better known as the East India Company, was a milestone in this respect. The East India Company had two governing bodies: a general assembly (Court of Proprietors) and a board of directors (Court of Directors). The Court of Proprietors comprised members with voting rights, granted by a certain minimum investment in the company. The Court of Directors functioned as an executive committee, and its decisions had to be ratified by the Court of Proprietors. The company was presided over by a governor and a deputy governor. This governance structure was quite similar to the structure in place in many countries today.

The British model of corporate governance has certain unique characteristics. One is that its financing system is very similar to the US model, with capital markets overriding banks in corporate finance and corporate control. Factors that helped make this financial system what it is today include the following: legislation that encouraged the growth of financial markets; banks' choice of specialization (focusing on their role as financial intermediaries rather than as direct investors in nonfinancial companies); and the sheer volume of investment required by companies (starting with the East India Company), which is well beyond the capacity of individual investors.

The deregulation of financial markets in the United Kingdom started in 1987 with the 'Big Bang', during which the British government took steps to promote market competition, speed up share and debt issues, simplify market mechanisms and reduce the cost of financial market transactions. In many ways, however, the system adopted in the United Kingdom was modelled on that of the United States. In fact, the Big Bang made the City and its institutions more like Wall Street and the large US financial institutions.

The British corporate governance system has other features in common with the US system, such as the importance of independent nonexecutive directors and the absence of controlling shareholders, a highly liquid capital market, an active market for corporate control, and a dynamic system for maintaining fair competition that favours rivalry over collusion within industries.

There are also important differences. The first is that in Britain the roles of chairperson and CEO are generally separate. This was already traditional before the Cadbury Committee, and, later, the Combined Code on Corporate Governance, made it official. In Britain the role of CEO has not achieved the status it has in the United States, and executive pay is lower. Basically, there is a better balance between the directors and chairperson, on the one hand, and the CEO, on the other.

The second significant difference is the importance of self-regulation, particularly since Sarbanes-Oxley. Britain follows the classic Anglo-Saxon tradition of 'comply or explain'. There are fewer legal requirements than in the United States and an emphasis on self-regulation and transparency in corporate governance.

The German model

The German corporate governance system is the polar opposite of the US or British system. The first major difference lies in the role that banks and capital markets play in corporate finance, corporate control, and, ultimately, corporate governance. As discussed earlier, until very recently the German financing model was the paradigm of the bank-based system (as opposed to the market-based system).

In the last decade, globalization of financial markets, fierce competition from the City of London and the precarious situation of certain German banks have wrought a profound change in the German financial system. Notably, capital markets have become more important, and the market for corporate control has become more active. It would be premature, however, to announce the demise of the traditional German financial system. Companies' financial behaviour, banks' formal and informal presence in companies and the slow growth of capital markets suggest that there will be a transitional period and that some of the historical characteristics of the German financial system will persist for years to come.

A distinctive feature of German corporate governance is that companies have two governing bodies with executive powers: the management board ('Vorstand') and the supervisory board ('Aufsichtsrat'). At first glance, this does not seem so different from British or US companies, with their boards of directors and executive committees. The differences are significant, however.

The management board in Germany has more say in decision making than the executive committee in the United States does, where more strategic decisions have become the prerogative of the board of directors. The management board in Germany tends to be more collegial than in the United States, where the CEO leads both formally and informally.

Another important feature of German companies, one that strongly influences their corporate governance, is the presence of controlling shareholders. These may be financial institutions or founding families who retained a significant interest in the company after it went public. The presence of controlling shareholders is a crucial difference between the German system and the US and British systems. Other Continental European countries, such as France and Spain, have systems more like Germany's, with concentrated ownership.

German companies above a certain size are also subject to 'co-determination', which means that employees are represented (in varying proportions) on the supervisory board. This has served to integrate employees in the company and get them involved in corporate governance. Today, however, it raises problems for corporate governance in terms of the capacity to reach decisions and in terms of professional expertise.

As discussed earlier, a large controlling shareholder can help to harmonize the interests and incentives of shareholders and management. Having a controlling shareholder can also create a virtuous circle of committed capital, especially if the controlling shareholder reinvests a substantial percentage of profits. In times of rapid change, however, controlling shareholders may find themselves in a more difficult position, owing to possible conflicts of interest or a lack of ideas for how to meet new challenges.

4.3 Are corporate governance models converging?

Our overview of corporate governance models shows not only the historical differences but also the similarities, which have been increasing in recent years. Those observations may suggest that corporate governance systems may be converging (Gilson 2000; Palepu *et al.* 2002).

Various reasons may explain why this convergence might be happening. The first reason is accelerated globalization. The World

Trade Organization (WTO) rules define a level playing field in international trade and foreign investment for all WTO member countries and others that would like to join this organization. One might assume that corporate governance standards are likewise bound to converge.

Second, firms' international expansion and their regional or global strategies might contribute to that convergence. Should a multinational company be subject to different corporate governance rules in each country in which it operates, it would be highly inefficient for companies and investors alike. Obviously, this is not just a matter of satisfying legal formalities. Governance mechanisms must genuinely enhance transparency, investor information and corporate decision making. The main challenge today is not a divergence of corporate governance standards between the United States and the European Union, but divergence among EU member states. There can be no international convergence until there is broad agreement within the EU. As we shall see, the legal mechanisms of corporate governance are rooted in each country's company law.

A third factor driving the convergence of corporate governance systems is pressure from capital markets. Having different systems is inefficient for investors and can give rise to significant information costs. Also, banks and analysts are increasingly required to include nonquantitative factors, such as the quality of corporate governance, in their valuations of companies. If universally accepted guidelines existed, companies and markets would be more transparent and investor information would be improved, boosting investment volumes in the medium term.

Finally, a significant driver of international convergence is the rapid spread of best corporate governance practices, led by auditing firms, consultancies, rating agencies and business schools. Better regulation helps to clarify what constitutes a conflict of interest between directors and shareholders, or between a parent company and its investees. In this as in other fields of management, good practices spread very quickly.

On the other hand, convergence faces certain obstacles. First, each country starts from a different legal, historical and business position. Certain social features of the way companies operate cannot be changed quickly. Two simple but illuminating examples are the strong leadership role of the CEO in US companies and the presence of trade union representatives on the supervisory boards of large German firms. None of these things are immune to change, of course. Yet they are so deeply ingrained in business and society that any change is likely to require a long transitional period.

Second, regulators play a decisive role in many sectors of the economy, notably energy, telecommunications and financial industries. Any changes to the law tend to be the result of long and complex negotiations; but such negotiations tend to be a desperate search for consensus rather than a quest for the best solution. Regulators seek minimum agreements to preserve their ability to influence the market economy.

Finally, convergence is impeded by the very different corporate ownership structures in the United States, Europe and other parts of the world. Corporate governance is neither the same for family and nonfamily firms, nor for companies that have a controlling shareholder who takes an active interest in day-to-day management and companies that do not.

In summary, there are significant forces pushing for the adoption of uniform corporate governance guidelines at the world level. At the same time, however, governments are determined to influence how firms operate. The result is that we can expect a gradual convergence, driven largely by the irresistible attraction of good practices in corporate governance and other areas.

5. ALTERNATIVE PERSPECTIVES ON CORPORATE GOVERNANCE

The corporate governance models dominant in different countries tend to shape the view that CEOs, board members, shareholders and regulators have on how to improve governance. In most cases, there is a prevalent view of governance focused around its legal and financial dimensions. This is a very relevant view, but we need to consider a more integrative perspective of governance.

5.1 A legal and financial view of corporate governance

Corporate governance can be viewed as a set of rules and processes that regulate the relationships between investors (shareholders), boards of directors and executives, as well as each party's relative ability to impose its point of view during company decision making. Shareholders choose board members and senior managers to manage the company. As a result, some corporate governance experts uphold the idea that corporate governance must ensure that these investors are duly protected from possible abuses of power by such managers. In a classic study on this issue, Shleifer and Vishny (1997) gave strength to this perspective, claiming that corporate governance is related to the means by which shareholders get legal protection for their investment. Without going into further detail, we can state that this perspective on corporate governance is closely related to the claim that a company's main goal is to maximize shareholder profit or its market value.

What is more, diversity in the structure of corporate ownership, the presence of banks as shareholders and companies' dependence on financial markets shape a financial model that influences companies and reinforces the financial perspective of corporate governance.

According to the financial perspective, corporate governance should try to prevent potential abuse by majority shareholders who can make decisions that directly harm the rights of minority shareholders when they exercise their voting power at the general shareholders' meetings or on the board of directors. In fact, as La Porta *et al.* (1997) point out, protecting investors' rights is an important feature of a sound system of corporate governance; this helps to explain one dimension of an economic system's efficiency, namely the development of its capital markets.

Still, when we take into account investors' interests and protecting the rights of minority shareholders, we shift the focus to a vision of corporate governance centred on the power and control relationships between shareholders and boards of directors. It becomes clear that corporate governance must include these issues. Nevertheless, reducing the goal of corporate governance to the management of these relationships would be tantamount to assuming that the relationships between investors and managers are the only important ones for the company in the long run.

The Cadbury Report goes further and views corporate governance as a system through which companies are managed and controlled.[3] In the report, the members of the Cadbury Committee put the emphasis on shareholders, stressing the fact that corporate governance is a system or set of processes through which companies must watch over and safeguard shareholders' rights.[4]

Without a doubt, these two goals are equally important and necessary in corporate governance. However, this vision of corporate governance has some limits, since it restricts itself to emphasizing the legal obligations to which those governing bodies are beholden and the boundaries within which they must operate. Yet it does not define a mission for corporate governance itself.

Likewise, the successive reforms of corporate governance proposed in several European countries during the past few years have not always been universally valid. In fact, some of the recommendations set out in various codes of good governance (such as the Higgs Report in the United Kingdom) assume that certain legal provisions or practices involving good governance have only advantages. In reality, there is still limited convergence in the practices of good corporate governance. The competition among the different systems has been flawed. The guidelines for governance in each country have

---

[3] Cadbury offers this definition in the first Cadbury Report (1992) and reformulates it years later. See Cadbury (2002).
[4] Demb and Neubauer (1992) described this approach.

Table 4.2. *Some principles of corporate governance*

Principle	Empirical support
Independent board members	Solid support
The board meets at least once a year without the CEO and without nonindependent board members	No evidence
Lead director	Mixed support
Some committees are made up solely of independent board members	Moderate support
No board member should act as a consultant	No support
Board members' compensation is a combination of fixed remuneration and purchase options	Moderate support

Source: Shivdasani (2004).

been adapted to different circumstances and crises, and they have yet to be fully unified (Gilson 2000; Palepu *et al.* 2002) . Shivdasani (2004) summarized the comparison between the empirical evidence available on the efficacy of some of the principles of corporate governance and the use made of these principles in certain codes of good governance (Table 4.2). The contrast between theory, empirical evidence and practice in this area is very significant.

Let us consider the proposition that the majority of board members should be independent – that is, neither executives nor shareholders. Whoever upholds this idea thinks that independent board members are better poised to defend the interests of shareholders than either shareholders themselves or the executive directors. This may be so in some cases, yet it is difficult to generalize this proposition for at least two reasons. The first is that it is not easy to define what an independent board member is. Ultimately, independent decision making is an internal, personal quality that is difficult to identify with external characteristics, such as how closely the person is linked to the company. The second is that, by definition, independent board members spend a limited amount of time and energy on the company and cannot be expected to either have exhaustive knowledge or be fully dedicated to it.

The propositions contained in some codes of good governance spark a similar degree of controversy over such matters as the wisdom of separating the function of the nonexecutive chair of the board from that of the chief executive, the age limit for board members, how many boards a member can belong to, how many mandates board members can hold, and the compensation systems for board members and senior executives.

Perry and Peyer (2005) presented a controversial argument. In response to the hypothesis that it is sound practice for board members to limit the number of boards to which they belong, these authors gathered empirical evidence to the contrary, showing that the number of board memberships directors hold can be an argument in favour of the company's market value.

Any proposal on corporate governance has both advantages and disadvantages, and it is important to weigh the various arguments carefully before suggesting blanket implementation of any of them. One model might work well in one company and poorly in another. The culture, values, managerial team composition and ownership structure may have qualities that constrain the universal validity of a given proposal. What is truly crucial is for each company to reflect on what model of corporate governance it should adopt.

Specifically, the ownership structure and level of shareholder concentration in the European Union differ vastly among countries, thus making it extremely difficult to set a single model for all countries, or even a single model for all the companies in a given country.

Ownership concentration and large shareholders may invalidate the purported advantages of having a majority of independent board members. In fact, the notion of independence is less relevant in companies where shareholders control the majority of shares.

The differing degree of shareholder concentration in public companies is a significant reason to exercise caution when discussing the supposed universal validity of certain corporate governance solutions. Likewise, it reminds us that the legal framework of corporate governance cannot be designed without taking into consideration a country's economic and business fabric.

5.2 An integrative perspective of corporate governance

Strategy scholars argue that a company should try to develop sustainable competitive advantages (Ghemawat 1991; Porter 1996). Competitive advantage makes a company more unique and special in the eyes of its customers; without it, its possibilities for success in the long term and survival are smaller, since easy imitation and competition will tend to erode its profitability.

The 1990s saw the emergence of models that explained a company's competitive advantage from the standpoint of its resources and capabilities. Hamel and Prahalad (1994), in *Competing for the Future*, focused on developing capabilities that allow companies to build competitive advantages related to the industry structure and the company's position within it. An important goal for good corporate governance is to help firms and its senior managers develop and grow those capabilities across the organization. This goal goes far beyond the legal requirements of governance.

In general, the most recent developments in the corporate strategy field have improved our understanding of the need for a more comprehensive view of corporate governance, a concept that includes not just financial dimensions, but also factors that make the company's long-term success possible. Some of these factors are clearly financial, while others are human, technological, organizational and strategic. In this sense, corporate governance must also include the mechanisms through which shareholders and the board of directors can assess and decide on issues that affect the company's long-term survival.

The notion of corporate governance we are proposing now shifts further in this direction and rests on the more integrative vision of firms. By corporate governance we mean the entire set of systems, policies, institutions, organizational processes and decision-making criteria that a company has designed with the aim of success and survival in the long term.

This perspective of corporate governance means that the company accepts its legal responsibilities and complies with its obligations to shareholders and third parties. It also includes management systems and policies that guide the company. Nevertheless, this notion does place the emphasis and purpose of corporate governance on the company's long-term development. This demands that the company develop sustainable competitive advantages and make strategic investment decisions that will help its development.

In other words, a well-governed company is not just a company that honours its legal obligations, takes account of shareholders' interests (including minority shareholders), scrupulously defines conflicts of interest and has a highly sophisticated risk management and control system. These and other functions would be merely secondary if they did not achieve what is vital for the company: its long-term success and survival as an organization and its continuity over time. With a handful of exceptions, a company that has no long-term prospects for survival is merely a business – not a company with a mission to fulfil in society. What is more, to survive in the long term, companies must attract and retain good professionals. A good system of corporate governance policies and practices will be futile without good professionals in charge of designing, executing and improving them. The long-term approach is at the core of this notion, and a host of studies and institutions underscore its importance (The Conference Board 2003).

The mission and values of a company also offer a clear pillar for governance in times of change. A. G. Lafley, former CEO of Procter & Gamble, explained that when he took over the company in 2000, in the midst of a slump in profitability and market value, he had to reassure employees that the changes in the organization and the firm's business model were necessary, but that one thing would not change: the company's mission to improve the everyday lives of the consumers the company served with products of superior quality and value. Nor did the company change its values: integrity, trust, a sense of ownership, and leadership. In this way, everyone knew that the purpose, values and principles were not going to change, since they were the very heart and soul of Procter & Gamble.[5]

At the same time, corporate governance expects the board and the executive committee to have an entrepreneurial, innovative attitude. A company can be successful in the long term only if it is unique, different from others – that is, if its value proposition for customers is different from what its competitors offer. This differentiation requires innovation, a willingness to take advantage of new opportunities that arise and a spirit of constant improvement. For this reason, the view of corporate governance as a set of legal norms or a system of principles and criteria still conjures up the idea of a closed space within which the company can operate. With an eye on the future, the company must use its corporate governance mechanisms for yet another purpose: to help drive its growth, innovation and investment, without which there is no long-term survival.[6]

The high turnover of top executives in recent years is a clear signal of just how difficult it is for a board of directors to engage in long-term thinking. Their natural tendency is to deal with the recommendations and pressures from financial markets, analysts and investment funds that own substantial shares in the company. However, without a sense of continuity and the ability to project into the future, the company is unlikely to survive in the long term. What is more, without this sense of continuity – without a business project – a company may find it difficult to attract and retain good professionals and good executives. And without a strong human

---

[5] Interview with A. G. Lafley, *The Focus*, Egon Zehnder, 9/2, pp. 4–10, 2005.
[6] Canals (2000) discusses the role of growth and innovation in a company's long-term survival.

team, long-term survival, as well as the ability to improve economic performance, is an incredibly complex challenge.

5.3 Corporate governance and other supervision and control mechanisms

The financial and legal perspective of corporate governance, as set out above, centres its proposals on designing rules for preventing conflicts of interest among board directors and CEOs, aligning the firms' goals with those of the shareholders, and preventing the abuse of minority shareholders by large ones. The clarity of the rules and the transparency of the company's governing processes are key factors.

However, the integrative vision of corporate governance that we just outlined looks to the long term and, without downplaying the contributions from the legal and financial approaches, suggests the need to consider how corporate governance can drive the company's long-term survival and the development of sustainable competitive advantages. This perspective is somehow broader, as it takes into account other mechanisms in the decision-making process and not just those that are directly related to the relationships between shareholders and boards of directors.

However, ensuring that a model of corporate governance runs smoothly, which should be the ultimate goal of the debate about improving corporate governance, does not depend solely on a precise focus on the perspectives described above. It is also necessary that the governing bodies of a company – the board of directors and the management committee – work properly and in a coordinated way. Other mechanisms, related to the company's ownership and financial structure and to certain aspects of the industry in which it competes, can also help improve the quality of corporate governance.

With regard to the ownership structure, the first factor is the presence of major shareholders who hold an important percentage of the company's capital. In theory, large shareholders have explicit incentives to make good decisions and guide the company as adeptly as possible in the long term. Conflicts of interest between shareholders and managers are less frequent. Generally speaking, the presence of large shareholders is a positive factor, as it means a clear commitment to the company's success.

The presence of large shareholders may at times be a stumbling block when a company attempts to implement significant organizational or strategic changes. The experiences of French and Japanese companies are quite telling. Prominent shareholders of many companies in these countries have not always contributed to implementing swift, effective action plans for change when the competitiveness of their companies was in jeopardy. This example suggests that while the presence of large shareholders may be positive when it comes to making decisions and grouping investors' interests, it also poses problems, especially in times of rapid change. In any event, it remains true that a shareholder who is committed to the company eliminates agency problems or delegation of responsibilities to the company's managers.

From an industry standpoint, two important mechanisms influence the quality of corporate governance. The first is the degree of rivalry in the markets in which the company competes. Generally speaking, it is logical to assume that a higher level of rivalry in the industry will force the executive team to weigh more carefully the decisions it makes and consider their consequences for the company's long-term competitive position. However, it is also logical to believe that high levels of rivalry can lead to inappropriate decisions from the standpoint of corporate governance, such as approving acquisitions of companies at overly high prices in order to outbid other competitors or blindly investing in new product development to follow competitors' behaviour. Rivalry in markets is a healthy way to prevent executive teams from resting on their laurels. However, it would be unwise to exaggerate its virtues, as rivalry can at times cause herding effects; unfortunately, evidence shows that this process tends to set off a mechanism of value destruction.

Another mechanism that can contribute to sound corporate governance is the potential threat of a hostile takeover. This threat is always an incentive for senior executives to manage a company as efficiently as possible. As a result, the existence of developed capital markets with clear rules for launching a bid and the absence of excessive blocking mechanisms or anti-takeover measures are factors that can help improve the quality of a company management and corporate governance.

Nevertheless, it can also be argued that legislation that makes it too easy to launch hostile takeovers forces companies to focus their attention not so much on their customers as on capital markets. While it is true that attention to one of these markets does not preclude attention to the other, the experience of takeovers, hostile or not, and mergers and acquisitions is, generally speaking, rarely positive. Empirical studies have proven the tendency for the acquiring company's market value to drop in these cases due to the high bidder's price. Consequently, although the disciplinary effect a potential takeover bid might have on a company's top management team is indeed worth bearing in mind, it would be wise not to exaggerate its importance.

The development of capital markets – in particular, of appropriate legislation that promotes investors' rights – has been identified as a key factor in the success of a corporate governance model. La Porta *et al.* (1997), in an analysis of forty-nine countries, pointed out that protecting investors and minimizing the risk of expropriation are the key factors behind the development of capital markets in a country and, ultimately, its potential for business development. Roe (1990, 1994) underscored the regulatory and legal origin of the differences between systems of corporate governance in a variety of economically advanced countries.

These legal and financial arguments represent a step forward in reflecting on the disciplinary effect that market rivalry or hostile takeovers may have on a company's managerial team, and empirical experience does confirm that these are important arguments.

However, just as the average profitability in a sector cannot fully explain either the profitability of a specific company within that sector or the differences in profitability among companies in the same industry, so the existence of appropriate legislation to protect investors is a necessary yet insufficient condition for improving corporate governance. Differences in the policies aimed at protecting investors may, however, be very relevant in explaining the differences among countries regarding indicators such as the development of capital markets or the volume of physical capital over the GDP. However, not even these factors can distinguish among the different qualities of governance in companies within the same country.

Table 4.3 shows some scenarios illustrating the importance that a company's corporate governance mechanisms should have depending on its external context, defined as the level of rivalry in the product market and the potential of the capital market to exert control over it. This table shows that the company's external control mechanisms, which come from product markets and capital markets, can play a more prominent role if they operate in the same direction in driving sound corporate governance.

Without strict discipline in financial markets or stiff rivalry in the product markets in which the company operates, the degree of discretion available to the executive team will be greater than in the opposite situation. As a result, in this scenario it is crucial to design internal governance mechanisms that help top management teams achieve the company's goals and develop a rigorous, serious decision-making system, as the product and capital markets themselves pose no significant challenges to the top management team. In the opposite case, when operating in more efficient product or capital markets, the executive team has less discretion when making decisions, since markets themselves impose greater rigour in the decision-making process.

However, it is important to underscore the fact that the external and internal mechanisms guiding the executive team and, ultimately, the governance of the company are complementary. They are

Table 4.3. *Interactions among mechanisms of corporate governance*

		Product market: rivalry	
		High	Low
Capital markets: efficiency	High	– Efficient external mechanisms – Internal mechanisms are less important	– Financial discipline – Nonfinancial decision-making mechanisms are important
	Low	– Stiff rivalry – Financial control and supervision mechanisms are important	– Insufficient external mechanisms – Comprehensive system of corporate governance is more relevant

not exclusive categories; rather, each of them can play a key role in improving corporate governance. Indeed, the efficacy of a country's corporate governance model will be determined largely by the coherence and coordination between the system's internal and external elements.

Ultimately, the control mechanisms we have just described, whether internal or external to the company, can help the company make more rigorous decisions and prevent the abuse of shareholders by the administrators. At the same time, they can condition or drive certain aspects of good governance. Nevertheless, their effectiveness cannot be taken for granted. The procedures and mechanisms of corporate governance that define the rules of the game are not determined *a priori*. Thus, having a reliable roadmap is not enough.

The drivers – a company's board and the executive team – must also know how to lead the organization to a safe haven while respecting the established criteria. The interaction among legal rules, the context in which the company operates, and the internal processes therefore contribute to a better explanation of the way governance works in a given company.

6. SOME FINAL THOUGHTS

In this chapter, we have examined some of the problems and challenges that the corporate scandals occurring in the early years of the twenty-first century have posed for corporate governance.

To understand these problems better, we presented separation between company ownership and management in modern economies. This separation has led to the emergence of professional senior executives whose interests do not always coincide with those of investors.

The concentration of power by the chief executive, the neglect of certain supervisory responsibilities by some shareholders and the increasing complexity of certain business decisions have all contributed to defining a context of corporate governance in which a handful of decision makers end up with heavy responsibilities that affect the future of the organization.

This situation has given rise to two possible solutions from a governance viewpoint. The first is a legal and financial view of corporate governance. This view includes the entire set of rules and processes that regulate the relationships among investors, directors and executives and delimits the functions of each. According to this perspective, the regulation of corporate governance must be aimed at preventing major shareholders from abusing their power and harming minority shareholders. The reforms in the governance of public companies can be understood in this context.

The second perspective considers an integrative framework for corporate governance that includes not only the legal, financial and regulatory dimensions but also other ingredients needed for good governance. In this chapter, we have espoused the view that corporate governance should consider the entire set of a company's systems, policies, processes and decision-making criteria that allow the firm to project itself into the long term in an entrepreneurial way and pursue its continuity and survival as an organization.

Finally, in this chapter we have also underscored the idea that other factors can help improve the quality of corporate governance. They include rivalry in the markets in which the company competes and the supervision that financial institutions and capital markets exert over the company's performance.

KEY LEARNING POINTS

- The financial and legal perspectives seem to dominate the current debate over corporate governance. The improvement in corporate governance around the world requires a more comprehensive view of what a company is and what governance is about. We argue that corporate governance is the set of policies, systems, processes and decision-making criteria that allow a company to project itself successfully into the long term in an entrepreneurial way and pursue its continuity and survival as an organization.
- Regulation can help define better mechanisms of governance, but without effective leadership and professionally led boards of directors, even the best regulatory systems could prove to be inefficient.
- There is no a single model of corporate governance that could be successfully implemented in all companies. Some country characteristics play an important role in shaping governance models. In particular, the financial system is a key determinant of the final shape that governance takes in different countries around the world.
- Besides regulation, a firm can use several mechanisms to improve its governance. Some of them are external to the company, such as pressure from investors and capital markets or rivalry in product markets. However, these can play an important role in improving the quality of governance provided by the board of directors and the board of management.

5   A mission-based view
of corporate responsibility

When the last technology bubble burst in 2000, many companies
began to realize that an exclusive focus on short-term financial performance and market value might erode their reputation among
customers, employees and even shareholders, not to mention public
opinion. Some of those companies – seriously affected by the quick
fall in market value after the stock market crash – started to rethink
the firm's goals and social responsibilities. Indeed, it seemed as if a
new day had dawned in the corporate world. Some people forgot that
some companies had been practising a clear idea of corporate responsibility for decades and graduate schools such as Harvard Business
School and IESE were already offering courses on the ethical dimensions of management and the social responsibility of corporations.

In a fiercely competitive industry like cosmetics, Henkel, a
German company, has always integrated a strong sense of social
impact with its business activities. Founded by Fritz Henkel in 1876,
when Henkel and two colleagues developed and marketed a universal silicate-based detergent, the company grew from a start-up into
a large family business. By early 2009, it was a global company with
revenues close to €10bn and operations in 125 countries. Moreover,
the company had managed to grow while maintaining corporate
values that were very close to the Henkel family, which has members of the fifth generation serving as board members.

Those values spring from Fritz Henkel's view: to create products that make people's lives simpler and easier. This sense of
mission and values (see Table 5.1) is key to understanding the transformation of a start-up into a global company that wants to maintain

Table 5.1. *Henkel's values*

- We are customer-driven
- We develop superior brands and technologies
- We aspire to excellence in quality
- We strive for innovation
- We embrace change
- We are successful because of our people
- We are committed to shareholder value
- We are dedicated to sustainability and corporate social responsibility
- We communicate openly and actively
- We preserve the tradition of an open family company

Source: Henkel.

an intimate spirit. These corporate values are the epitome of what a responsible company should aim at.

Several aspects highlight the fact that Henkel is a truly remarkable company in terms of its social commitment. The first is the preservation of a family business tradition with strong roots in its community. This tradition started with Fritz Henkel and continued through five generations, and today it effectively serves Henkel's shareholders and, at the same time, conveys an admirable professionalism in firm management and governance. The second idea is Henkel's pioneering role in promoting ethical values and corporate responsibility, starting with a clear notion of competition with other firms but also of cooperation with suppliers and trade unions.[1] Henkel has always been a leader in this area, as evidenced by many recognitions. Henkel was ranked among the top companies in the world in the 2008 Dow Jones Sustainability World Index; it was the 2009 leader in Germany in *Fortune*'s Most

---

[1] Henkel as a cooperative partner is discussed in 'Henkel Ist Kooperativster Handelspartner', *Handelsblatt*, 6 September 2006.

Admired Companies; and it ranked second worldwide, behind Procter & Gamble in the 2009 survey on the World's Most Ethical Companies run by Forbes and the Ethisphere Institute. The third idea is that those achievements arrived during a period of strong growth for Henkel in revenue, business units and geographies. Moreover, Henkel's top managers shared the belief that this growth process was enhanced by those values.

A final quality of the Henkel values that should be highlighted is that they have a holistic meaning. The Henkel family and the board of management interpret them not as individual factors worthy of consideration but as ingredients of a system that makes Henkel stronger, frames what is and is not important, creates a demanding yet open and friendly culture, and makes Henkel one of the most respected companies in Europe for its commitment to those values and the way it puts them into practice.

A risk when dealing with corporate social responsibility is overselling its importance in order to hide an organization's intrinsic weaknesses. A true indicator of how committed a firm is to those admirable objectives is not how much money it spends in philanthropy or supporting valuable social causes, but how committed it is to its people, clients, shareholders, suppliers and society, beyond public relations purposes. Henkel has proven this over many decades and provides a good starting point for thinking about corporate social responsibility in broader terms.

2. CORPORATE SOCIAL RESPONSIBILITY AS A REACTION TO CORPORATE CRISIS

The current financial crisis in the United States and Europe has prompted the need for additional regulation. However, this may not be enough to restore corporate reputation. The development of respected companies calls for a deeper reflection on companies' mission, purpose and role in society. It is true that in the past few years, numerous social-oriented initiatives have emerged in the business world with goals that clearly extend beyond the company's basic activity. These initiatives include philanthropic activities and social projects that aim to awaken companies' social awareness – or, at least, to socially legitimize their behaviour and strengthen their reputation.

There has also been a surge of society's interest in companies' social activities. All stakeholders seem to have the right to suggest, and even demand, that companies take certain actions to demonstrate their commitment to corporate social responsibility. Governments study and sometimes pass legislative measures. Nongovernmental organizations (NGOs) vacillate between acting as watchdogs of companies' good intentions and benefiting from the funds that companies earmark for social actions.

Thus, a strong movement has emerged in the business world around what is known as corporate social responsibility. This is how some companies refer to the responsibilities a company takes on related to social issues, and for which they wish to be held accountable. The importance of the relationship between firms and society and the need for accountability are not in question. However, this movement, which is brimming with good intentions toward society, does have certain shortcomings, as we shall see. First of all, this orientation leads one to think that only actions with direct links to social issues should be classified as expressions of social responsibility. This is a serious misunderstanding, since any company's main responsibility is to fulfil its mission and purpose in society. And a company's mission in society consists of producing goods and services for its customers, generating added value and promoting the development of the people involved in this process. A company that fulfils this mission is by definition a socially responsible company.

This view supports the idea that a socially responsible company should not be separated from the company's mission as if it were a different phenomenon. One company might be involved in more philanthropic activities than another, or one might allocate more resources to projects with a clear social content. But we must not lose sight of the fact that a company that fulfils its mission plays an extremely valuable role in society.

This perspective helps us focus more sharply on a company's so-called social activities. Philanthropic activities are clearly voluntary in nature, and even though they are important for resolving certain social challenges and problems, they make sense within the realm of companies for three reasons: they help solve certain immediate problems, thus fostering a connection between the company and the society in which it operates; they help develop company employees; and they allow companies to share experiences with government and NGOs, such as valuable resource management, project management and the efficient achievement of goals.

Likewise, the concept of companies' social responsibility might also outline an artificial distinction between the idea of a company's responsibility and, ultimately, the responsibility of the company executives. This might lead to the conclusion that if a company focuses on the quality of its products, employee training and development, customer satisfaction and continuous improvement but fails to undertake social development projects, it cannot possibly be considered socially responsible. Projects of this sort are invaluable for society due to their exemplary nature, the problems they contribute to solving and the development of capabilities and broadened horizons for employees. However, a company is equally responsible when it fulfils its primary mission – serving customers, developing people and creating economic value. A company that performs numerous social projects yet does not fulfil its primary mission is a less responsible company from a social standpoint.

Thus, a company's commitment to social responsibility does not depend primarily on the number and scope of social projects in which it is involved. Rather, it is determined by its responsibility in fulfilling its mission and its role in society in all spheres, beginning with those activities that are specifically its own and that only the company itself is capable of performing.

These remarks are not an attempt to downplay the importance of companies' social responsibility. On the contrary, they aim to reinforce the idea that a company's social commitment is not limited to those having to do with meeting social needs outside the sphere of the company itself. This would be tantamount to acknowledging a type of schizophrenia that is good for neither people nor firms. Companies fulfil an extremely important role in society and are consequently socially responsible when they fulfil their mission within the bounds of legality, generating not just economic value but also human and social capital by training and developing the people working in them.

The idea of a company's social responsibility is useful, but unfortunately it is too often bandied about erroneously. A company's positive impact on society demands several different levels of action, all of which are worth examining; one of these is the social dimension of its activities.

In this chapter, we will try to reassess the notion of a company's responsibility to society, which includes all the interactions between a company and society. We will not only discuss actions that are defined *a priori* as social, but also strive to simultaneously relate the content of their responsibility to corporate governance. On the basis of this perspective, we try to reframe certain aspects of the corporate responsibility notion and its connection with the goals of corporate governance. We will see that this approach is important in strengthening a firm's reputation.

3. THE RISE OF CORPORATE SOCIAL RESPONSIBILITY

3.1 Some contributions to the notion of social responsibility

The emergence of corporate social responsibility in recent years has occurred in parallel with the growing influence of financial markets in the world economy and, more recently, the scandals sparked by the dishonest behaviour of executives in prominent companies.

Friedman's (1970) formulation, which claimed that the first and exclusive social responsibility of any company is to maximize shareholders' profit, had the significant effect of spurring reflection on the argument that was used to justify companies' actions in society. This reflection is the starting point for several authors when exploring the relations between companies' economic and social dimensions more deeply.

During the 1970s and 1980s, the idea of corporate social responsibility shifted from exclusively encompassing actions whose motivations went beyond the economic interests of business to a broader notion that opened up new perspectives. One notion that has exerted and continues to exert a great deal of influence on management, not to mention on public opinion, is the stakeholder theory as formulated by Freeman (1984). Stakeholders are people with interests in a certain company: shareholders, employees, customers, suppliers or other people who may affect a company's results, or who may be affected by the company's actions. This formulation defines different levels of responsibility for different groups of people. Thus, the primary stakeholders are those whose contribution to the company is indispensable for its very survival. This includes employees, shareholders, customers and suppliers. A second group comprises stakeholders who influence the company, although their presence is not strictly necessary for the company's survival.

An important perspective suggested several layers of distinction within corporate responsibility, based on the image of concentric circles.[2] The first circle includes companies' obligations in the economic, commercial and labour dimensions when performing their day-to-day activities. The second circle, called the intermediate circle, includes all activities in the first circle plus an interest in, and concern for, certain social activities, such as respect for and defence of the environment. The third circle includes the obligations in the

---

[2] For one of the earliest original approaches to the perspective of concentric circles, see Committee for Economic Development (1971).

first two circles along with social duties that are somehow related to the company's mission and nature, which the company must perform in order to fulfil its role in society more satisfactorily.

In a simple, practical formulation, Carroll (1999) proposed a notion of social responsibility that includes four different types of dimensions: economic, legal, ethical and philanthropic. This and similar notions that were developed over the past decade have the advantage of simplicity, yet also the serious disadvantage mentioned above: the splitting of companies' and leaders' responsibilities into different parcels. Carroll's definition has yet another disadvantage. It regards certain ethical responsibilities as distinct from economic and legal ones, as if the latter were not or could not be ethical in nature. The risk of a schism between the efficiency and ethical dimensions in this context is enormous.

More recently, the idea of corporate citizenship has attempted to frame the classic issues of corporate social responsibility within the context of the company's activities and interactions in society. This formulation points to a notion of a company as a social institution that behaves in society, focusing on more than just its strictly social actions; it is based on the principle of a company having rights and obligations similar to those of a citizen – that is, a physical person. This concept demonstrates one way of integrating a company's various responsibilities, which include legal obligations as well as duties that, though not required by law, underscore and reflect the nature of the company as an essentially social entity.

This brief discussion about various ideas of the nature of corporate social responsibility brings to light two issues. The first issue is the clear risk of a rupture between one type of responsibility – economic, legal and so forth – and another that is more social in nature. This rupture is not serious *per se*, but it can become so in that it entails omitting the positive social impact inherent in an effective company.

The second issue this discussion reveals is that the idea of a company as an institution with an economic goal is in itself insufficient. We need a broader notion of what a firm is, its nature and its mission, a concept along the lines of the definition proposed in Chapter 2. Ultimately, much of the current discussion of corporate social responsibility has a redemptive angle. Some authors have tried to evade the traditional importance of the profit maximization criterion as the guide to companies' social actions (in accordance with the Friedman (1970) formulation mentioned above). In emphasizing a company's responsibility and social dimension, the authors' aim has been to foster the perspective of companies in interaction with society.

The exclusive focus on economic factors, including finance, and executives' neglect of ethical values are at the root of the recent corporate crisis. Some companies have reacted to this phenomenon by spearheading improvements in their corporate governance system and adding social programmes that highlight the company's responsibility to society.

This chain of events, however, betrays several weak links. A company's social actions must encompass not just social programmes but also the entire set of interactions between the company and society. The economic and legal aspects are just as important as social actions. In fact, what society expects of a company is the efficient provision of goods and services. Employees expect fair compensation and opportunities for improvement and development based on reputation and excellence. And investors expect a return on their investment. Socially oriented programmes are important, but the core dimensions of a company's mission are more critical.

3.2 What lies behind some notions of corporate social responsibility?

This flood of ideas about corporate social responsibility betrays an underlying confusion about the very idea of a company's mission. If a company's sole mission is to maximize its market value, it would be logical to try to add all kinds of deal-sweeteners for those who view this goal as less than noble. When a company's mission is viewed in a broader context, however, social action takes on a clearer meaning, as we will see in the sections below.

In fact, as Garriga and Melé (2004) point out in a benchmark study that traces the roots of diverse ideas about corporate social responsibility, the different philosophical notions of a company, its mission and its goals also include different notions of social responsibility. The authors distinguish among four major categories of theories that explain corporate social responsibility.

The first category includes instrumental theories, which propose an idea of companies as instruments for creating economic value. From this perspective, firms' social responsibility is limited to generating wealth. Furthermore, any reference to companies' social responsibility leads to the conclusion that it must be subordinate to the goal of generating economic value. Friedman (1970) pointed out that any activity involving social promotion or investment should be conducted only if it generates shareholder value. The central argument is illustrated by the example that Friedman himself used: part of a company's interest is to act within the context of a local community in order to help develop that community so that the company, in turn, can attract the best workers, increase productivity or lower the total production costs.

In this same category, we could also include theories that base their arguments on a company's contribution to society. One example, especially popular today, is social marketing. The value of these marketing actions results from the brand image that the company may develop by associating its products and services with certain actions, projects or social concerns. In theory, these actions can stimulate awareness of certain social problems, yet the social impact of these programmes is highly mediated by achieving economic results through the mechanisms used.

The second category includes political theories. Their common denominator is the emphasis on the social power a company has in the society in which it operates. One upshot of this power is the acceptance of rights or duties in order to actively participate in the life of this society. Davis (1960) asserted that a company is a social institution and, as such, must use its social power responsibly. The more social power a company has, the greater its social responsibility.

The social contract theory, within this political notion of corporate social responsibility, has had an enormous impact. It frames the relationship between society and firms as an implicit social contract that generates rights and responsibilities on both sides. This formulation has the initial advantage of grouping responsibilities toward society in an integrative way. However, although it aptly describes the type of responsibilities a company may have, it does not properly justify either how these obligations arise or, in the case of obligations that are not legal in nature, who holds the company accountable for fulfilling or neglecting these obligations.

The third category of social responsibility theories claims that companies operate within a certain society, owe their existence and possible growth to this society, and thus must accept the demands that the society makes at any given time, depending on the prevailing social concerns and values. This is a practical approach that drives companies to continually consider the factors that might have a special social interest and potentially impact the company, and that the company might be poised to address successfully.

Perhaps the best-known theory within this group is based on the notion of stakeholders – that is, different groups of people who have an interest in the company or are affected by the way it is managed. This approach does not limit itself to distinguishing between the various agents in the company's activities and other passive agents who are affected by the consequences of any given business action. Stakeholder management entails ensuring that the managerial team promotes the utmost cooperation possible between the various stakeholders and management in order to achieve their goals (Freeman 1984). This theory also upholds the wisdom of involving stakeholders in managing the company, setting goals, resolving conflicts between goals and finding possible ways of overcoming these conflicts. In the end, the advantage of this theory is that it provides a simple approach to recognizing the legitimate interests that different stakeholders might have in the company. The downside is that it may not conclusively determine what should be done to resolve conflicts and what criteria should be used to assess the available options.

The fourth and final category encompasses ethical theories, which address the relationships between enterprise and society based on ethical principles. One of these notions is that of universal human rights, which in its richest and most ancient tradition is regarded as a natural law upon whose foundations individuals' rights and responsibilities are based. One of its most explicit formulations is the Universal Declaration on Human Rights approved by the United Nations in 1948. More recently, the United Nations approved a declaration called the UN Global Compact (2004), which is aimed at international companies and includes nine principles that companies can pledge to uphold in the realms of human rights and environmental protection.

Under this category, the common good perspective has a great deal of potential. Common good is defined by a set of conditions that enable individuals to develop their potential and excellence as human beings. According to this notion, companies have an obligation to society, just as any group of individuals does, and they must contribute to its common good via their specific mission, since they are part of a society and can operate and develop within that society.

This brief survey of the theories justifying certain models of corporate social actions offers a complex and, at times, contradictory vision of the idea of social responsibility itself and the different levels of responsibility for companies. We shall return to this contradiction in Section 4 of this chapter in order to provide criteria that can help to better formulate this responsibility and put it into practice. However, first it would be wise to survey how companies have interpreted the content of their social responsibilities in their strategies.

3.3 Corporate social responsibility in practice

Business initiatives in the area of corporate social responsibility have reached as intense a boiling point as those aimed at improving corporate governance. In fact, these two phenomena should be studied together for reasons related to the nature of the problems they attempt to resolve; we shall address this idea at the end of the chapter.

The definition of corporate social responsibility provided by the Green Paper on Corporate Social Responsibility, prepared by the European Commission (2001), offers a useful starting point for examining the practical aspects of the field. It includes companies' voluntary involvement in social and environmental concerns in both their commercial transactions and their relationships with their stakeholders.

This definition comprises three dimensions. First, a company is not accountable for its activities merely through its economic results; rather, a profit and loss statement that properly expresses a company's activities must also take into account the social and environmental aspects of these activities. Second, relations with stakeholders should not be viewed as an add-on; they are part of the company's core activities. Third, concern for social and environmental factors goes beyond what might be stipulated by law and involves companies' voluntary decision to focus on these issues as a distinctive capability, as a chance for their employees to build skills and competencies, and as a show of their commitment to society.

Snider *et al.* (2003) attempted to classify the actions through which companies strive to show their commitment to socially responsible behaviour. To accomplish this, they asked a simple yet key question: what concerns of the different groups of stakeholders do leading companies take into account in the realm of social responsibility? Using a sample of ninety-three of the world's largest companies, the authors presented the following results of companies' expressions of this type of concern. The issue of the answers' credibility is always important, and the changing perception of companies in different economic contexts is undeniable, but the outcome deserves some comments.

The first dimension includes a declaration of principles regarding the companies' mission and values, through which some companies attempt to explicitly set forth the ethical principles that are to govern their employees' work and attitudes. In these cases, companies tend to spotlight values such as transparency, integrity, respect, professional excellence and a spirit of cooperation.

The second explicit expression of social concern refers to a commitment to preserving the environment, defined through specific policies related to the company's activities or a system of rules and criteria that the company's employees must bear in mind.

The third expression of social concern is directed at a company's customers. In this case, companies strive to outline their commitment to their customers in terms of product and service quality; aspirations to ongoing improvement, innovation and cost reduction; and the constant quest for customer satisfaction, which in some cases includes clauses guaranteeing product or service quality.

Employees and associates are the target of yet another explicit object of social concern. For decades now, many companies have been declaring their desire to put people first, at the core of the organization, although they do not always manage to achieve this in practice. The importance of attracting, developing and retaining talent in the era of the knowledge society is greater than ever. As a result, the explicit efforts and commitments that companies implement to achieve these aims have multiplied in recent years. These actions' main shortcoming is that they have been based on a belief that employees' commitment can be enhanced by articulating performance-based incentives. However, when managing people, incentives, although necessary, are never sufficient by themselves; at times, if they are poorly devised, they can even yield disastrous results.

One increasingly important aspect of companies' commitment to their employees is the active quest for diversity. In close connection with this goal, studies and practices relating to companies' responsible behaviour toward people's private life have cropped up in recent years, including family-friendly policies.

Generating economic value and pursuing fair returns for investors should also be regarded as an expression of a company's commitment to society. Today, when companies formulate these criteria, they focus less on achieving or ensuring appropriate capital yields during a certain time period; instead, they focus on the quality of the explanations offered to shareholders about the company's behaviour, the impact certain measures or phenomena may have on company value, and the way the company plans to address its challenges. Today, many investors seek not just yields but also a way of interacting with companies that is based on trust and truthful, appropriate, timely and sufficient communication.

Finally, an increasing number of companies wish to express their commitment to certain aspects of social life or to certain social actions that are beyond the scope of their operations. To do so, companies earmark resources for certain activities, raise funds and promote volunteerism, thus expressing their commitment to the educational, cultural and economic development of the societies in which they operate.

The range of social actions companies promote is vast and has expanded in recent years. Clearly, many companies believe they must commit to social actions that go beyond their business activities, perhaps with a heterogeneous set of motivations that are not always consistent.

This range of actions raises important questions. The first is the coherence between companies' declarations and their actions. In some cases, social actions may be the expression of a genuine, authentic interest in social problems; in other cases, they may simply be a way of enhancing corporate image while concealing the company's underlying problems with society, such as promoting unsafe products or pursuing sales or investment policies with high human or social costs. When companies reflect on their social actions, they should consider whether their level of coherence directly affects their reputation and their ability to attract talent, customers and investors.

As companies assume new commitments beyond their specific mission, they may well be entering unknown territory where they cannot effectively handle the challenges they will face. On occasion, the company's very nature may keep it from achieving certain goals that require people to cooperate voluntarily. Companies are institutions that have a high social impact, but they cannot be all things to all people; otherwise, they could end up sacrificing their ability to effectively fulfil their central mission.

Some questions stem from this observation: How should a company's social actions fit into its mission, policies and internal corporate governance system? What role should the firm's mission play in company governance? Should a company have different codes of good governance with disparate contents, some aimed at the generic good governance of the company and others at underscoring the development of a socially responsible or sustainable company? We address some of these critical questions in the next section.

4. TOWARD RESPONSIBLE COMPANIES

A company is an organization made up of people who provide goods and services for customers in an efficient way, and, in this process, they create economic value – otherwise this organization would not be a company – and offer employees opportunities to learn and improve. This is the company's primary mission, from which its main responsibilities are derived. As a result, creating economic value is necessary yet insufficient for a company to fulfil its mission. Nor, on the contrary, would it be enough for a company to produce goods and services with a business model that did not generate profits.

In this sense, Argandoña (2006) distinguishes among three dimensions of corporate responsibility that are especially useful and mutually complementary. The first is the economic dimension, by which a firm aims to achieve the greatest possible efficiency. The second is the social dimension, which includes the company's inward-looking (employees) and outward-looking (customers, suppliers and so forth) relationships and responsibilities beyond strict economic efficiency. The third is the ethical dimension, which underscores the quality of individual and corporate learning in their ongoing inter-action, and in turn allows for personal growth and helps generate trust. The distinction among these three dimensions of responsibil-ity allows us to focus the debate on this issue more clearly.

Every company is founded within a specific society, influ-ences this society and develops alongside it. Companies must also fulfil their mission within this society. Good business leaders are interested in bettering their society. Thus, it is natural that in their interactions with employees, customers, suppliers, financial institu-tions and local organizations, companies serve as a positive focal point for spreading solid professional and personal relationships that are based on the dignity of each individual. As a result, it is logical to think that companies should not neglect the problems that each society is grappling with, especially those that their competencies uniquely position them to address.

Consequently, this idea of a company's mission hints at the firm's commitment to society. A company that meets society's needs with quality goods and services while generating economic value, contributing to the development of the people who interact with it, and respecting the legal framework and ethical values, is a socially responsible company. This is the first tier of a company's responsibil-ity to society, directly derived from its specific mission and aimed at achieving the goals that society expects of any company.

Ultimately, this conception is the counterpart of economic freedom. Individuals have a natural right to freedom of enterprise, and exercising this right provides an opportunity to contribute to society. This freedom would be incomplete if it did not go hand in hand with the responsible exercise of it. In both the corporate world and in society, freedom and responsibility are inseparable. As a result, the freedom to do business entails certain demands for acting responsibly toward others. Thus, at a primary level, the realm of a company's responsibility to society encompasses the specific areas of its mission.

Nevertheless, companies do business in the broader context of a society. Each society has its challenges, problems and plans, many of which may be related to companies. All companies benefit from a stable social and political setting, an educated population and a fair, efficient legal system, with relationships based on ethics and trust; these are just a few important factors for determining the quality of life beyond the material aspects in any advanced society. The question that arises is this: to what extent should companies get involved in projects that are outside their realm of responsibility as economic institutions but that either directly or indirectly affect them as social stakeholders?

The answer to this question should come within the framework of a specific context, in terms of both the company and the society in which it operates. Nevertheless, one could formulate a more general criterion: a company may contribute to social projects beyond those strictly derived from its mission as long as those projects do not prevent it from fulfilling its specific mission, and provided that the extent of its obligations to society do not hinder it from fulfilling its other primary obligations.

Following these criteria, it is logical to think that companies should have an interest in a country's educational system or social welfare system. Thus, it is natural for them to become involved in projects related to these social needs. However, they should not do so if these initiatives result in a reduction in the excellence with which they must fulfil their own mission. We are not talking about the cost of the social actions that the company undertakes, which might be a certain percentage of overall profits. Rather, the goal is to avoid committing to projects outside the company when the required resources might be better applied inside it. It would make no sense for a company to help resolve a housing problem for third parties without first resolving an urgent social need among its employees. Nor would it make sense for it to foray into specialized areas where it has no expertise. Consequently, a company's mission can help its executives channel social actions in one direction or another.

This criterion can also be formulated another way. Companies must be involved in social projects that are coherent with their mission and that involve developing their employees' personal and professional qualities. In the end, in this scenario companies act as a repository of professionals' knowledge and experience. Companies may be unable to directly solve certain social problems; however, they can mobilize the talent, experience and commitment of their employees, those who may have the capacity and experience to help. Companies that do so know they are enhancing their social capital in different ways: by giving people who participate in the social project the opportunity to learn and improve, by developing the intrinsic value of the project itself, and by helping the company learn through its exposure to new problems and challenges.

In fact, the modern corporation has made important contributions to humanity beyond the efficient organization of the production of goods and services, among others. One of them is the ability to organize groups of people, professionals from different backgrounds, into complex structures in order to undertake projects that clearly go beyond the individual contributions of the people involved. Efficient companies are made up of people whose work generates an output that is clearly superior to the mere aggregation of individual outputs. The organized work that takes place inside a company multiplies the efficacy of the employees' individual efforts.

In this sense, companies can contribute to the good of society through projects to which they bring their ability to resolve complex challenges, innovate and generate new solutions to tricky problems. For over a century, companies have shown that they can provide answers to complex problems, create an organization to do it efficiently and change when conditions demand a new approach.

Likewise, in a knowledge-based society, companies offer a critical context where investment is made in research and development and where people do not just learn a trade but also acquire knowledge, experience and a perspective of working with other people. Today, companies are the leading clients of universities. Their ability to assimilate new knowledge is vast. Additionally, companies today are one of the major driving forces behind continuing education. As a result, lifelong learning is not only necessary for companies – it is a critical dimension for which they must feel especially responsible.

A company is also a school of capabilities where people can learn about the process of living with others in society. It is not the only such school, but it is extremely influential, especially in a context in which companies are assuming a more prominent role in social life. Deep down, companies are communities of people with the ability to organize individual work and enhance its value through cooperation. Firms should be schools where individuals learn not just knowledge and skills but also personal and social values that are key to the common good, such as the value of professionalism, the spirit of service, the work ethic, cooperation, trust and lifelong learning.

Companies are institutions that demand trust and cooperation from their members. Without trust, companies as a collective project vanish; they can neither survive nor reach toward the future. In this sense, companies can be outstanding schools that integrate people into society, not from the utilitarian perspective of their economic contribution, but from the perspective of learning to live harmoniously with others. In fact, in many countries, whatever is regarded as proper in the business world is also regarded as socially acceptable, such as professionalism in one's job. Companies help to set a benchmark and perform a role that, unfortunately, families and schools do not always fulfil and in areas where governments do not dare intervene due to a lack of resources as well as a lack of conviction about the issues' importance.

As a result, companies must undertake some primary responsibilities related to fulfilling their mission: producing useful, quality goods and services; generating economic value in the process; and fostering opportunities for learning and improvement for whoever participates in its activity. These responsibilities have both personal and social components.

Likewise, companies are in a position to make contributions to society that no one else could make – or, at least, that no one else could make as skilfully. Among these contributions are fostering innovation, research and continuing education and creating a context where indispensable social virtues can be promoted.

As a result, social actions, which may be aimed at meeting social needs that are of interest to the company, could make sense for a firm as long as they do not distract it from its main mission, nor from the indirect social contributions that only the company can make. As social institutions, companies and their executives in particular, must be concerned with the relevant problems and challenges facing their society. And they should simultaneously explore how they can contribute to resolving these problems from the most efficient perspectives – specific and functional – they have to offer.

For this reason, it may be preferable to use the idea of a responsible company as an alternative to corporate social responsibility, while still preserving the intrinsic value of the latter. The notion of a responsible company must clearly include a variety of factors, such as economic efficiency and a contribution to developing people, innovation, education and the environment. The notion of corporate social responsibility, understood as those activities or processes through which a company voluntarily includes social projects in its operations, might remain restricted to isolated projects that are of keen interest to the company yet do not necessarily fit into its mission. Under no circumstances do we wish to insinuate that these social projects are not important: they are important inasmuch as there is a societal need to which the company can contribute its people or resources. However, we should not lose sight of the fact that a responsible company can tackle these challenges through these projects while primarily fostering the initiatives that are part of its specific mission in society.

Within this context, it is crucial to organize the company's priorities regarding different types of responsibility. Melé (1998) distinguished among the following areas of responsibility. At the top of the list are primary responsibilities. These include the company's specific activities as defined by its mission and the goals derived from this mission: to serve customers in society with useful products sold under fair conditions; to achieve the greatest possible efficacy in the business activity and create wealth; and to strive to secure the company's future and achieve reasonable growth. Companies also have responsibilities related to the means used to achieve these goals: to respect human rights and foster their workers' development; to respect the environment; to obey laws and honour legitimate contracts and promises; and to distribute equitably the wealth they generate.

Next come a company's secondary responsibilities, which encourage it to seek the most favourable effects possible within the social groups with which it interacts, depending on its specific activity. A company's responsibility to these groups will vary according to the links binding the groups to the company. Thus, it may include *core* groups (executives, permanent employees, committed shareholders), *peripheral* groups (short-term employees, passive shareholders, customers, habitual suppliers), and *external* groups (occasional customers and suppliers, competitors, local communities).

Last come the tertiary responsibilities, the company's actions aimed at improving certain aspects of its social environment that are not directly related to its specific mission and that it performs as a good citizen. These actions include initiatives such as sponsorship, charitable aid, advice on or management of social affairs, and contributing either time or money to social programmes.

A company's primary responsibility is to do what it is supposed to do well in order to fulfil its specific mission. Supporting social action programmes or patronage falls within a company's tertiary responsibilities: if these things are done, society will welcome them, but under no circumstances should a company believe it is fulfilling its social responsibilities just because it is participating in social action programmes. Nor should it believe that these actions can justify a hypothetical neglect of the purposes inherent in its mission, which none other than the company can fulfil. As Melé (1998) pointed out, the closer business responsibilities are to the specific activity of each company, the more binding they are.

Friedman (1970) criticized executives who dip into companies' profits to donate them to social activities rather than distribute them to shareholders. His argument is that executives must maximize profits and that it is shareholders who, if anyone, should be the ones to earmark dividends for social purposes. Friedman is partly right when he says executives are responsible for ensuring that companies fulfil their purposes, although he errs when he confuses a company's purpose with just making money. A company must be asked to fulfil its primary responsibility; however, this responsibility is more nuanced than short-term profits.

At times, the notion of corporate social responsibility has been viewed as a way of including ethical considerations within the dimensions of efficient management. The concept of a company's mission that we have set forth includes the efficient provision of goods and services with an economic profit. The company must perform such a mission with meticulous respect for the law and ethical criteria – the latter regardless of whether or not they are legally compulsory. Social responsibility is not a substitute for ethics. Ethics must be present in all of a company's dimensions and operations; it cannot be regarded as an add-on to be borne in mind when an efficient decision has been reached or as a restriction in the process of seeking the best possible decision. In this way, economic efficiency and ethics reinforce each other and enhance corporate reputation.

5. SOME FINAL THOUGHTS

In this chapter, we have presented an overview of corporate responsibilities that emerge from the specific notion of the firm that we introduced in Chapter 2. We have also examined the place that corporate social responsibility should have in the firm's mission, its practical development during the past few decades, and its connection to corporate governance. The increasing importance that corporate social responsibility has recently assumed is, unfortunately, due not so much to an intrinsic appreciation of its wisdom by firms and society as to the fact that it has often arisen as a counterpoint to scandals in the business world. When compared to the efficiency dimension that dominates many aspects of business life, corporate social responsibility has somehow emerged as a purported condition of equilibrium in the system that helps highlight the ethical dimensions of the business world. In fact, the notion of corporate social responsibility often seems like a replacement for business ethics.

The concept of corporate social responsibility that we have explored in this chapter is built on a company's mission in society and impacts its perception by society. Without this mission and a specific way of developing it, there can be no talk of responsibility. Responsibility requires freedom. As a result, it is wise not to sever the link between the notions of responsibility and company mission – a mission that will be pursued on the basis of freedom to undertake new business ventures, create and invest. Without this mission, the responsibility would lack a solid foundation. It would be unprotected, at the whim of diverse interpretations or interests. With a mission, firms are more accountable and can become more respected institutions.

A company's mission as we have framed it includes the ethical dimension, which should be present in any human or economic activity. Ethics is not a restriction but a condition that ensures the equilibrium of a system. An efficient solution without ethical criteria would be neither wise nor balanced. At the same time, a responsible company is one that fulfils its mission and ensures its long-term survival on the basis of professionalism and trust. Investment in both variables requires a company to interact with society in a variety of ways, thus helping to address social problems and challenges as a core part of its mission.

Likewise, corporate governance, understood as the entire set of procedures and policies that contribute to a company's long-term survival, is aimed at fulfilling a company's mission. Some of these means relate to social actions that the company's executives prudently deem appropriate, but they also go beyond them.

Finally, responsible companies are those that contribute to develop responsible people, both its employees and those who interact with the company in a variety of ways. Companies are an outstanding school for citizens; without downplaying the other actions companies can take in the field of social work, the contributions they can make to our society by helping to educate people in the knowledge age are unique and extremely valuable. In the near future, this contribution may become one of the most formidable drivers of corporate reputation.

KEY LEARNING POINTS

- The increasing influence of corporate social responsibility is positive because it highlights the importance of better connecting the firm with society. But it is useful to review what a firm is responsible for.
- The firm's primary purpose is to produce and/or sell goods and services that could be beneficial for its customers, generating sustained economic value in the process and helping its people develop their professional and personal potential while doing their job. A company that tries to achieve this is already having a great social impact. A company that tries to keep investing, educating its people, innovating and developing new entrepreneurial ventures is a socially responsible company.
- It is useful to distinguish among the firm's primary responsibilities, which concern the firm's mission; the firm's secondary responsibilities, by which firms try to develop closer relationships and social initiatives with the groups with which it usually interacts; and the firm's tertiary responsibilities, aimed at improving social dimensions not directly related to the firm's activity.

- The notion of corporate social responsibility is useful, but it may have a restrictive meaning: it could consider only some of the firm's activities to be social. On the contrary, a firm that does what it is expected to do (invest, educate its people, innovate and so forth) is already showing a high degree of social responsibility. For this reason, we prefer to use the notion of corporate responsibility in general because it includes also social dimensions.

Part IV Leading and growing a respected company

6 The board of directors at work: impact beyond regulation

1. BANKS' BOARDS OF DIRECTORS MISSED THE CRISIS

The collapse of US investment banks in the autumn of 2008 was one of the most remarkable events in modern economic history. While the responsibility of senior executives in that outcome is clear, what was the role and responsibility of boards of directors and their members? For many years, the boards of directors of leading US banks were collections of remarkable individuals, among the best and the brightest: well-known CEOs, former CEOs, or government officials, successful investors and brilliant entrepreneurs. So why did these boards, encompassing so many intelligent people, fail to prevent the current financial crisis? Why did they fail to stand up and oppose the aggressive investment bets and leverage decisions made by senior managers? Why didn't they stop compensation practices that were inducing traders to assume even more risk at the expense of shareholders and other employees? Why couldn't they prevent at least some of those disasters? Why couldn't the board of directors better monitor top executives at large banks? And why have very few board directors stepped down over the past few months in recognition of their failure to deal with these serious issues in their organizations?

These events in the financial services industry in the United States are unique: no other industry has imploded this way in any other country. It is reasonable to ponder why banks' boards of directors did not act quicker and wiser to stop those developments that severely damaged the world economy.

Board directors were supposed to be a firm's backstop. Unfortunately, in the US banking industry, many of them missed the crisis. It is true that the problem was complex. In mid-2000, the leverage of the US economy was ballooning, as a result of a very lax regulatory framework and a very expansive monetary policy. At that time, lending risk was not a problem; the problem seemed to be growth. Boards, like regulators and almost everyone else, missed the looming crisis. Unfortunately, besides the complexity of the crisis, it may also be true that many boards of directors were not working efficiently. In some cases, they were using processes that had been shaped a few decades earlier, when stability dominated the banking industry. Most board members simply did not have the capabilities to deal with those new challenges.

On the other hand, recent corporate governance reforms, including Sarbanes-Oxley in the United States, focused on establishing formal procedures and standards rather than improving the quality of governance. After Sarbanes-Oxley, it was more difficult to hire board members with deep financial services expertise because the law required independence and absence of conflicts of interest. Board directors had neither the knowledge nor the expertise to evaluate investment decisions or risk positions.

The expectations around board directors' performance have also increased over the past few years. The legal responsibilities are also bigger, and they may discourage good professionals from serving on boards of directors. At the same time, directors' professional qualifications and expertise – as well as their willingness to serve – should be indisputable. What is clear is that a board of directors should not be a place of retirement for senior executives or entrepreneurs.

More importantly, it is imperative to understand that boards are central instruments in firms' long-term health. They are not just the CEO's backstop but stewards of the firm's reputation and progress over the years. For this reason, anticipating the financial crisis was probably a very complex task for most board directors in the banking industry. Nevertheless, a better understanding of the tasks and responsibilities, beyond the legal ones, that board directors must assume is a very important step in improving governance, avoiding too much risk and helping firms become successful in the long term.

2. WHOSE RESPONSIBILITY?

In recent years, an increasing number of boards of directors of some listed companies have made headlines for very publicly disagreeing with their CEOs. In many cases, these clashes ended with the CEO's dismissal. The painful replacement of many prominent chief executives, such as Michael Eisner at Disney, Carly Fiorina at Hewlett-Packard and Charles Prince at Citigroup, is symptomatic of a wider phenomenon.

On one level, these news stories reflect the fact that boards of directors are taking a firmer hand in corporate governance in an effort to regain some of the decision-making power overtly or tacitly ceded to CEOs in the past. Various factors contributed to this change, including the mistakes made during the financial bubble, the scandalous behaviour of some CEOs and the skyrocketing pay packages some of them received, especially in the United States.

Hiring, supervising and, when necessary, firing the CEO are undeniably some of a board's main tasks. In fact, as we saw in Chapter 1, capitalism has been dominated by CEOs in recent decades rather than shareholders or boards of directors. For many years, boards were content to simply rubber-stamp the decisions made by top managers. Board meetings were not always conducted with the necessary professionalism, competence or commitment. This pattern of conduct is no longer acceptable. Today, shareholders know their right well, are more organized than ever, and are willing to trust managers and directors only insofar as they perform their duties with professionalism in a climate of trust and transparency.

Governments are also stepping in, hoping to regulate board structure and membership. But regulation is not enough here. The challenge is how to build outstanding boards. In these new circumstances, the functions of the board, beyond what laws require of directors, must be reconsidered. It is no longer enough for the board merely to accept or reject the CEO's proposals. A board of directors today is expected not only to exercise more effective oversight of the work of the top management team, but also to know the company and its industry intimately so as to be better qualified to assess, ratify or amend the strategy chosen by management.

The numerous changes in strategy at Sony over the past ten years offer some insight in this regard. In 2005, the world's best-known consumer electronics manufacturer was struggling. Sales growth was virtually flat, margins were rapidly shrinking, the company's stock price was being battered and the innovation initiative seemed to have passed to other companies in the industry.

To make things worse, Sony was in the middle of a major identity crisis. In the 1980s, following the failure of its Betamax technology, which lost the battle against the rival VHS format, Sony had decided to move into the content industry. Accordingly, it had invested in movie and music production, as well as software companies. For more than fifteen years, Sony had tried to combine its traditional strengths as a consumer electronics manufacturer with the capabilities of a content producer.

But the world seemed to belong to specialists. On the consumer electronics side, companies such as Samsung, Canon and Nikon had an advantage in certain new products and offered lower prices. Meanwhile, Apple, with its iPod, seemed to have taken the lead in the twenty-first century's successor to the Sony Walkman, the MP3 player. On the content side, Sony faced an increasing number of traditional competitors – Hollywood studios and music producers, such as EMI and Universal – as well as newcomers, such as Pixar. With increasing rivalry on all fronts, problems integrating hardware manufacturing with content production, and a complex and costly organizational structure, Sony found its potential diminishing. In 2005 the board of directors opted for a change of strategy; and they were convinced the company needed a new CEO, with different qualities, in order to formulate and execute this new strategy. On 7 March 2005, Howard Stringer, a Sony veteran, replaced Nobuyuki Idei as Sony's CEO. Nevertheless, by 2009, four years later, neither the change in the top leadership position nor the firm's strategy seemed to have worked properly, and a new board reshuffle took place. How much of the failure can be attributed to a deteriorated environment, how much to a more competitive industry, and how much to a mediocre board leadership and smooth execution?

This episode illustrates the environment in which boards of directors must operate today. Global competition is increasing, and directors must focus their company's strategy and operations more precisely, explain them clearly inside and outside the company, implement action plans swiftly, change plans whenever circumstances require and know their business inside out so they can judge what the company needs at any given moment. In addition to these capabilities, directors must have the ability to oversee, advise and develop executive talent so that the company's management is up to the circumstances.

With the CEO taking a new role inside and outside the company, directors' attitude toward the CEO must also be radically different. After a period in which it was the CEO who proposed the names of directors to the board, the pendulum has swung in the opposite direction. Selecting a new CEO is now considered one of the board's most crucial responsibilities. Whenever a change of CEO occurs, directors put their reputation and credibility on the line. Their standing depends on how effectively they handle the incumbent's departure and how successful they are in their choice of a new CEO. As the boards of companies like AIG, Morgan Stanley or Disney have discovered over the past few years, boards of directors' decision to allow a CEO to remain in the post despite unsatisfactory performance and behaviour can seriously damage the directors' reputations. Shareholders and public opinion will begin to question the directors' right to sit on the board of a company that demands special care.

In recent decades, we have moved from a scenario of inactive boards that avoided any challenge or upheaval to one in which directors are expected to demonstrate radically different qualities, competence, dedication and commitment. These qualities clearly go beyond what regulation pursues or can achieve.

Directors today must understand, approve and, where necessary, change their company's strategy. They are expected to participate in shaping the company's mission, vision and culture; monitor the internal control systems; cultivate a transparent and fluid relationship with shareholders; select the CEO; oversee top management succession and executive development; and, lastly, extend the company's influence as an institution in society. In a word, the task of the board of directors has become complex. It now requires a greater sense of responsibility to shareholders, employees and society as a whole, as well as greater professionalism, dedication and commitment than in the past. This means that a directorship entails a serious professional responsibility, with clear legal consequences in the event of negligence. The challenge boards of directors must meet today is clearly very different from what they were accustomed to until the end of the twentieth century: more complex and demanding, but also more stimulating for board members and more critical for business.

Given this context and the new expectations for firms, the board of directors must enhance the company's mission and establish the necessary corporate governance processes and mechanisms so that the company grows and survives in the long term. The functions of the board of directors are independent of neither the purpose of the company as an institution, nor the mission of each company in particular. Shareholders, employees and other stakeholders expect the board to help the company do better, build a viable future, become more efficient and contribute to society.

3. THE BOARD OF DIRECTORS AT WORK

According to the notion of corporate governance outlined in the previous chapter, the board of directors[1] must work to ensure the company's long-term development and survival. This perspective is essential for the company's future, as nobody else in the firm has this mission. Although there are certain international good practices for boards in general, every board must try to answer certain basic questions: What role should the board play in this particular company? What functions should it perform – beyond its legal obligations – in order to add value? How should its work be organized so as to have the greatest possible impact? How can it contribute to the company's long-term survival?

These questions may seem simple, but they have no simple answers. Boards must give them careful consideration if they really wish to benefit their companies. The following ideas and suggestions are intended to help directors marshal their thoughts on these matters. Our intention here is to structure some questions to stimulate reflection on how the board of directors can help improve corporate governance beyond regulation. It should be borne in mind, however, that a good practice for one company may not be good for another. It is also important to remember that imitating good practices is not enough to change a company; the important thing is to adopt a management system built on consistent, harmoniously integrated practices, not just a random collection.

Before we consider the tasks of the board of directors in detail, we must define some basic principles that should govern everything the board does.[2] These principles are not rigid rules; rather, they are

---

[1] Boards of directors are different from boards of management. A board of directors' members are chosen and/or confirmed by shareholders. The board of directors is led by its chairperson. The board of management, which in some countries is called the executive board or the executive committee, is led by the chief executive and made up of the full-time senior executives.

[2] For a more extensive discussion of these matters, see Canals (2003).

Table 6.1. *The board at work: some basic principles*

- Transparency
- Specialization
- Collegial decision making
- Unity

guidelines for designing good corporate governance mechanisms that will allow the board to fulfil its purpose (see Table 6.1).

The first principle is transparency. Transparency does not require the company to disclose all the information it has, but it does require the disclosure of any information that may be of legitimate interest to shareholders, including information about the company's situation and evolution and possible conflicts of interest. The demand for transparency follows logically from the principle of self-regulation in corporate affairs. Today, it has become a pillar of every company's reputation.

The second principle is specialization and the division of functions, both within the board and in the board's relations with the board of management. The division of functions demands that the work to be done by committees within the board of directors be carefully planned and each director be assigned clear responsibilities. Ultimately, these committees are essential if the board is to have a sufficiently in-depth understanding of the company as a whole.

The third principle is collegial decision-making. This demands that the chairperson and the CEO use the board's deliberative and decision-making capacity to its fullest potential in order to find the best solution to the company's challenges. Collegial decision-making counterbalances the power of the chairperson or the CEO and is indispensable if the board is to work as a team.

The fourth principle is unity. The board of directors must work for the long-term good of the company. Each director must bear this in mind and refrain from considering only the interests he happens to be representing at any given moment. A company is unlikely to survive for long if its board is divided and if each director thinks only of his own interests, or the interests he represents, as opposed to the interests of the company as a whole. This is undoubtedly a major challenge for the chairperson, but board unity is essential if the company's long-term goal is to be achieved.

These principles underlie the board's working philosophy and the way the board should work as a team. At the same time, they help address certain issues regarding relations between the board and the executive committee. The board cannot be a rubber stamp for the CEO's decisions nor an arena in which to settle disputes among shareholders. However, the board cannot be everywhere and do everything; if it tried, it would soon be incapacitated.

4. TASKS AND RESPONSIBILITIES OF THE BOARD OF DIRECTORS

The tasks of the board of directors do not follow a simple pattern, and there is no traditionally accepted definition of board duties, beyond certain legal requirements.[3] Practices also differ enormously among countries, and even within the same country or industry. Moreover, good corporate governance practices are not mutually exclusive. In other words, two companies may have different practices yet both be admirable.

Based on the notion of the firm's mission presented in Chapters 2 and 3, and with the aim of helping directors reflect on the role and functions a company's board of directors should have (beyond strict legal obligations), we shall now briefly describe the main tasks of the board of directors (see Table 6.2). These tasks include the following: defining the company's mission and values; approving the strategy and critical investment decisions; establishing an effective control and information system; fostering the company's

---

[3] Some authors have given an admirable account of the work of the board of directors, notably Conger *et al.* (2001); Stiles and Taylor (2001); Cadbury (2002) and Carter and Lorsch (2003).

Table 6.2. *Board of directors: activities and tasks*

– Corporate mission and values
– Strategy and resource allocation
– Control and information systems
– Institutional development
– Executive committee oversight
– CEO selection
– CEO compensation

institutional development; guiding and monitoring the executive committee; and selecting, evaluating, and paying the CEO. Naturally, another task deriving from these is periodically assessing the board's own performance, its contribution in each area and, in particular, its contribution to the company's long-term survival. We should make it clear from the outset (although we shall address this later in more detail) that the board of directors and the board of management both have responsibilities in many of these areas. However, overlaps in their scope of action are not incompatible with a proper division of work, as we shall see. That is why, when detailing the board's tasks, it is important not only to specify the areas in which the board must act, but also to describe specific actions it must take in each area.

4.1 Corporate mission and values

The process of developing companies into great institutions, as we have seen in Chapter 3, 'The firm as a respected institution', requires a mission, a sense of purpose for what the companies can do. Most companies are established with the idea of selling goods and services and creating economic value in the process, on the assumption that it is in business for the long term. In some cases, the company's founders, explicitly or implicitly, have a mission in mind – that is, a legitimate purpose for which the company exists, beyond that of making money or building a successful business.

After a company has been in existence for a while, its mission and values must be renewed and implemented throughout the organization; otherwise they risk becoming obsolete. Both the founding shareholders and the board of directors must continuously redefine and reaffirm the company's mission and values. This is a key function of the board of directors: to redefine or become the custodians of the firm's mission.

Likewise, the board of directors must define or confirm the values that are to shape the company's existence and mould its culture. In some companies, this task is left to certain divisions, such as organizational development or human resources. However, strengthening corporate values is so important to the company's future that the board of directors must necessarily take part in it. The mission gives meaning and purpose to the efforts of every person who works in the company, lends consistency to each person's contributions and is a rallying cry to mobilize the entire organization. The mission also gives the organization an orientation that goes beyond any particular strategic triumph or defeat. As Collins and Porras (1994) point out, companies that have survived for many years have a very clear sense of purpose and mission.

An important dimension of a company's values is how it considers corporate governance. The above-mentioned guidelines – transparency, division of functions, collegial decision making and unity – should therefore be taken into account when defining the values that govern the work of a board of directors.

4.2 Strategy and resource allocation

The CEO and the executive committee must analyze short- and long-term prospects; develop market, product and business strategies; and make important decisions that will influence and shape the company's future development. But because these are such far-reaching decisions, the board of directors must have the last word. That means not just approving or rejecting a strategy but engaging in a strategy dialogue with the top management team. The board of directors must act as a sounding board, promote second thoughts and reflect on different scenarios. Diverse, informed opinions are always enriching, and the board of directors is the natural source of such opinions.

If the board is involved in strategy formulation, it is more likely to approve the resulting investment decisions. This follows from the board's role in corporate strategy, which translates into decisions to allocate resources to particular investment projects. Thus, the approval of individual investment projects must be given within the framework of an overall allocation of the company's resources, not just for the immediate future but over several years. This framework must be very flexible, allowing the company to adapt and react to changes in the environment without unnecessarily tying its hands. At the same time, the framework must serve as a reference so that overall resource allocation is taken into account in every individual investment decision.

The board of directors has a duty to think long term and help management do the same. It is not the directors' job to run the company on a day-to-day basis, and they may not even be particularly good at it; after all, this is not their mission, and they would be treading on management's toes if they attempted to do so. But they do have an obligation to think about the long term, for the good of the entire organization. Thus, at regular intervals, the board must set an agenda that includes anticipating and assessing changes in the environment and the industry, and it must ask the executive committee to consider the consequences and possible responses to different future scenarios. Regular discussion of these matters will help to re-evaluate the company's strategy, pinpoint its weaknesses over time and weigh new challenges and ways of meeting them.

4.3 Control and information systems

The board of directors cannot do a good job and contribute to the company's mission and long-term survival without effective control and information systems. Many of the recent corporate governance problems have to do with ineffective disclosure mechanisms and control systems.

When designing control and information systems, a balance must be struck between two extremes: completeness of information (implying ever-larger quantities of data as a company grows in scale and complexity) and simplicity (so that directors can understand the information and use it in their decision making).

Traditionally, boards of directors have tended to focus almost exclusively on economic and financial information. Such information is essential, but it is not sufficient. If, as we discussed earlier, profit maximization as a criterion is not enough, clearly the board of directors must have information about other aspects of the company.[4] The board must construct its own set of indicators, which will certainly include financial variables as well as others. A good balanced scorecard for the board should include indicators of competitive positioning in the company's various businesses and markets; financial position; innovation and new product and service development; employee attraction, retention and development; customer acquisition, retention and satisfaction; and productivity and operational efficiency.

Every company must assemble its own set of indicators, depending on its industry and the type of company it is. Indicators mean different things to different companies. The important thing, however, is that the board of directors must be able to track changes in each indicator over time in order to detect areas for improvement and emerging challenges for the management team and the organization as a whole.

4.4 Institutional development

In order for a company to succeed in the long term, it must have the right financial structure and a financially sustainable business.

---

[4] Kaplan and Norton (1996) introduced the balanced scorecard as a tool for the company's top management team. Following this framework, boards of directors may design their own roadmap, with indicators covering a range of areas that are critical to the company's long-term future.

Yet a sound financial structure and a successful business model, on their own, will not ensure continuity and survival. Companies are groups – or communities – of people who provide good services in coordination with others. To do this, people in companies must develop their creative, executive and entrepreneurial potential and deploy it in the service of the company and its mission.

Firms also play a decisive role in society. Besides their classic role as providers of goods and services, companies today have a growing influence on society and individuals. As social agents, they create enduring patterns of behaviour and affect the lives of millions of people worldwide.

Accordingly, the firm as a social institution may take a variety of forms, in addition to those it may adopt as an economic entity. It is the board of directors' task to plan the company's institutional development and its embedding in the societies in which it operates. Indeed, companies' growing concern for social responsibility is a response to this challenge. However, developing a company as an institution goes beyond what is understood by corporate social responsibility.

Institutional development includes a company's policies, criteria and values with respect to specific stakeholders and business areas. Together, these policies, criteria and values determine a company's institutional profile – that is, the particular way of interacting with society that makes this company different from others. Key stakeholders include the following: shareholders and capital markets; employees and associates; customers; suppliers; communities in which the company operates; regulatory bodies; and, lastly, the media (see Table 6.3).

Institutional development requires that the board of directors nourishes new initiatives, defines policies and principles of action, and monitors compliance. The executive committee is responsible for the details of the action plans, following guidelines laid down by the board of directors.

Bundling under one heading issues as diverse as the company's relations with capital markets and its relations with employees,

Table 6.3. *Institutional development: some key stakeholders*

- Shareholders and capital markets
- Employees
- Customers
- Suppliers
- Local communities
- Regulatory bodies
- Media

customers and the media may seem strange. The common thread is that in each of these areas the firm acts as an organization toward a particular group of people, demonstrating a pattern of behaviour and particular policies, values and principles – in other words, it shows a particular institutional profile. This profile is ultimately what determines a corporate identity. Corporate identity is sometimes presented as if it were the product of a sophisticated marketing campaign. Surely, marketing has a role here. But corporate identity is projected through the firm's policies, which are conveyed in a large variety of ways, only some of which are covered by marketing.

The quality of a company's identity and the consistency of its policies in each area produce a corporate reputation – that is, a certain prestige as an institution that goes beyond the prestige of the company's products. There can be no sustainable corporate reputation without good products; but good products are not enough to sustain a solid corporate reputation.

In a world in which the power of image and reputation is intensifying, the board of directors must oversee the company's institutional development and make sure that the end product is consistent, not merely the result of an assortment of generally sound but otherwise disparate policies. The value of a company will increasingly depend on the value of its corporate reputation – that is, its reputation as an institution that not only creates economic value but also adds other kinds of value to the societies in which it operates. That is why this area deserves the board's serious attention.

4.5 The board of directors and the board of management: some basic relationships

The board of directors and the board of management, or the executive committee, are the two lungs of good corporate governance. With only one of its two lungs, corporate governance will obviously be much less effective. Both lungs are needed to drive the company's long-term success and survival.

The board of directors must act as mentor, supervisor and driving force of the executive committee. It must not interfere in the board of management's functions, as this would betray its role and the board of management's mission. But it must be a mentor to the board of management, helping it develop its members' managerial capabilities and providing a testing ground for their ideas, concepts, plans and proposals for the company's future. It must be an effective supervisor of the board of management's tasks, serving the interests of shareholders and other stakeholders. And it must be the engine that drives the executive committee to take on new projects and set itself new challenges.

For the two lungs to work together efficiently, there must be a steady pace, coordination and empathy, all of which are difficult to describe in writing. It is like creating a work of art where the artists (the chairperson of the board and the CEO) must work together, sometimes making no visible progress or even slipping backward, yet never losing sight of the ultimate goal.

The relationships between the board of directors and the board of management must be built on certain principles. The first is a balance between initiative and control. The board of directors must promote and encourage initiative, while at the same time exercising oversight and control. These two functions tend to go in opposite directions. It is the board's job to harmonize the two so that the company is not hamstrung by excessive supervision nor torn apart by unbridled initiative.

The second principle is the delegation of functions to the board of management and a clear division of competencies in accordance with the principle of subsidiarity. This means that nothing should be done by a higher-ranking body that is more naturally or effectively done by a lower-ranking body. The executive committee obviously cannot supervise itself. And because it cannot supervise itself, it cannot approve the company's strategy or budget. This criterion points to a possible division of roles between the governing bodies, which the board of directors must respect and enforce.

The third principle is transparency. Among the board and the executive committee there may be differences of opinion or perspective. However, provided that all parties seek the long-term good of the organization as a whole, such differences enrich the decision-making process. For that to be the case, relations between the two entities must be conducted in a spirit of transparency of objectives, positions and opinions. The board must set an example of transparency. Here, too, the principle to be followed is that the higher authority must set guidelines for the lower authority, showing how the company's mission is best served. At the same time, transparency in relations between the board of directors and the board of management must be matched by transparency in the company's dealings with investors and society. These are two sides of the same coin; there cannot be transparency on one side if there is not also transparency on the other. Without transparency, the company would lose a capital asset.

Transparency both requires and reinforces trust. Trust is a rare quality of relations among people that flowers or dies for reasons that are not always understood. It cannot grow without a combination of at least three ingredients: professionalism, honesty and respect. All three are necessary, and it would be dangerously reductionist to think that honesty is enough. Honesty is indispensable, but without professional expertise, without the skill to effectively address problems and frame solutions, trust would soon wither and die.

The fourth principle is initiative, another important quality of relations between the board of directors and the board of management, and both bodies must demonstrate this quality. Good governance is not just about defending legitimate interests, but also about organizing the continuous improvement and pursuit of opportunities that are the foundation of any organization that aims for long-term success. Continuous improvement demands fresh initiatives and new approaches that help the board and the executive committee to properly plan the company's future. Initiative must, of course, be organized and structured – otherwise, it leads to organizational chaos. And the best way to organize initiative is by clearly defining competencies and dividing functions among the two governing bodies.

Assigning roles and responsibilities to the board of directors and the board of management is one of the board of directors' main tasks. This task is never completed: the division of functions must constantly be improved, refined and perfected so that the relationship between the two bodies is permanently fruitful and effective. Every company has a history, a mission and its own ways of doing things. That means it is difficult to establish *a priori* what functions each body should perform and then generalize this division of roles to all organizations. Thus, every board must make its own decisions in this respect.

There are, however, certain generic functions that can be clearly attributed to either the board of directors or the board of management. Table 6.4 shows a possible division of responsibilities between the two bodies, including some of the key tasks of corporate governance: mission strategy, control, institutional development, development of talent, investment decisions and resource allocation, and mergers and acquisitions. In each of these fields we distinguish between deciding the action to be taken and actually putting the decision into effect. True to the principles mentioned earlier, however,

Table 6.4. *Responsibilities of the board of directors and the board of management*

Function/task	Board of directors	Board of management
Mission and values	Define	Implement
Strategy	Approve	Design
		Implement
Control	Strategic	Strategic
	Financial	Financial
		Operational
Institutional development	Promote	Promote
	Approve	Execute
Development of leadership talent	Board of management	Overall company
Investment decisions and resource allocation	Approve	Propose
		Implement
Mergers and acquisitions	Promote	Propose
	Approve	Implement

these fields and role assignments must not be viewed as watertight compartments. The principles of initiative and trust demand that the delegation of tasks and the division of labour be always accompanied by a determination to seek what is best for the company's long-term future so that this framework of relations is governed by initiative, not inaction.

4.6 The CEO selection process

The principle of trust that should govern relations between the board of directors and the board of management is upheld by several pillars, one of which is CEO selection. It is the CEO who assembles the management team and organizes the work of the board of management. The CEO implements and executes the decisions approved by the board, proposes decisions or policies to the board that will decisively affect the company's future, and ultimately serves as a liaison between the board of directors and the board of management.

A good CEO can make all the difference to corporate governance in various fields. To start with, the CEO can shape and direct the way the executive committee works effectively and implements board decisions and applies decision criteria. Second, the CEO can help design the information and control system that is genuinely useful to the board of directors. Third, the CEO can promote transparency between the board and the executive committee, and between the executive committee and all the other people who work in the company. The bottom line is that in a company, each person should be accountable for his or her performance. The CEO, however, should lead by example, setting the tone and direction for the rest of the organization.

The CEO should be able to answer the company's most pressing questions in the medium and long term. In the United States, it has become common practice to appoint CEOs based on how financial analysts are expected to react, even though some analysts are liable to criticize or applaud the board's choice for no good reason, based on little actual knowledge about the candidate. Although the tendency to seek charismatic leaders with a high media profile seems at last to be on the wane, there is no guarantee that it will not re-emerge. This would not be good news; such a bias constrains and distorts the board's efforts in this area, which is so decisive for the company's future. A charismatic CEO may be inclined to pay more attention to short-term results and relations with analysts and the media than to the company's long-term interests.

Selecting the CEO is therefore not only one of the board's basic responsibilities, but also one of its most critical tasks. It is a complex process that demands great professionalism. We would like to point to some of the issues and principles the board of directors should bear in mind when selecting the CEO.

Table 6.5. *The CEO selection process: some challenges*

– Reasons for replacing the CEO
– The new CEO's profile
– Managing the CEO recruitment process
– CEO's pay package

The CEO selection process involves some important challenges (Table 6.5). The first is that the board must define some clear reasons for replacing the CEO.[5] The second is determining the expected profile of the new CEO. The third challenge is managing the selection process and dealing with the executive search firm, if one is used. The fourth and final challenge is determining the CEO's compensation.

The directors' professional and personal reputations are very much at stake in the CEO selection process. Mistakes can be very costly for the organization in both the short and long term and can cast doubt on the board's professionalism. Some issues and potential risks of the CEO selection process deserve explicit mention.

Replacing the CEO

The first challenge of the CEO selection process is to develop a clear understanding of the reasons why the current CEO must be replaced. Boards of directors must be very sure of the criteria by which they evaluate their CEOs; and the criteria must be precise, known and subject to regular review. In order for a CEO and a board of directors to work closely with each other, each side's expectations must be clearly defined. Otherwise, in complex situations there may be confrontations that lead to deadlock and a loss of focus on the business, customers and innovation, sowing discord among the management

[5] Some people define CEO tenures as life cycles. Top managers learn quickly during their initial time in office, but they may lose touch later on (Hambrick and Fukutomi 1991). But circumstances change in each industry (Henderson *et al.* 2006) and boards should be prudent enough to articulate well the reasons for a change.

Table 6.6. *The CEO's key competencies*

– Assume, communicate and implement the company mission
– Long-term perspective, strategic thinking
– CEO's values, beliefs and interpersonal skills
– Management of complexity
– Cross-cultural skills, international mindset
– Implementation and change

team. In Morgan Stanley in 2005, the infighting around the figure of then-CEO Philip Purcell, the dissent within the board over his performance and continuance in the job, and the purge of top managers who did not accept Purcell's line highlight the kind of discord that destroys the unity, efficiency and reputation of a company and its board.

The CEO's competency profile
The board of directors must define the competency profile the CEO must have in order to succeed in the post. The actual competencies will depend on the company and the industry, but there are some that are commonly regarded as best practice (see Table 6.6). First of all, the candidate must be capable of assuming, communicating and implementing the company's mission. If the mission is the compass that guides the company's long-term ambitions, the CEO must not only be compatible with the mission; he must also represent it, share it and make it his own.

A second essential competency for a CEO involves the ability to think long term or strategically, to grasp the various aspects of a problem as a whole, and to comprehend the company's positioning in the context of its interactions with competitors, customers and suppliers. This ability has sometimes been called strategic vision or strategic thinking. Despite appearances to the contrary, many recent business crises that seem to arise from strategic issues in fact derive from a short-term view of the company – the pursuit of spectacular

results in the shortest time possible and, in the case of listed companies, the attempt to constantly surprise investors. Many companies
forget to consider the industry's long-term future and the steps they
should take to position themselves appropriately in this context.

Another dimension, one that the board of directors must watch
very closely, is the set of values that a potential CEO brings to the
company. These values have many nuances, and every company will
need a different combination. As a rule, however, companies need
CEOs who will be an example to the entire organization in their
professionalism, integrity, ability to admit mistakes, perseverance,
commitment, attention to detail, preference for effectiveness over
image, and ability to build personal relations and foster teamwork at
all levels of the company.

The ability to manage complexity is another key CEO competency. Complexity is a feature of twenty-first-century business that
derives mainly from three broad trends: market globalization and
firms' internationalization; the impact of technology on companies,
society and individuals; and the challenge of attracting and retaining valuable professionals and managing their careers in an organization. In a nutshell, corporate decision-making has become more
complex because of the many variables to be taken into account, the
uncertainty and risk involved, and the direct or indirect impact the
decisions will have both on those who make them and on others. A
CEO must have the intellectual, practical, moral and physical capacity to manage complexity.

Managing complexity is particularly relevant in dealing with
the internationalization process and leading global companies. Cross-
cultural issues are extremely relevant and CEOs need to have the right
capabilities to handle them, especially, when the challenges of the
top management shift from strategic thinking to implementation.

Managing the CEO selection process
When a board seeks a new CEO, there is the risk of a badly organized or nontransparent selection process. Though the CEO selection

process should be discreet and open to only a select few, there should be no doubt that it has been fully open and professional at all times. The selection process conducted by Accor, Europe's largest hotel chain, during the second half of 2005 illustrates the need for consistency and transparency. Founded by Gérard Pelisson and Paul Dubrule, Accor had appointed Jean-Marc Espalioux CEO in 1997. Accor's financial performance in recent years had been good enough, but not all investors were convinced that the company had the right strategy. The board decided to replace Espalioux with Gilles Pelisson, a nephew of one of the founders. The Accor board considered Pelisson the right man to make the changes the company needed. To avoid the appearance of nepotism, however, the board hired an executive recruitment firm – *after* they made their decision about the new CEO. The recruitment firm tried to do its job and proposed a number of candidates. But then the name of the preferred candidate, a clear rival to Pelisson, was published in the media, and the company for which he was then working dismissed him. In the end, the Accor board appointed Pelisson CEO. Incidents such as this not only waste time and energy, but also discredit the board of directors and the company itself.

Transparency is also important when deciding whether the replacement should be a senior manager from inside the company or an outsider. Casual observation suggests that the proportion of outsiders is likely to increase in the future. There is a growing market for CEOs, a peculiar, somewhat closed market in which supply dominates demand and intermediaries (headhunters) play a unique role, as Khurana (2002) has masterfully described.

4.7 Some reflections on CEO compensation

In the United States in recent years, outrage over CEO pay has been fuelled by apparently unjustified golden parachutes, poor financial performance and the damage caused to companies by CEO behaviour. In a company that is in financial difficulties or has recently undergone major restructuring, the board is skating on thin ice if it is too generous to an outgoing CEO who has not thoroughly fulfilled his duties of diligence and loyalty.[6]

In deciding a CEO's salary and benefits package, the board of directors must demonstrate rigour and professionalism, as its reputation is at stake. Top management pay is probably one of the most complex issues in corporate governance. The decision is as much philosophical as technical. For this reason, despite the proliferation of consultants specializing in executive pay, public opinion, particularly in the United States, strongly believes that executive compensation is too high (Bebchuk and Fried 2004). The reason why many people in the United States have lost faith in business is not so much companies' strategic errors as the belief that some boards of directors have allowed top executives to appropriate corporate profits through extravagant – some would say unfair – compensation systems. In Europe, the problem has not reached the same proportions, simply because CEO pay in the United States is so much higher than in Europe.

In 2003, for example, the profit growth of the five hundred largest companies in the United States was 9.6 per cent. Over the same period, average CEO pay in these same companies grew 22 per cent, twice as fast as in 2002.[7] The problem is not just the relative increase in executive compensation, but the absolute amount. William McDonough, president of the Public Company Accounting Oversight board, in testimony before the US Congress in June 2004, explained that in 1980 the average Fortune 500 CEO made forty times more than the average person under his charge. By 2000, it was between four hundred and five hundred times more, and the gap was expected to widen still further in 2004. In 2003, CEOs of the ten largest companies in the United States earned upward of $30m.

---

[6] For an excellent discussion on the different arguments around executive compensation in recent years and the question of whether CEOs are overpaid, see Bogle (2008) and Kaplan (2008).

[7] 'Off the leash: What will bring executive pay under control?' Source: The Corporate Library, quoted in *The Financial Times*, 24 August 2004.

This is a lot of money, and the amount may undermine the commitment and motivation of other people who work in the company. Boards of directors therefore need to think carefully about executive pay. CEOs are expected to assume huge responsibilities, and the demands are much greater than in most other professions. Furthermore, leading, managing and changing an organization, especially a large and complex one, is a huge task. CEOs must have knowledge and experience, but they must also be able to listen, decide, influence, motivate and give way or make demands at the right moment, knowing all the while that such decisions may affect thousands of people. Clearly, this requires very special qualities. Also, if the CEO does a good job and the company achieves good results, the CEO's share of those results will always be a small or even negligible percentage of the total profits.

If we agree that being a CEO is a very demanding and influential profession that calls for exceptional qualities, can we make an analogy between CEOs and elite athletes or artists? The CEO job market certainly has some similarities with those markets. But is this the right analogy? Can we apply the same criteria? There is absolutely no doubt that in all cases we are talking about people with unique abilities. But there is also an obvious difference between the types of organizations involved – that is, the social context in which each profession is exercised.

In the case of athletes and artists, the achievement is almost exclusively individual – except in the obvious case of team sports – and history has very little role to play. It is the individual who performs, and the public admires him or her as an individual.

The teams that support these individuals are important, but they are relatively small groups. In contrast, think of the CEO of a large company, with subsidiaries in many countries and tens of thousands of employees and associates. The performance of a company like this is obviously not entirely the work of the current CEO; it is also partly the work of his predecessors. The seed of today's achievements was sown in the past. Also, if a CEO lives, say, on the East Coast of the United States, the performance of subsidiaries on other continents is more likely to be the work of employees in those regions.

By saying this, we do not mean to detract from the CEO's work; we aim merely to clarify the terms of a potentially misleading analogy. In any case, a good company must pay competitive salaries; otherwise it will be unable to attract good candidates. At the same time, it is important to bear in mind that recruiting people by offering outlandish pay packages may foster an undesirable culture in which financial performance is completely divorced from the spirit of service that should prevail in management, as in any other profession.

Our aim here is merely to emphasize the important role the board of directors has to play in determining CEO compensation, not to set out the precise steps to be followed. Lastly, whatever benchmarks are used to establish a compensation system, the system must meet two basic criteria: it must be reasonable, and it must be transparent. Executive compensation must be reasonable for the company, the industry, the country and the context. Boards of directors are free to decide what they think is best, but they must take into account the repercussions certain decisions may have.

A second, complementary criterion is that whatever the legal obligations are regarding the disclosure of CEO pay, the board of directors must always act and decide with an attitude of complete transparency. In all matters, especially with respect to CEO compensation, the important thing is that the board acts impartially and equitably, rewarding excellence without being unfair. In other words, the decision about CEO pay may be debated, and there may be arguments for and against. What is not acceptable is a lack of professionalism, lack of transparency, favouritism, unjustified discrimination or unfair appropriation of what may be due to other people.

5. SOME FINAL THOUGHTS

In this chapter we have addressed a central issue regarding corporate governance: the role of the board of directors and its contribution to the company's long-term survival and success.

Current thinking on corporate governance and corporate governance reform holds two dangers. The first is the risk of putting too much emphasis on legal reform, strict guidelines and regulation in general as a means of improving corporate governance. As we have argued, legal reforms that set limits in certain critical areas, such as conflicts of interest or duties of loyalty to the company, are welcome. But good governance, understood as the mechanisms and norms that guide a company's long-term development and ensure its continuity and survival, cannot be achieved solely, or even primarily, through legal reform. What is needed is a deeper understanding of the role that the board of directors and, on a secondary level, the board of management can play in this process.

The second danger of the current debate is the temptation to create strong boards of directors at the expense of weak chief executives. This is a reaction against the era when so many boards of directors were subservient to the CEO. The opposite situation is equally undesirable, however: having an executive committee that is a puppet of the board of directors is not the best way to improve corporate governance.

This delicate web of relationships between the board of directors and the board of management reveals some other dimensions of corporate governance. The first is the need for a climate of trust between the two bodies. Without this, it is impossible to build trust in the rest of the organization, or in relations with investors and the community at large. And without trust it is impossible to create a sustainable company, however efficient the organization and however strong its short-term competitive position may be. There must be trust, first of all, among the directors, and then between the board of directors and the board of management. The second critical dimension is that this set of intangible assets, which comprises the principles according to which the board of directors operates, is naturally difficult to quantify and, occasionally, even to specify. Yet the parties involved know when these assets are present and have been put to work to improve governance; conversely, they know when the assets are impaired or ineffective. These intangible assets are located beyond the scope of even the most sophisticated legal system.

In fact, the role of regulation is similar to the role of the track in a railroad system: it provides a framework and sets guidelines that prevent the train going off in the wrong direction. But in order for the train to actually go anywhere at all, it first needs a good locomotive. The same is true of companies. There must be laws to ensure that the company stays on track, that people's rights are respected, and that conflicts of interest do not harm third parties. Rules of good governance go some way toward achieving these objectives. But we must not forget that behind any business activity lies entrepreneurial initiative, a desire to innovate – and this should not be regulated any more than is necessary. By overregulating, we could make a wonderfully straight and level track with clear limits and gradients; however, the really important thing is to have companies running along the track at high speed, creating the future. This is the challenge for the board of directors.

The board of directors legitimizes itself inside and outside the company by creating conditions that will enable the company to continue successfully in the long term and by interacting with the board of management to achieve its goals. The board of directors must consider whether it truly adds value to the company's decision-making process and whether it is a model of professional and personal excellence for the entire organization.

The company is one of the leading social institutions of the twenty-first century. It is not just an instrument of wealth creation but an agent of change, a repository of knowledge, a driver of innovation, and a creator of rules of social behaviour. It makes an essential contribution to social well-being and progress and needs proper governance. Our proposals for raising the expectations of the board's contribution to the company are intended precisely to serve that purpose.

KEY LEARNING POINTS

- After many decades of quiet and sometimes not very effective work, boards of directors have become more active over the past decade. Understanding the nature of their job and responsibilities is essential for the firm's long-term success. More importantly, clearly defining the board's functional responsibilities, beyond the legal duties, is key to developing a good working relationship with the management team and the rest of the stakeholders.
- The work of a board of directors should be inspired by four basic principles: transparency, specialization, collegial decision-making and unity.
- The main activities and tasks that a board of directors is responsible for are the following: defining and approving the firm's mission and values; approving the strategy and the allocation of financial resources; defining effective control and information systems for the board and shareholders; fostering institutional development of the firm; overseeing the board of management; selecting the CEO; and establishing and approving guidelines and specific decisions for CEO compensation.
- A clear challenge of any board of directors is to discover a good way of working with the CEO and the senior management team. A delicate balance between control and oversight on the one hand and delegation and trust on the other should be developed.
- A well-performing board of directors should clearly distinguish between the functions and responsibilities that the board of directors and the board of management have regarding the following areas: mission and values; strategy; resource allocation; investment decisions; control; institutional development; talent development; and mergers, acquisitions and alliances. Both board members and the senior management team should know who is responsible for what and when. Ambiguity should be reduced so that a clear sense of responsibility can be attached to any important managerial decision.

7 The chief executive: reputation beyond charisma

I. INTRODUCTION

By the early 1990s, Walt Disney was already one of America's corporate icons. Under Michael Eisner's leadership, Disney had delivered solid financial performance, had an influential voice in defining the future of media and entertainment, attracted great talent, and combined solid organic growth with bold acquisitions, such as Capital Cities/ABC. Unfortunately, in the late 1990s the firm's shining performance started to fade. The death knell arrived on 11 February 2004, when Comcast, America's largest cable TV company, launched a hostile bid for Disney, valuing it at $66bn. Disney's board of directors, former directors (including Walt Disney's nephew) and angry shareholders complained about Disney's increasing lack of focus and Eisner's slow reaction in tackling the challenges created by the new digital world.

The fight between Eisner and some shareholders and board members became acrimonious. Eisner felt besieged on all sides and retrenched to protect his turf. Just as people gave him credit for the company's growth and success in the 1980s, they now accused him of leading the company toward the abyss in the early 2000s. Eventually, the board of directors fired him; in October 2005, Bob Iger, one of Disney's senior managers, took over as the new CEO. Blaming Eisner for Disney's failure to reinvent itself in the early 2000s was only partially justified, just as it was not completely fair for Eisner to get full credit for Disney's success in the 1980s.

As the new CEO, Iger brought a new leadership style and strategic approach to Disney. He boosted employee morale; accelerated innovation with the concept of product and service platforms for cross-channel distribution; strengthened the Disney brand, which was damaged by the deteriorating economic performance and the infighting; restored confidence with shareholders; and established a new, more cooperative working relationship with the Disney board.

Nevertheless, what emerges from Disney's experience, and also from other companies' initiatives, is that the influence of the chief executive and his team on the firm's performance could be very important or, at least, be perceived as such. Shareholders, boards of directors and public opinion seem to think so. And the academic experience tends to confirm it, as we will see later.

However, amid the increasing awareness of the decisive role that CEOs play in developing successful firms, shareholders' concerns in recent corporate crises and failures have focused exclusively either on ousting CEOs or on reforming the board of directors. Some shareholders and experts have called for tighter regulation of board structure and composition in areas such as the number of independent directors or the separation of the roles of chairperson and CEO. Nevertheless, a serious consideration of the CEO's job and responsibilities is more necessary now than ever.

The current economic crisis highlights the idea that the goal of improving corporate governance and performance does not rest only with the board of directors. The firm's successful long-term development and the effort to save a company from a corporate crisis require the commitment and leadership of the chief executive and his senior management team. The primary aim of good governance is to contribute to the company's long-term success and survival. Good governance implies that the firm must be competitive, serve its customers well, attract good employees, reward shareholders appropriately, meet all its legal obligations and be fully integrated in the society in which it operates. All these dimensions directly impact companies' transformation into respected institutions. Clearly, ensuring that these conditions are met is something neither shareholders nor the board can do on their own. They can neither get involved in day-to-day management nor find solutions to many of the problems the company must address. These are the responsibilities of the CEO and his management team.

In this chapter we shall look at some of the functions of the chief executive (and, indirectly, the other members of the executive committee) and how these stakeholders can contribute to developing a respected firm. And we shall consider how the CEO – and the board of management or the executive team, or the senior management team – relates to the board of directors to develop a firm in the long term and contributes to its growing reputation. In this area, as elsewhere, there is no one solution that will work for every organization. Entrepreneurs and senior managers need sound judgement to make the right decisions in light of the company's challenges. The reflections presented here are intended to help design a conceptual framework that can be used to organize the work of the CEO and the board of management, define some of their responsibilities, coordinate their efforts with those of the board of directors and contribute to the company's long-term success and respect. This is not intended to be a systematic study of top management tasks and responsibilities, which Drucker (1974) undertook, but rather an examination of the tasks and functions related to good governance that are specific to a CEO[1] or a member of a company's executive committee in the context of developing respected companies and corporate reputation.

The CEO has a central role in affecting corporate performance, a fact that is recognized in both theory and practice.[2] Here, however, we aim to extend the focus beyond the CEO to encompass the entire top management team. The reason for this is that the CEO acts as the head of a team that he has very likely helped

---

[1] For simplicity, we shall use the terms chief executive and CEO interchangeably.

[2] See, for instance, Selznick (1957), Child (1972), Donaldson and Lorsch (1984) or Schwenk (1988). Research results are not unequivocal in this respect, due to factors such as the evolution of the external environment and organizational inertia, but there is strong evidence for the view that top managers play a decisive role in their organizations (Tichy and Devanna 1986; Bower 2007).

build. Every team will have its own way of doing things, examining issues, tackling decisions, implementing them and relating to other company bodies.

A member of the top management team, other than the CEO, has a dual mission. First, he has the mission that derives from his senior functional or corporate responsibility (marketing management, human resources management or financial management, for example). And second, he has the mission that derives from being a member of the company's top management team, which, as a team, must achieve certain goals, perform certain tasks and generally assume certain specific responsibilities.

2. DO CHIEF EXECUTIVES MAKE A DIFFERENCE?

With the rise and growth of the modern corporation, chief executives have gained a higher public profile. Sam Palmisano, CEO of IBM; Steve Ballmer, CEO of Microsoft; Franck Riboud, Chairman of Danone; and Narayana Murthy, founder and co-chairman of Infosys, are only a few of the many chief executives whose influence exceeds the boundaries of their firms. They also shape public policy and influence perceptions about their companies and the future of their industries. Previously, with few exceptions, their names would have been known in their industry but not to the general public. Today, in many countries, the CEOs of large companies are featured in the media, voice opinions on a variety of issues, and, in some cases, are active in politics.

Traditionally, management has been a specialized and highly respected profession, comparable to liberal professions such as medicine or law. With the growing influence of companies in society; their central role in promoting research, innovation and new technology; the spread of entrepreneurship; and the rise of the business media, CEOs have become more like famous artists or athletes than the anonymous professionals they were in the past. Perhaps the main difference between CEOs and celebrities is that CEOs do not have as large or as loyal a fan base.

Unfortunately, the model of charismatic leadership that emerged in the 1980s and 1990s lost its shine (Khurana 2002). Former CEOs such as Sandy Weill of Citigroup, Jurgen Schremp of Daimler and Hank Greenberg of AIG, among others, were consummate deal makers who helped grow their firms in good times; however, it is less clear whether they left a strong organization behind once they left their firms. Today, rethinking CEOs' critical role – apart from the charismatic aura that seems to be intrinsically tied to their relevance – is vital. After all, charisma is not a critical attribute for a successful CEO, even if it may help him.

The idea of a chief executive coming to prominence is nothing new. In fact, it is implicit in what Chandler (1977) described as the managerial capitalism that characterized the United States and, to a lesser extent, Europe in the second half of the twentieth century. What is new is the scale of the phenomenon.

It is only fair to say that part of CEOs' prestige comes from the very demanding role the chief executive of any reasonably complex company must play. The job requires exceptional knowledge, experience and abilities. Although CEOs sometimes may talk about their work in superficial terms, being a CEO is, in fact, one of modern society's most demanding and complex professions. A CEO is expected to be prudent and competent; to have knowledge and experience of the company and its industry; to be a skilled salesman and communicator; to be a good judge of people and situations; to be a good listener and motivator; and also to be virtuous – that is, the sort of person who strives to improve and help others improve through their work, becoming a role model. In a nutshell, the CEO's knowledge, intellectual ability, capacity to get things done, people management skills and conduct are expected to be exemplary.

This combination of knowledge and capabilities, reflection and action, analysis and synthesis, and long-term and short-term perspectives characterizes the general management, holistic perspective that any good CEO must have. The CEO's main job is not to analyze but to understand problems in their context, think long term, build the organization and draw action plans. He is a general-ist, not a specialist, which distinguishes the CEO from a functional manager. The chief executive is a politician in the classical sense; he sets goals and formulates policies and action plans to achieve them. And he does all this by working with other people. It is an inter-disciplinary, cross-functional role in which excellence in any one dimension is perhaps less important than a balance of competencies across the spectrum of capabilities.

Furthermore, a CEO must deploy these abilities continuously over time.[3] A CEO is always on the job, dealing with colleagues, customers, suppliers, shareholders, regulators and other authorities. This demands considerable physical and mental energy, an ability to prioritize and focus on what is most important, and a capacity to switch almost instantly from analysis and reflection to action and motivation. A CEO must also have almost unlimited availability and commitment. Therefore, it is not just a matter of cultivating a set of rather sophisticated qualities, but of acquiring the vital bal-ance that enables a person to consistently perform diverse tasks at a high intensity with unvarying effectiveness. The increasing com-plexity of the business environment and global operations further add to the heavy demands of the job.

When the news is not about how well companies are perform-ing but about how badly some have failed, or when corporate scan-dals – a perennial feature of corporate life – erupt, public opinion is inclined to overlook these multiple dimensions of a CEO's role. Today, a chief executive is more likely to make headlines for some-thing he has done wrong than for something he has done right. We must not forget that the recent corporate scandals are few and far between compared to the total population of companies. However, the few companies that break the rules make a much bigger impres-sion than the vast majority that continue to grow, innovate, invest,

---

[3] A CEO's tenure in a firm can be seen as a sequence of life cycles in which learn-ing takes place. See Henderson *et al.* (2006).

create jobs and contribute to social well-being. Unfortunately, the two types of companies are often lumped together. The same problem affects CEOs. A scandal involving one particular CEO, or the awarding of an arguably excessive pay package, quickly becomes an excuse to demonize the entire profession.

A relevant theme in the leadership literature is whether the CEO's role in a company really is all that decisive. If it is, why don't companies try to devise a simpler, more systematic way of assessing CEO performance? While some experts maintain that the CEO's contribution is indeed decisive, others contend that it does not matter who is CEO – the important thing is the company's management team and workforce. Experience shows that, in some instances, the CEO has crucially influenced an organizational change, restructuring, turnaround or new capability development. Few will doubt the differential impact that CEOs such as Roberto Goizueta at Coca-Cola or Bill George at Medtronic had. One need not agree with everything they said or did to acknowledge that they have had a positive impact on their companies. Conversely, one cannot deny the negative impact that some CEOs have had on their organizations due to incompetence or unethical behaviour.

At the same time, let's not forget that a CEO, unlike a pop singer or athlete, must manage people, secure their commitment, build teams, coordinate units and divisions, and ensure that the company's many functions work together to serve the end customers. In short, this is an objectively complex, yet absolutely vital profession in an age dominated by knowledge-based organizations.

The fact that a CEO's ability to make the right decisions has never been so in doubt as it is today is cause for concern. Recent corporate scandals and alleged excesses in executive compensation have prompted many boards of directors to clip their CEOs' wings. In itself, this is not a bad thing, partly because the pendulum had swung too far in the other direction. Yet a CEO must have the means to perform the functions that the company and society expect of him.

It may not be a fair comparison, but given the choice between an excellent CEO and a mediocre board of directors, or a mediocre CEO and an excellent board, many investors would probably opt for the former. Excellent steering (by the board) is not going to be much help if the firm is seriously underpowered with a weak CEO.

In this chapter, we will examine the main functions a CEO must perform in an organization – in particular, those related to good governance and corporate reputation. Numerous academic and not-so-academic studies have described the CEO's functions and ideal qualities in the abstract. We shall take a different approach. Starting from the company's mission, which should be the focus of everything a CEO does, we shall define the qualities a CEO should have. A start-up is not the same as an established firm in a mature industry. A local company is not the same as one that is internationally active. Managing a low-tech company is not the same as managing a high-tech one. Therefore, expecting a CEO to be able to handle any and every situation may mean expecting the CEO to have every possible capability. Yet it would be unrealistic to expect CEOs to be supermen or superwomen. It would be unrealistic because people acquire capabilities by practising them, and a chief executive is unlikely to be able to develop all possible capabilities during his lifetime or career.

Nevertheless, it is fair to say that any CEO must develop capabilities in three basic dimensions: strategic capabilities, related to business development; executive or organizational capabilities, which help build an organization that is capable of fulfilling the company's mission; and leadership capabilities, which are essential for managing people and engaging them in any business venture.[4] A CEO need not be excellent in each individual dimension, but he should be minimally competent in all three. Otherwise, his suitability for the job would be questionable.

[4] See Pérez-López (1993).

Strategic capabilities involve understanding the company's business, customers, products and markets; knowing how to serve customers better; and knowing how to innovate or restructure when necessary. Organizational capabilities involve dividing up tasks and functions, assigning responsibilities, combining competencies, delegating tasks and setting up compensation systems, all of which are vital to creating the organizational infrastructure that will enable a good business idea to thrive. Leadership capabilities involve more than just managing other people; they also involve working alongside them, offering them a view of the future, and share with them ways of doing things that foster learning and commitment to the firm. These things are done not out of necessity but by choice; it is an opportunity to learn, improve and share this progress with others. A person does not acquire these capabilities easily. Most professions demand many hours of learning and a good deal of knowledge, and top management is no exception. Yet few other professional activities demand these personal capabilities, which help not only a CEO's own reputation but the overall firm's reputation.

3. A CHIEF EXECUTIVE'S MAIN TASKS

The CEO and his team are as essential to corporate governance as the board of directors. In recent years the pendulum of corporate power has swung away from the CEO toward the board, and today, very often a strong, charismatic, entrepreneurial CEO is confronted with a strong board of directors.

This is a mistaken approach, for several reasons. First, the key to good corporate governance and leadership respect is not power but a combination of professionalism, entrepreneurship and integrity. A company is not a political territory to be conquered but a wealth-creating social institution that needs to be developed. Like any other institution, it must work efficiently and harmoniously, which means that its members – both individuals and governing bodies – must fulfil their mission. Therefore, to view the company mainly in terms of power is a dangerous and simplistic reduction.

Table 7.1. *The CEO's tasks and challenges*

– Embody and implement the company's mission and values
– Develop a point of view about the company's future
– Leadership development
– Resource allocation and investment decisions
– Operational efficiency
– Organizational design

A second reason is that though good governance requires a balance of power, it is also about driving the company forward, serving clients extremely well, developing people and building the company's long-term future. Historically, leading the company has been the CEO's task. In fact, a company with a strong executive committee and an ineffective board of directors – ineffective by today's standards – may be weak, but it will still have a future. The opposite situation may be worse. A company with a superficially effective board of directors but an ineffective executive committee is likely to be structurally just as weak.

In today's economic climate, companies need a very professional board, a very competent CEO and a strong executive committee to guarantee their future. Hence the need to define and outline some of the tasks and challenges a CEO must address in order to improve corporate governance and build respect for the firm. These tasks must be aimed at achieving the financial and nonfinancial goals set by the board of directors and ensuring the company's long-term survival (see Table 7.1).

3.1 Embodying the company's mission and values
Very often, a company's mission is defined by its founder or a CEO who left his stamp on the organization at some point in the past. At other times, such as when a company is turned around after a major crisis, redefining the mission may give meaning to a new stage in the company's life. In such cases, the mission statement may be drafted

by a top management committee. Though the strength of a mission will depend on its authenticity and ability to engage all employees in an enterprise that goes beyond each individual, the mission must be approved by the board of directors. The CEO and the top management team must help define and embody the mission, and put it into practice in the company's various activities and initiatives.

A mission statement may be a living and inspirational set of ideas, but it also has the power to mobilize hearts and minds and define what a firm should do. This is the case of Medtronic, a leading medical technology firm, whose mission is clear:

> To contribute to human welfare by the application of biomedical engineering in the research, manufacture and sale of instruments or appliances that alleviate pain, restore health and extend life...To make a fair profit on current operations to meet our obligations, sustain our growth and reach our goals. To recognize the personal worth of employees by providing an employment framework that allows personal satisfaction in work accomplished, security, advancement opportunity and means to share in the company's success. To maintain good citizenship as a company.[5]

Novartis, one of the world's leading pharmaceutical companies, provides another clear example of a company led by a sense of mission: 'We want to discover, develop and successfully market innovative products to prevent and cure diseases, to ease suffering and to enhance the quality of life.'[6] The focus here is not on shareholder value, which all firms must try to generate, but on great products that can serve a social need and improve the lives of thousands of people.

It is true that in many cases, the firm's mission may be no more than a literary curiosity. The difference lies not so much in its style as in its content. In companies like Novartis, Medtronic and

---

[5] See www.medtronic.com.
[6] See www.novartis.com.

many others, the CEO and a group of senior executives strives continuously to make the mission the basis of everything the company
does, while in other firms the mission is there to be admired but not
applied in daily activities. One of the critical tasks of the top management team is to put the mission into practice in their own lives
and bring it to life in the eyes of the rest of the organization. There
lies one of the pillars of corporate reputation.

A mission is actualized when it is presented, discussed and
included in corporate agendas. It can be said to be embodied, however, when it actually inspires the decisions chief executives make
in specific circumstances. The Johnson & Johnson credo was already
famous, but its reputation increased in 1982 when the company
decided to recall millions of bottles of Tylenol (one of the company's
top-selling drugs) after it was discovered that some bottles had been
criminally adulterated with cyanide. This decision was worth more
than a thousand words about respect for customers, and it was also
the most consistent with the Johnson & Johnson credo.

Negative examples are equally plentiful. Every time a company
with a mission acts in a way that harms an employee, customer,
shareholder or other stakeholder and makes no effort to prevent or
remedy such harm, it instantly undermines its mission. Embodying
or destroying the mission clearly is a responsibility that falls within
the remit of the top management team, and both actions impact corporate reputation and performance.

The behaviour of a company's chief executive can have a
significant impact on the value of the company's mission. We frequently hear about the visionary leader or the charismatic leader.
Sadly, we do not hear so much about the leader who serves and who
sets an example by serving others. The primary responsibility of any
chief executive is to serve the people under his responsibility. And
this service must be exemplary – that is, it must set the tone of the
melody that the rest of the company must play in order to serve customers and create economic value. The idea of service is central to a
company that wants to be respected.

An exemplary CEO embodies a broad range of virtues and qualities: professionalism, fortitude, fairness, respect, humility and perseverance, to name but a few. A good CEO must exercise these virtues in order to do his job well and help the company survive and succeed in the long run. These virtues will also make him a better professional and a better human being, and they are implicit in many companies' missions. Without these virtues, and without an effort by chief executives to live them, the mission will be ineffective. It is not a matter of major decisions affecting employees or customers; it is more a matter of working style, a person's way of doing things, the consistency between what a person says and what he does. It relates to a person's manner and affability, the demands a person makes on himself and others or his ability to listen. For a chief executive, these are small details, but for the people who work with him, they can be very significant. These details may not directly affect the company's mission, but they do generate a working climate or atmosphere that can either assist or hamper the fulfilment of the corporate mission and objectives and the chief executive's own personal development.

The mission is positively actualized when a company's chief executive helps the divisions or business units relate their various initiatives and actions to the corporate mission so that the mission is not merely window dressing, used from time to time whenever there is a major crisis. The mission must be alive. Chief executives must ask themselves – and encourage their employees to ask themselves – whether a particular decision reinforces or weakens the company's mission. In some cases, the answer will be impossible to anticipate, or inconclusive. In others, however, it may be a useful compass, showing the way forward or the steps to be taken before reaching a final decision.

The company's mission should never threaten individual freedom or professional responsibility. Otherwise, it would be a shackle rather than a compass. The mission must be ambitious in the challenges it poses, and respectful of the freedom and dignity of every person. Management needs a corporate context in which a person is best able to develop his abilities and realize his potential. A senior manager is not expected to show blind obedience; he is, however, expected to identify with the company's mission and values. In the short run, a senior manager may need to remain within a company, but if he does not identify with its mission, staying for any length of time will impoverish him as a person and as a professional.

Extrinsic motivation grounded in economic incentives is necessary, but it is clearly not sufficient for creating dynamic, living institutions. The CEO and the executive committee must have the ability to inspire and motivate those who work in the company, using the company's mission to spur them on. This task is like the work of an artist: it is never finished and can always be improved. Moreover, it should be a standing item on the executive committee's agenda.

3.2 Strategy: developing a point of view about the company's future

In any company, most employees are engaged in functional activities (marketing and sales, purchasing, manufacturing and so forth) at different organizational levels. Every day, problems and challenges arise in the areas of purchasing, selling, manufacturing and financing, and the functional organization provides clear advantages of scale and specialization. However, the company also faces an equally important challenge that is rarely identified as a management priority: the need to ensure the company's long-term survival and success as an institution. This goal requires a readiness to think and act with a long-term view, without neglecting more immediate challenges and problems. The company's top management must systematically manage both the short-term and the long-term dimensions, though at times they may seem contradictory. These are some of the paradoxes of management: making the firm profitable and keeping its sense of fairness and organizational culture, preserving the old while building the new, being both efficient and fair, thinking long term and solving day-to-day problems. By addressing these challenges successfully, a firm becomes a respected institution.

When Iger was named CEO of Walt Disney in 2005, the stock price of this legendary firm was falling; margins were decreasing; and many managers, employees and shareholders did not believe in the firm's strategy. Iger quickly redefined how the company would become unique in a competitive, challenging digital world. His solution was franchises, or platforms of products and services that could create value across multiple businesses or countries on a recurring basis. Instead of relying only on the great value of traditional franchises like Mickey Mouse or Winnie the Pooh, Iger encouraged his team to think about new ones. The recent success of the Jonas Brothers,[7] a young and already very successful musical group, effectively demonstrates this strategy.

This group sells thousands of CDs; their songs can be downloaded via Disney's Hollywood Records label; they have performed live, before audiences of many thousands of people; they have already released a book published by Hyperion (a Disney subsidiary); and a show on the Disney Channel has already been designed. Developing new franchises and strengthening the different avenues for creating and growing a brand had been, for many years, among Disney's core capabilities. Nevertheless, Iger and his team clarified these tasks, mobilized the firm's different divisions around this concept, and pursued this objective systematically. The outcome so far has been extremely good in terms of profitability, talent attraction and competitors' admiration. After the frustration with Eisner in the early 2000s, investors and critics see that Disney has a clear strategy, a point of view on how to compete and be unique.

Having a long-term view of the company's future is crucial for all concerned. Without it, neither employees nor shareholders nor customers will know where the company is going. Worse, they will have no idea what criteria should prevail. It is the top management's

---

[7] See *Fortune*, 19 January 2009.

job to think long term, because nobody else will do it systematically. There will always be people in the organization who will make marketing or financial decisions; but if chief executives do not consider the long term, nobody will make decisions for them. In a sense, they are the guardians of the company's future.

One way to respond to this challenge is to develop a vision of the company's future and long-term development. Defining the company's strategy offers an opportunity to develop scenarios regarding its future as an organization. The company's future must be built into its strategy. Any strategy must contain the following ingredients: a view of the company's future, a perspective on the present and future needs of its customers, an understanding of how the industry value chain activities are organized and may evolve, a map of the company's operations (its internal value chain), and selected key competitive variables that should show in what way it is unique.

The strategy must also provide answers to certain questions: what products or services the company will sell, what customers and markets it will serve, in what geographical areas it will operate and, lastly, what type of competitive advantage it aims to develop.

Top management must govern the company in order to shape its present activities and influence its future. To succeed, the company must know what it wants to do and exactly how to do it. The company's mission defines what it wants to do and why it exists. The strategy – and, in particular, the vision of the company's future – will describe in various ways how that mission is to be carried out.

The strategy must be flexible enough to adapt to changing circumstances. The corporate mission, by contrast, will be fixed, provided it has been properly formulated and the customer needs that the company proposes to satisfy are meaningful. The strategy, however, must adapt to changes in the environment. Top management must decide when a strategy is no longer valid or when external threats or opportunities call for a change. In fact, one of top management's critical tasks is to identify new opportunities and foster entrepreneurship within the organization. To that end, the strategy must serve as a conceptual framework to make all the company's activities consistent and meaningful; it should not be a straitjacket that prevents the company from fulfilling its mission, adapting to new circumstances or responding to day-to-day challenges. Strategy alone does not guarantee corporate reputation, but no respected company lacks a good, tested strategy process.

3.3 Leadership development

A company is, first and foremost, a group of people who collectively undertake to carry out a mission that none could take on individually. People with entrepreneurial initiative and team spirit are the basic building blocks. At the core of any company is a group of people with a plan and ideas. A company may have few financial resources yet still be a company. It may have no technology and still be a company. But a company without at least one entrepreneur with a plan and ideas cannot exist. Also, in many cases, the distribution of tasks and responsibilities means that the entrepreneur will need the help of other people to carry out the company's mission. Financial resources are indispensable, but the primacy of people in business is logically irrefutable. Morally speaking, moreover, the acknowledgement of the primacy of people is a precondition to building efficient, humane companies and societies that respect and promote personal dignity. It is also a central pillar of corporate reputation.

In practice, however, people are not the primary concern in all companies. Sometimes they are treated simply as means to an end. But the full realization of every person's potential is one of the goals driving any activity a company must undertake.

One of the most interesting experiments in leadership development over the past two decades is the emergence of many corporate universities around the world. Well-known companies such as GE, Allianz and Goldman Sachs established their own universities or learning centres to help develop their firm's new generation of leaders and send an unequivocal signal that talent development is key. Corporate universities are a heterogeneous body of institutions. Some of them organize formal learning around business functional topics, from managerial disciplines and subjects to leadership; others use the context of the so-called university to share experiences and foster reflection and learning on how to do things and how to make companies better. While many corporate universities have been successful in this learning process, there have also been failures along the way. Moreover, corporate universities often tend to be too inward-looking, restricting the dialogue and reflection to what insiders think about their firm, without exposure to outsiders. Nevertheless, corporate universities are a clear signal that senior managers are concerned with the development of talent and, more specifically, leadership capabilities. Corporate universities are very important, but developing leaders involves more than just sharing knowledge and good practices, forcing innovation and raising the level of aspirations.

One of the core tasks of the CEO and the company's top management team is to reconcile economic efficiency with a sense of fairness so that each person is treated in accordance with his or her dignity. In other words, top management must strive for the greatest possible efficiency while at the same time promoting the professional and personal development of those who work in the company.

This is one of the biggest challenges for chief executives. In the context of globalization, technological innovation and changing customer needs, companies need to be very flexible and responsive. Amidst this uncertainty, chief executives prove their worth – as professionals and as people – by managing for people, rather than against them; by involving people in their decisions, rather than alienating them; by eliciting their contribution, rather than rejecting it. This is no easy task. Yet it is one of the most exciting challenges facing top management today: how to build organizations that are both truly effective and full of humanity.

This notion of management and personal development is built on two principles. The first is practical: unless people are treated fairly, they will not get involved in a company. A firm may aspire to have willing collaborators, or it may choose not to. The latter is invariably the worse option. The company's people are in contact with its customers. They produce and sell, and they are a source of ideas and initiatives for improvement. Clearly, efficiency requires willing collaborators. In the short run, an organization may get by with people-unfriendly policies and attitudes; but it is unlikely to succeed in the long term. Furthermore, if it does not show respect for people, it will not be trusted, either by its own employees or by others. And if it is not trusted, it will acquire a bad reputation and will be unable to attract talent in the future.

The second principle is moral: people deserve to be treated with respect, and it is wrong not to treat each person with dignity. A chief executive who does not respect the people who work with him shows no respect for himself as a person and risks personal self-destruction. Aristotle made the point that the first victim of injustice is not the person who suffers it but the one who inflicts it.

People development is a task for top management, one that cannot be delegated. The human resources department must do the bulk of the work, but the commitment of top management is critical for several reasons. First, the company must attract the right people in order to survive in the long term. Without the right people, there will be no ideas and no action. Second, decisions about people and their contributions to the enterprise always have a special connotation: we all perceive a sense of fairness, or the lack of it, in what companies do and how they do it. Third, the way people are treated is an essential ingredient of the company's mission and values. A fine mission will be weakened if top management fails to treat people in accordance with their dignity.

An essential element of top management's task of building the company's future is to develop the next generation of leaders. Strategy formulation is important, and to effectively plan and execute a strategy, companies need good professionals: senior managers who are capable of thinking holistically, who develop new talent and who have the necessary competencies to execute decisions and plans. Consequently, people development requires a qualitatively larger commitment of time and money by the executive committee than regular investment decisions. In other words, this task has top priority.

In developing the company's new leaders, the CEO and the top management team should bear in mind certain basic guidelines that are valid for most people (there will always be exceptions) and that go beyond the usual human resources policies and techniques. First, economic incentives are important, but they are not the most important thing. Most people expect reasonable pay, but they also require a solid career plan, a sense of purpose, opportunities to learn and improve, and a positive working atmosphere.

Second, every person wants to make a contribution; and it is top management's job to ensure that every person is in the position in which he is best able to realize his potential, for his own benefit and for the benefit of the company. Third, people want to align their expectations and aspirations with the company's needs and purposes, and so contribute to fulfilling them.

Companies with great products or services are good performers. But to become legends, they need to excel at leadership and people development.

3.4 Resource allocation and investment decisions

A company's long-term future depends not only on the strategic choices made by its top management (the decision to compete in a particular market with a particular product, and so forth), but also on the resources it commits to this objective. Chief executives determine the company's future through certain key decisions. One such decision is the allocation of financial resources among alternative investment projects. This decision strongly affects the company's performance and very often is irreversible in the short term (Ghemawat 1991). The choice of a particular technology for a new manufacturing plant, the selection of alternative distribution channels, a new product launch or the establishment of a foreign subsidiary are all decisions that shape and constrain the company's future choices.

Walt Disney's recent evolution provides compelling evidence for the importance of investment decisions. One of Iger's first strategic moves was to strengthen Disney's animation units. In October 2005, he asked the board of directors to consider acquiring Pixar Films, an animated film company founded by Steve Jobs, CEO and founder of Apple. Disney had been distributing Pixar releases under a deal that was about to end. Iger not only convinced his board to make a $7bn offer for Pixar, but he also convinced Steve Jobs and other senior executives from Pixar, including John Lasseter and Ed Catmull, to sell to Disney and join the company to oversee the new, larger animation unit. With this bold move, Iger got new top talent on board (Jobs, Lasseter), a great brand (Pixar) with great products, new capabilities and more confidence in what Disney could achieve.

As the Pixar acquisition highlights, strategic investment decisions must be based on an overall understanding of the company and be consistent with its mission and strategy. An investment decision that is not aligned with the company's chosen strategy makes no sense. Nor does it make sense to consider an investment decision in isolation. Every decision must have one or more action alternatives. Every plan should have a rival plan, competing for the same financial resources. Therefore, top managers must thoroughly explore all the options before settling on one. In practice, however, many investment decisions are based entirely on financial criteria. Financial considerations are important, but they are not sufficient in and of themselves. Financial resources are a means, not an end.

Consequently, investment and resource allocation decisions cannot be made exclusively from a financial perspective. They must be weighed in the context of the company's strategy; its resources and capabilities; the positioning it aims to establish; and the foreseeable reactions of customers, suppliers and competitors.

Because resource allocation is so important to a company's future, it behoves chief executives to also consider worst-case scenarios. What should the company do in such situations? The ability to improvise is very valuable. But top management's first obligation is to anticipate, and only then to improvise, as circumstances permit or require.

The CEO is not obliged to know all the technical details of an investment project, but he should have an informed opinion about its nature, its goals, its expected impact on the company and its financial and qualitative value compared to other projects. In other words, resources must be allocated based on the needs of the company as a whole, the relative merits of all the options and what is best for the company in the long run.

The resource allocation process itself may be considered a procedure. Nevertheless, respected firms learn to manage this process masterfully and gain investors' trust in the efficient use of resources.

3.5 Operational efficiency

The board of directors cannot and should not interfere in the day-to-day running of the company. That is the realm of the chief executive and the executive committee. We have stressed the importance of long-term development and survival as a firm's primary goal when establishing guidelines for corporate governance. However, we must not forget that long-term results are built on short-term decisions. Top management needs to know where the company is heading; but it also needs to ensure that the steps taken each day are in the right direction and that they help reach the long-term goal. Operational efficiency (doing well what has to be done) is different from strategy (deciding what has to be done). Yet it is indispensable to achieving the company's goals.

Zara, one of the decade's fastest-growing and most successful retailers, may be best known for its stylish fashions, sophisticated outlets, product diversity, strong brand name and good price-to-quality ratio. What is less known is that behind the phenomenal success of the Spain-based retailer is a relentless effort to make the

company's operations very efficient and the time-to-market decisions very quick. Moreover, for a company that still manufactures
more than half the products it sells worldwide in Western Europe
instead of outsourcing them to low-wage countries, success depends
very much on operational effectiveness. Zara's inbound and out-
bound logistics and the real-time sales information for every product
in every outlet in more than one hundred countries are the paradigms of operational efficiency. More importantly, they also show
that manufacturing in high-wage countries is still possible if logistics and operations are efficient enough to yield high productivity.
The Zara case shows very clearly that even in the fashion business a
focus on operational efficiency should be a priority in any successful
firm.

Day-to-day operational efficiency, effectiveness and excellence
in the company's various functions and departments are crucial to
the company's long-term survival. They are equally vital in order to
make clear to all concerned that the company's mission and values
are enacted not through abstract definitions but through daily effort,
excellence and commitment in the service of customers who expect
the best of the company. Good chief executives are strongly results-
oriented and determined that plans be implemented and goals be
met. They do not tolerate cost overruns when they could have been
avoided, or loss of business opportunities due to inertia or apathy.

To achieve operational efficiency, every task, function and unit
must perform well and contribute to the efficiency of the organization as a whole. At the same time, tasks must be coordinated and
functions integrated to serve customers as efficiently as possible. It
is not enough to be excellent in just some operations. A company
that aspires to excellence must strive to coordiante its functions and
activities. The company as a whole must be perceived as more than
the sum of its individual functions.

In fact, operational efficiency is a means of manifesting a company's mission in everyday tasks, a way of embodying the organization's values and asserting its character. Operational excellence

is often a reflection of excellent individual performance, backed by even better team organization and a focus on serving internal and external customers. Excellent operations are also a reflection of personal effort and capability deployment, which are the true foundations of personal growth for every member of an organization. This is not to say that inefficient companies have no intention to serve; merely that they do not serve as well as they could. Ideally, companies must simultaneously maximize efficiency and develop people's potential.

Therefore, the executive committee's concern for operational efficiency does not preclude higher considerations of strategy or long-term survival. The challenge is to strike a balance between these two management dimensions, in the conviction that mistakes in short-term execution can thwart the long-term vision. Nevertheless, an outstanding reputation will not be achievable unless a company learns how to operate efficiently.

3.6 Organizational design

A company's top management must organize the work to be done, set goals and measure achievement. The purpose of organizational design, whether in functional areas, such as marketing and sales, finance or technology, or in business or geographical units, is to split the business enterprise into more manageable sub-enterprises in order to assign them to specific people, set goals and coordinate and supervise units over time.

An organization may be structured in different ways and according to different criteria. The chosen structure (functional, divisional, matrix and so forth) must meet certain requirements. First, the organization of work must facilitate performance of the tasks required to achieve the goals. Second, the organization must be simple and use simple procedures to accomplish its objectives. Third, the organization must be flexible and adaptable to the needs of customers, suppliers and markets. Fourth, the organization must promote hard work and initiative. Fifth, companies need specific goals. Without clear and specific goals they cannot improve, and without proper measurement they cannot know the extent of any improvement.

Organizational design also requires appropriate control systems. These are procedures that help chief executives evaluate the degree of achievement of the objectives derived from the company's mission and strategy. Designing and selecting control systems is one of the executive committee's essential tasks. In this section we shall reflect on some guidelines for the design of control systems.

A company's control system reflects, or discredits, its culture and values. The decision as to what variables to assess and how to measure them can either strengthen or weaken the values that top management wishes to embody.

Control systems must ensure that every person, division and department in the company knows what top management expects of them, as well as encourage them to accept that responsibility for the benefit of the company and every person in it. Such systems must be a permanent reminder to each person of the contribution he or she is expected to make, and serve to garner a commitment to his or her responsibilities. Basically, the control function must heighten people's sense of responsibility and transparency and make them accountable for the assignments they accept and the resources they receive. A good control system, therefore, must strengthen an organization's atmosphere of trust so that people feel duty-bound to do what they have undertaken to do, accept the need to account for their actions and be confident that their efforts will be rewarded.

Top management's job is not only to design a good control system, however. It faces a greater challenge: to ensure that every person in the company is willing to account for his or her actions, and that the organization is completely transparent and able to explain to employees and external stakeholders exactly what it does and why. Companies are not legally obligated to explain everything they do. But when a company needs to clarify certain events or defend itself against a false accusation, senior managers should be able to explain in sufficient detail why the firm did what it did, and in so doing reinforce its institutional prestige and reputation. Top management must put the company in a position where a focus on internal policy, decision or circumstance will actually boost the company's reputation.

Consequently, when designing a control system, it is important to include the right variables without losing sight of the fact that the ultimate goal is to improve transparency. Control systems must also help the company's employees grow and develop by ensuring that their objectives and challenges are clear, the means of measuring performance are accurate and fair, and the organization's members trust one another.

4. SOME WORKING GUIDELINES FOR THE BOARD OF MANAGEMENT

A company's board of management should be a team, led by the CEO, whose ultimate goal is to contribute to the company's long-term success and survival. In its work, the board of management, like any other team, must draw on a basic philosophy or set of values or principles that strengthen its cohesiveness and effectiveness. Simply having such values does not guarantee that the company will achieve its goals, but it may mean that top management works better and contributes to strengthening a firm's reputation. We shall focus on some criteria that should inform the board of management's work (see Table 7.2): building a team, collegial decision-making, accountability, efficiency, and global, integrative perspective. All of these criteria help a firm's management achieve higher levels of efficiency and excellence.

4.1 Teamwork

In decision making, the board of management should act as a single team, headed by the CEO, rather than an assembly of individuals or an appendage of the CEO, hiding the fact that the CEO makes all the decisions. Its primary mission is to ensure the company's long-term survival, even though some or all of the company's activities are sure to change over time.

Table 7.2. *The board of management: some guidelines for its effectiveness*

– Teamwork
– Collegial decision making
– Accountability
– Efficiency
– Global, integrative perspective

The board of management must act as a team, not as a mere sum of individuals. It must have a clear sense of the company's mission and goals. It must be an example to the rest of the organization: an example of professional excellence, personal worth and, above all, teamwork in the service of a collective enterprise. Diversity of opinion is perfectly legitimate; but the unity of the executive committee, once a decision has been made, is good for the organization as a whole, so any disagreements must be confined to committee meetings. Any sign of disunity in the committee almost instantly affects the rest of the organization and saps energy and enthusiasm from the collective enterprise.

4.2 Collegial decision making

The board of management must be chaired by the company's CEO. His role is analogous to that of the chairperson of the board of directors: the CEO must conduct the orchestra, but need not – and probably should not – play all the instruments.

The CEO will naturally influence the committee's decisions, but he must primarily ensure that matters are debated in an orderly and open manner so that all committee members adhere to the final decision. The aim is to ensure that all members of the board of management are able to judge whether a particular action alternative will work in favour of the company's long-term survival and debate the various viewpoints openly and impartially.

Certainly, diversity of people and profiles is an asset in any work group. In the board of management, it should be actively pursued. The fact that committee members usually have knowledge and experience of different areas of the company means that they will examine problems and solutions from different perspectives; it also means that any options they consider will take the whole company into account, not just one functional area. This cannot be taken for granted, however.

As with the board of directors, collegial decision-making requires other ingredients. First, it requires that the issues the committee must decide be known in advance. The agenda should be put forward in due time. Collegial decision-making will soon break down if the issues to be discussed are not announced in advance or board members are not properly prepared to discuss them.

The collegial model also demands that if the board of management should handle an issue, that issue should not be withheld from it. This underlines the importance of having good decision-making routines. Such routines should clarify which issues must go to the executive committee, which are for the CEO to discuss with each committee member individually, which are the responsibility of the board of directors, and which are for each person to decide for himself or herself.

4.3 Accountability

The accountability of the board of management has several dimensions. The first is the obligation to report problems, solutions and results to the board, employees, shareholders and stakeholders, in accordance with the company's obligation to each party. This obligation demands transparency of information and decisions. Most of the decisions made by a board of directors must be based on information and recommendations supplied by the board of management, particularly those concerning the company's performance, business threats and opportunities, organizational structure and good workplace atmosphere. Consequently, the quality of the board's decisions will depend on the depth and rigour of the preparatory work done by the board of management and the information it supplies to the board.

Another dimension is transparency *vis-à-vis* the rest of the organization. The board of management is not obligated to disclose all the information it has. Indeed, it would be imprudent for it to do so. However, it is obligated to report to its employees, in reasonable detail and depth, on the company's progress, the risks it faces and any relevant facts that may have arisen. It must also report to employees on any major changes and strategic decisions before the employees find out by other means. This obligation is all the more pressing when it is a matter of informing the people who will suffer the direct, sometimes painful consequences of changes or decisions.

At the same time, the board's work and any decisions it makes must be such that, if they are exposed to public scrutiny, people's trust toward the committee members will not weaken. In other words, the committee must work for the long-term good of the company as a whole, not for the particular good of a certain stakeholder. Whenever the board's decisions are made public, officially or unofficially, they must inspire in employees a sense of belonging and trust, rather than one of suspicion or disaffection. For that to be the case, decisions must be transparent, as a safeguard against the tyranny that power or money may exercise over chief executives.

Transparency, collegial decision-making and unity foster a working culture within the board of management that encourages responsibility, open debate without entrenched positions and a rigorous approach to issues. These intangible dimensions of the committee's work are clearly just as important as committee structure and composition. They help the board of management act as a team, with clear goals and responsibilities and a clear distribution of functions.

4.4 Efficiency
The efficient assignment of tasks and priorities and a strict adherence to the company's goals and agenda are vital principles of the

board of management's work. The legitimacy of power rests on two pillars: the source of power, and whether power is exercised prudently and effectively. To have legitimacy in the organization, chief executives must prove themselves effective in what they do. Power is not enough; they also need authority. Moral authority requires two ingredients: professional competence and moral integrity. A CEO needs both.

These qualities are equally necessary in the top management team as a whole. All the work done in a company is organized around projects and initiatives that are planned, driven and executed by working teams. The board of management is, in a sense, the first of these teams. This being the case, we should add that it is not enough for board members to be excellent professionals. They must also work as a team, plan projects as a team and implement solutions as a team, notwithstanding their individual accountability. Basically, the board of management must also be a model of good teamwork for the rest of the organization.

4.5 Global, integrative perspective

The job of a CEO demands careful scheduling of tasks to be completed, issues to be reviewed, and goals to be achieved, covering every area of the company. At the same time, all problems, challenges and alternatives must be analyzed in their overall context, considering every aspect of the company and properly identifying the role of each function, task or division within the organization as a whole.

One of the defining characteristics of the work of a CEO is, precisely, the general management perspective; that is, a way of addressing problems, challenges, alternatives and solutions that takes the company as a whole and every interested party into account. The general management perspective encompasses the diverse tasks and functions as part of a greater whole. It is not a matter of avoiding conflicts but of elevating them to a higher level and resolving them. It requires an ability to make the short term compatible with the long term. In a nutshell, it assumes the ability to manage paradoxes or contradictions between different parts of the company so that they never become an obstacle to the company's progress.

The general management perspective puts its stamp on any organization. The idea is that the company as a whole is more than the sum of its parts. From this we may infer that top management must always pursue the common good of the company above the private good of any individual. This is a condition of economic efficiency and moral legitimacy.

5. SOME FINAL THOUGHTS

In this chapter we have discussed some of the challenges and responsibilities of chief executives, their relationship with corporate governance, and their potential contribution to corporate reputation.

In this respect, some theories highlight the importance of regulations and legal reforms in improving corporate governance and reputation. Others make the case for a radical change in the structure, profile and functions of the board of directors. The importance of those institutions in corporate governance is decisive. Nevertheless, a thesis of this book is that chief executives and top management teams have a central role in making governance work and strengthening a firm's reputation.

This thesis has two direct implications. First, corporate governance reforms cannot be designed or implemented as part of a battle between boards and chief executives to grab more power. They complement and need each other, like the two wings of a bird, in order to make governance work.

Second, it is important to reflect on the work, challenges and responsibilities of chief executives in the wider context of corporate governance and a firm's long-term success and reputation.

Many people consider good chief executives those who implement changes and get things done, ultimately reaching the goals they set. Indeed, these things are good. Nevertheless, we must integrate those objectives with the firm's long-term development; otherwise we would live with companies that are like pure machines, without a soul. But building respected companies requires some additional ingredients, beyond short-term success. This is the nature of the challenge for chief executives that we have explored in this chapter.

KEY LEARNING POINTS

- Chief executives can have a lasting impact on their companies, their people and society at large. In many countries, some CEOs have become public figures and help shape the views of public policy and society, a status that attaches new responsibility to their job.
- The effectiveness of chief executives is not related to the level of public charisma they display. Charisma can help, but chief executives are professionals who must constantly demonstrate a unique blend of knowledge, capabilities, attitudes and virtues. Charisma is neither a necessary nor a sufficient condition for successful chief executives.
- The main functions and tasks of a chief executive are the following: embodying and implementing the corporate mission and values; developing and structuring a point of view about the firm's future; investment and resource allocation; developing leadership and management; and improving operational efficiency and organizational design.
- Most of the chief executive's tasks must be developed and executed by and in cooperation with the board of management. Choosing the right people for this board, developing them, giving them clear responsibilities and goals, and making them a real team are some key challenges for a chief executive.
- When working with the board of management, the chief executive could consider some basic principles to facilitate this task. They include team spirit, collegial decision making, accountability, efficiency, and a global, integrative perspective.

8   The CEO's role in developing the firm as an institution

In an industry dominated by US companies, Bertelsmann, the German media conglomerate, stands out as one of the most innovative firms in this sector. It is neither the largest nor the most profitable firm in the industry, but it has certain qualities – beyond its business model and performance – that make it very unique in the business world. In fact, it is one of the most respected companies in Europe, both for its business activities and it social impact.

Bertelsmann was founded by Carl Bertelsmann in 1835 in Gütersloh, Germany, as a publisher of Christian books and songs. It is a family business, controlled by the Mohn family (the fifth generation of the Bertelsmann family) and the Bertelsmann Foundation. After the collapse of the German economy in World War II, Reinhard Mohn started to rebuild the firm in 1947; he changed it into a global player in the media world and took it to new levels of excellence.[1]

The growth of Bertelsmann after World War II and its transformation into a huge media conglomerate and a respected institution cannot be explained without acknowledging the work, leadership, charisma and ideas of Reinhard Mohn, one of the most successful European entrepreneurs of the twentieth century and the driving force behind Bertelsmann's development.

Bertelsmann is known worldwide for a number of important dimensions. It is a media company committed to the creation and

---

[1] For a more detailed view of the history and evolution of Bertelsmann and the emergence of its culture and values, see Cardona and Wilkinson (2008).

diffusion of culture at all levels, but it also sees itself as a responsible member of a society and is recognized by that society. This German firm has developed very important ideas in the area of people development and corporate culture. The family atmosphere still permeates Bertelsmann's professional context, even if the company already employs thousands of people round the world. Visitors can sense the spirit of the place as soon as they arrive at Bertelsmann's headquarters. Its values permeate everything: it is an entrepreneurial firm with a cooperative atmosphere among employees, a culture of partnership and a strong sense of citizenship.

Its model of corporate social responsibility is also extremely innovative. For Bertelsmann, social responsibility is not just a fad of our times. The company has been practising it for decades, targeting its efforts at the societies in which it operates. Social responsibility is closely tied to Bertelsmann businesses so that these companies and their senior managers can get more involved with social initiatives. Their efforts focus on both short-term and long-term results.

In many ways, Bertelsmann reflects not just Reinhard Mohn's personality, but also his ideas, attitudes and values. Among them, we could highlight his interest in building not a powerful business but a social institution, a firm that could have a strong impact on society. For Mohn, profitability was not the most important criterion. Mohn's indisputable entrepreneurial drive was also reflected in the way the firm was organized: autonomous business units and a very decentralized organizational structure. Mohn also had an interest in the long term. This is the reason why he wanted to preserve the firm as a family business, but he was generous enough to give 69 per cent of his Bertelsmann stock to the Bertelsmann Foundation, becoming the company's largest shareholder. Liz Mohn, Mohn's wife and vice president of the Bertelsmann Foundation, has also promoted Mohn's basic notions about companies and their role in society through the many initiatives that the Foundation has organized and spread around the world.

Reinhard Mohn's notion of professional work in companies was also very creative.[2] His ideas on the nature of human work, the role of people in companies and the foundations of firms' success fostered his belief in positioning cooperation as the linchpin both inside firms and between firms and society. He was more interested in the progress of individuals through his company than in accumulating power or money. He also thought that business leaders must work and encourage others to do so through personal example.

Like any other company, Bertelsmann has challenges and problems; but it remains a respected company, a firm that has become a social institution. It did not achieve this status spontaneously. Rather, it is the outcome of many decisions, big and small, made over the years by Mohn. It is a clear case for the potential impact a chief executive can have on a firm's performance. We can also observe that basic attitudes and qualities – beyond professional competence – help a chief executive shape his company in unexpected ways. Mohn's case highlights the potential that senior executives have in creating lasting organizations with deep values.

2. CAN A CEO TURN A FIRM INTO MORE THAN A SIMPLE ORGANIZATION?

In Chapter 7, we examined the tasks, duties and responsibilities of the CEO and the senior management team and their contribution to corporate governance. Having introduced the notion of the firm as an institution in Chapter 3, here we shall focus on the CEO and his challenge in leading and developing the firm as a respected institution. Our perspective here is different from (and complementary to) the one adopted in Chapter 7. Here we are concerned not with the capabilities and responsibilities of CEOs or senior executives in general, but with the attitudes and values a CEO must develop to go beyond business success and help make his company a respected institution.

---

[2] Some of his ideas were discussed in Mohn (1996).

The focus on leadership and the role of business leaders in corporate growth and development has steadily gained momentum in recent years. The booming leadership industry publishes books, holds seminars, develops educational products and creates specialist leadership education institutions. There has been a tremendous proliferation of studies on leadership from various disciplines. CEOs with proven track records, such as Lou Gerstner of IBM, Bill George of Medtronic and Andy Grove of Intel, have authored or inspired works on leadership.

This outpouring of ideas should not surprise us. Leaders can play a very decisive role in business, just as they can in politics. Leaders' professional and personal excellence makes a real difference. In a study of critical success factors for firms, Noria *et al.* (2003) showed that a significant proportion of a company's performance is directly attributable to the work of the CEO. If we could quantify the indirect impact of leadership, the proportion might be even higher. Conversely, counterproductive leadership can wipe out human, moral and economic value on a vast scale, as we have seen in the current financial crisis. Companies, organizations and countries need good leaders. As a matter of fact, lack of good leadership both in politics and in the business world seems to be considered one of the major weaknesses of modern society. The current financial crisis has made the need for good leadership even more striking.

The common denominator among most leadership studies is the group of features they consider: the distinctive qualities and attributes of business leaders; how they exercise leadership; how they develop over time; and the impact they have on their organizations. Many of these studies are simply the result of more or less rigorous empirical observation. Others are more solidly grounded in sociological or psychological theory. Some of the earliest works on the role of chief executives, such as those of Barnard (1938) and Drucker (1954), are interdisciplinary studies drawing on managers' practical experience.

This is a very useful approach for determining what corporate leaders are like; what qualities, skills and competencies they possess or acquire; and even what mistakes they tend to make. But the approach has a limitation: it sees leadership exclusively from the perspective of the leader – that is, the person who exercises the leadership responsibilities – or from that of the leadership function in general. Very few authors have given in-depth consideration to the particular type of leader a given company might need to make companies sustainable in the long term. In other words, there is abundant knowledge about the supply of leadership and the broad range of leadership options, qualities and style. Nevertheless, there is not strong evidence about the type of leader and the leadership qualities a company in any given circumstances is likely to need, not only to survive, but to be turned into a more respected institution. We may go back to Reinhard Mohn and the development of Bertelsmann and ask a simple question: what are the qualities of his leadership that made it possible to transform a small publisher into such an influential and respected firm?

Recent decades have brought a growing interest in management as a profession. In fact, several business schools came into existence in the United States with the aim of turning the managerial job and the activities of entrepreneurs into a respected profession (Khurana 2007), on par with medicine or law. Leaving aside the regulatory dimensions of the access to some professions – like medicine or law – the definition of the management profession should help highlight the specific tasks of a senior manager: the type of problems a manager deals with, the social needs he addresses, and the knowledge and skills he needs to be professionally competent. In some cases, the definition of a profession can exclude outsiders and protect the status of insiders. Yet the professions that have earned social recognition are those that are necessary to society, and it is only reasonable that members of these professions – and society as a whole – should want to safeguard their quality and the impact of their service to societies.

The professionalization of management is an important trend. At the same time, however, a dangerous phenomenon has become apparent: the disconnect between what society expects of managers, how companies understand what is expected of managers and how they themselves respond to these expectations. To appreciate the seriousness of the problem, imagine what would happen if the supply of doctors and medical training were independent of society's health needs; if the education of medical doctors were divorced from people's real needs; or if the policy debate were focused on the teaching styles of different medical schools, without any thought for the patients or their health problems.

The analogy between medicine and management can be taken only so far, but both professions share a need to combine science, art and practice. Both also have a huge impact on the lives of many people and, ultimately, on the life of society. Basically, the analogy shows the sort of problem that can arise if leadership is not also considered from the point of view of what companies and society need. And this analogy can be also applied to other relevant professions, such as law or architecture.

A first approximation to this dilemma suggests that the demand for management professionals is highly influenced by what financial analysts think companies need, even if some of them know companies only from their financial statements. For many boards of directors of listed and unlisted companies, such analyses are important references.

Headhunters hired to recruit CEOs take the briefs from their clients, refine them and search for managers who display qualities consistent with analysts' opinions. Many of them assume that CEOs must deliver results quickly, get things done and implement change. These abilities are important, often indispensable qualities for many firms. Yet the main challenge for CEOs who meet these requirements is to manage dilemmas, conflicts and paradoxes. Some of these qualities are more important than others. Some are core competencies; others are peripheral. Also, some qualities are praised to the skies at certain stages of the business cycle or on the wave of a management fad, only to disappear as quickly as they came and return to oblivion. A significant limitation of those lists of expected qualities for CEOs and senior managers is that they do not include prudence, a classical virtue that serves precisely to help senior managers exercise other qualities or virtues in the right measure. We will discuss this later in this chapter.

Every company has its own leadership needs, which may change over time. But the great majority of companies that are in business for the long haul have one essential need: they must constantly improve their reputation as social institutions that offer useful goods and services to their clients and, in so doing, create economic value and develop their people. In a nutshell, their goal is to become respected institutions.

This objective, associated with the willingness to survive in the long term, goes beyond product and service quality, market access, innovation capacity or brand image. It calls for a careful thought about the role of the firm as an institution that creates economic wealth and promotes human and social development by providing goods and services. Therefore, leadership cannot be considered merely in terms of leadership style or personal qualities; it must also be considered in terms of what firms and society need and expect from CEOs and senior managers.

Our core thesis in this chapter is that CEOs must contribute to accomplishing the company's mission, which means, among others things, enhancing the company's social legitimacy and working to ensure its long-term development and survival. These goals can be achieved only if the firm becomes a relevant and good provider of goods and services, if it allows its people to develop, and if it generates economic value.

A central task of any CEO, therefore, is to help create and improve the company as an institution that is capable of developing and surviving in the long run by accomplishing its mission, both external (vis-à-vis customers, shareholders and society) and internal

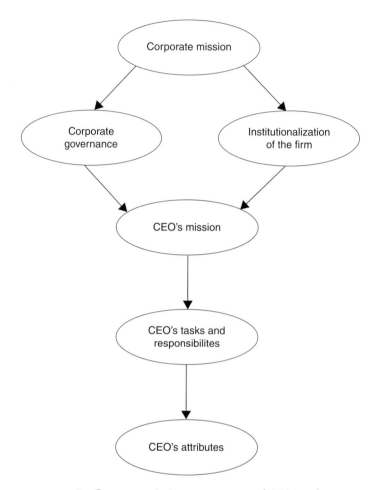

FIGURE 8.1 Corporate mission, governance and CEO attributes

(*vis-à-vis* employees). A company that does this becomes a respected institution.

A chief executive or senior manager must strive to develop a set of essential qualities and attitudes to achieve this goal. These qualities constitute the backbone and basic profile of any senior manager who aspires not only to build a successful business but also to create and develop a respected institution. This is the subject of this chapter. Figure 8.1 summarizes the relationships among the company's mission; its development as an institution; the CEO's mission, tasks and responsibilities; and the qualities a CEO must develop in order to contribute to that mission. As we said previously, our aim is to relate the company's mission to the CEO's mission and identify the qualities a CEO must have in order to accomplish his mission.

3. THE CEO'S MISSION AND THE FIRM AS AN INSTITUTION

If the company's mission and function in society are as we have described them, then the CEO's role is to display her or his professional and personal qualities at the service of the company's mission. Whether business leaders should be charismatic or not, whether they should be great communicators, whether leaders are born or made, whether companies need executive leaders or visionary leaders: all these are relevant issues, but not the most relevant one. The important thing is that the CEO, with his experience and qualities, be suitably equipped to help the company achieve its goals and carry out its mission.

The CEO must do his part to ensure that the company accomplishes its mission, becomes a respected institution, and develops and survives in the long term. This means that the CEO must ensure that the company is efficient, attracts good professionals and achieves good financial results by providing good products or services for its customers. He will do this by building a management team whose members find the company's goals attractive. Also, the CEO will try to ensure that the company is not a foreign body in the society in which it operates by leading it to interact with society on levels beyond the strictly economic dimension.

This view of the CEO's role contrasts with the one that is, unfortunately, still present in the market for CEOs. Too many people still try to assess CEOs in terms of short-term financial performance or stock price gains. These could be good achievements – but only if they are sustained in the long term.

After two decades of excessive praise for CEOs' qualities such as drive, charisma and ambition, the current financial crisis and the spate of corporate scandals have prompted a more sceptical view of the firm, its mission, its role in society and the role of the chief executive. In the wake of this crisis of confidence, rather than praising CEOs' strategic vision or capacity for quick restructuring, investors and public opinion have voiced their indignation at the abuses committed by some top managers, the outsize pay some of them receive, and the huge disparity between CEO pay and that of other employees. Executive pay is obviously a very complex issue. Executives do a very special job, and what they do can affect the entire organization. But team spirit and trust evaporate when the pay gap becomes too wide and a sense of fairness and decency is lost.

The erosion of confidence in large companies and the discredit of top management cannot be overcome simply by weeding out a few 'bad apples'. The firm's legitimacy in society cannot be founded on economic efficiency, wealth creation or job creation alone. Such factors are important but insufficient. Companies achieve legitimacy by becoming exemplary economic and social institutions that combine efficiency with humanism, and wealth creation with respect for human dignity and the communities in which they operate, while seeking long-term viability. In a word, firms must become respected institutions, and CEOs must work toward this end.

The long-term perspective is an essential part of the CEO's mission. The challenge is not only to achieve short-term economic success, but to make the company a respected institution, ensure its long-term survival, and help everybody in the company take a forward-looking approach that strengthens the firm's future viability. Good financial performance is necessary, but it is not the only indicator of a CEO's success. The company must also have something special that attracts customers and employees. Short-term success often has a stifling, disorienting effect. Developing a legendary company demands not only good financial performance but also certain qualities in the organization and its people that inspire social respect.

4. ATTRIBUTES AND QUALITIES OF AN INSTITUTION-BUILDING CEO

Beyond well-known professional competencies, the job of a CEO differs from that of a functional manager in various ways. A CEO must cultivate a comprehensive, integrative view of the organization and avoid taking a partial, functional or divisional approach to problems, challenges or solutions. He must orient the organization toward the long term, beyond short-term fluctuations, and contribute to the enterprise's long-term success and survival, beyond any failures in individual business units. A CEO does not need to know more about finance than the CFO or more about technology than the CTO, but he must be able to engage in a rigorous debate on any of these subjects. A CEO must be capable of leading and working with the top management team and securing its commitment to the company's purposes: this is one of his core tasks. A CEO must also be capable of raising the necessary financial resources for the enterprise and directing the business and the organization so that it wins the respect of society.

The notion of building, developing and strengthening an institution encompasses and defines the qualities and capabilities required of a business leader who helps a company's long-term growth. A person who builds for the future or reinforces what has already been built thinks naturally in terms of long-term successful growth and survival. The above considerations suggest some competencies and qualities of an institutional leader (see Figure 8.2).

4.1 Long-term perspective, short-term execution

The first attribute that a CEO should develop is a long-term perspective not only of markets, customers, products or competitors, but of all the areas and functions that help a firm become an institution: a mission, a set of values, a group of professionals, an organization and, of course, customers who have needs and who expect goods or services, which must be provided as efficiently as possible and at a profit.

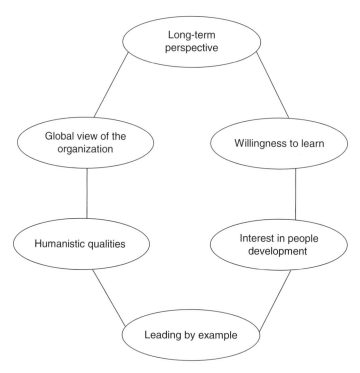

FIGURE 8.2 Some of a CEO's attributes

Senior executives are under enormous pressure to deliver short-term results. Analysts demand not only results but also quarterly earnings forecasts. Analysts and media tend to magnify performance announcements, talking some firms up while running others down, often for reasons that have little or nothing to do with what firms have actually done. Any experienced executive knows how difficult it is to manage for the short term, as many of the most important decisions have an impact only in the long term. And however good analysts may be at anticipating events, they often lose sight of what a particular decision means for the company's long-term future.

None of this will be of any use if the CEO does not strive to ensure that the company as a whole is efficient. A good long-term strategy must be executed efficiently day to day. The CEO must be capable of looking to the long term and, at the same time, ensuring the proper quality in executing the different plans and policies.

4.2 Global view of the organization: the general management perspective

The concern that a CEO or a senior manager should have for the long term is associated with other qualities that he should develop. One of these is an integrated and holistic view of the organization, as well as a good knowledge of its various functions, divisions and people. A CEO must combine an understanding of each of the company's units, divisions and functions with a thorough grasp of the whole organization. This is a necessary step in order to develop the firm as an institution. We refer to this view or vision as the general management perspective.

This perspective goes beyond the boundaries of the different functions (like marketing, operations, finance or technology, among others) and is by definition cross-functional. It takes into account and combines the relevant external factors regarding social and economic trends, markets, competitors, technology or product innovation, and puts them in contrast with the firm's positioning, people and internal capabilities. The general management perspective looks at the long term while managing the short term. A good CEO constantly thinks about the firm's future, how the firm has to change over the next years and how this change has to be implemented. At the same time, long-term plans have to be considered simultaneously with the design of new plans and ideas and their implementation in the short term.

CEOs with this general management perspective are interested not only in sales growth, financial performance or productivity, but in the development of the company as a whole. In this respect, they design a group of indicators of performance – similar to those that we presented in Chapter 3 when speaking about the firm as a respected institution – that help them develop a more comprehensive and holistic understanding of the firm. In fact, one of the greatest challenges for a functional manager when assuming the CEO role is to leave aside his former functional role and perspective, and focus instead on the grey areas of general management, like thinking about the long term, developing the top management team, understanding the external environment or how to deal with shareholders and other external parties. In particular, solving the conflicts among divisional functions and priorities, where the important thing is not to plough ahead in any direction but to advance in a direction that enables the company to develop as an institution, is a key challenge for the transition from a functional managerial job to the chief executive job.

The general management perspective requires experience, which is only natural in this profession. It also requires proper development and education. Without thorough knowledge and experience of the company's various functional areas, a person cannot have a general management perspective. A good CEO or senior manager must have a sound grasp of finance, marketing, operations and technology. Above all, he must know his people and know how to work with them, lead them and help them grow. Indeed, the CEO's primary task is to manage people. A sales director must sell, and a financial director must optimize the use of financial resources and raise the funds the company needs to operate. But a CEO is like the conductor of an orchestra. He has no instrument to play and does not need to be an expert in each one; but he must know what each player can and has to do and bring it into play at the right moment when the orchestra is performing a particular piece.

This global view also relates in a particular way to the firm's financial and strategic health. The CEO must have the ability to make a good global diagnosis of the firm and its problems and challenges, ensure that plan execution is good, that the company makes money, and that it has a healthy and sustainable financial position. The CEO must also assess the various investment options and decide which projects are to be undertaken and which are not. The various possible projects (any healthy company must be capable of generating enough project proposals to be able to turn some of them down) must be classified and prioritized. Economic value is an important factor to consider when setting priorities and evaluating business decisions, but so is the impact that each project will have on other dimensions of the company (human, organizational, strategic, social) and on the company's long-term development and survival. Very often, the projects merely exploit opportunities, which are always welcome. Yet the CEO must always be on the lookout for projects that will help to consolidate the company's long-term objectives. The firm's financial dimensions are very relevant, but they should also be understood in the wider frame of the general management perspective.

4.3 Humanistic qualities

The CEO's long-term outlook opens new perspectives in some qualities that business leaders need to develop. Short-term performance is always important, but long-term performance is what makes a difference in a senior manager's professional life. Some of those qualities require technical expertise, but many others have to do with the ability to face complex situations in professional life and, in particular, are related to working with and leading people in an atmosphere of trust. Some of them are related to what can be defined as the CEO's character. Collins (2001) and Llano (2004) identified humility as an essential virtue for any CEO, that should be combined and developed together with a determination to achieve agreed objectives.

Bennis and Thomas (2002) stressed the importance of courage, fortitude, resilience and drive to overcome the difficulties that any CEO must deal with. Llano (2004) described the tenacity of leaders whose characters are forged in adversity and their efforts to overcome external and internal difficulties of all kinds as a source of personal growth. This may seem like a surprising choice of virtues or qualities, but as soon as one thinks seriously about it, it is obvious that they are decisive if a CEO is to meet the challenge of promoting the company's long-term development and survival. They are essential to the making of a CEO.

In fact, humility and courage to face difficulties and challenges belong in a more general framework, a core set of virtues initially developed by the Greek philosophers and later refined by the Christian tradition. Some of them are also important in other cultural and religious traditions. They are virtues based upon a notion of the person that has some basic pillars: unique dignity, unquestionable rights, individual freedom and responsibility to assume one's duties, among others. These characteristics help define some cardinal or core virtues in a person's life: fortitude, fairness, prudence and temperance. These virtues are habits that enable a person to accomplish his or her purpose as a human being, and live a meaningful and fulfilled life. It is interesting to note that while areas like finance, marketing or operations are considered indispensable in the education of managers, character development, which is so important in the making of a good manager, has received very little attention. Moreover, a CEO's character is key in developing companies that could eventually become respected institutions. In so many cases, like in Reinhard Mohn's story in relaunching and developing Bertelsmann after World War II, the character of the chief executive or the firm's founder is in some ways reflected on the soul of the corporation that he helped create or develop.

In the case of a CEO, however, these virtues have a specific profile. They are important and relevant in any profession, and the qualities associated with them are always useful. A CEO, however, must deploy these virtues in a special way, not only for his own personal development but also because they will make him more effective in the job and, eventually, help gain the respect of colleagues, employees and competitors.

In his work, a CEO constantly deals with other people (employees, customers, shareholders and so forth), motivating them, engaging them, promoting their rights, reminding them of their duties, and always keeping their development and the common good in mind. The job of a CEO or senior executive is to pull everything together. The job is oriented to action, to transforming the world, with the collaboration of other people. For a CEO, the requirement to exercise these and other virtues is not merely a matter of convenience, utility or corporate reputation. It is not that in current circumstances head-bowing humility goes down better than tall ambition. No; there is a deeper reason. If a CEO does not exercise these virtues, he will not be able to do his job well, fulfil one's personal mission or help accomplish the company's potential in the long term.

A CEO cannot grow professionally without practising the habits of temperance, strength, fairness and prudence in the exercise of his profession. To neglect these habits is to encourage negative learning and allow mediocrity to take over, obstructing good intentions, undermining good will and deleting the potential impact of leading by example.

Without these core virtues, a CEO is unlikely to be able to contribute effectively to achieving or developing the firm's mission. As professional qualities, some of them are at least as important as knowledge of finance or marketing, or experience of corporate change processes. Good CEOs need to be professionally competent, but also have a sense of integrity and be people of character. Without a sense of justice and fairness, or the strength of character to seek what is good and do what needs to be done, for example, a CEO cannot possibly ensure the company's long-term survival. And this is a limitation that will most likely prevent him from carrying out well his own mission or contributing to that of the company as a whole.

A CEO who does not strive to live by and develop these habits is failing to improve his own development and performance as CEO. His conduct ceases to be exemplary, and the relationship of trust with his colleagues becomes impaired.

The CEO's role considered in this context is associated with a clear willingness to serve. The CEO is a professional whose work is at the service of customers, shareholders, employees and the society in which the company operates. In fact, there can be no leadership and no legitimate exercise of power without such a commitment to serving others. Nor is there any point in being spectacularly effective as a manager if such effectiveness does not have a positive impact on other people, and enhance other people's well-being and growth. Without service, the leader's power becomes narcissism, selfishness or complacency. And the legitimacy of such a power will be called into question. Only if he shows a spirit of service can a leader become a model for others and help build a respected company. Imagining otherwise – for example, that it is others who must serve the CEO – would be a huge mistake. In certain recent business cases we have seen how some CEOs made their companies serve their own goals and purpose. Anyone can make a mistake, but persisting in error and not correcting it disqualifies a CEO from occupying this position.

Top management's responsibility requires strategy, vision, team management, mobilization of people's effort, and a sense of entrepreneurship and innovation to serve customers better. All these activities will eventually affect top managers themselves. How this actually happens will depend on the professional competence with which they carry out their activities and the habits and qualities they acquire in this process. Aside from short-term results, what remains after a CEO has spent several years in the top position is the impact that his work has had on the company, on the people who have worked with him, on customers and shareholders. This impact is obviously richer and more diverse than any measure of financial performance can encapsulate. A person may have grown rich and, at the same time, may have ruined his life. Or he may have attained a fulfilled life in accomplishing his mission.

In addition, as discussed in Chapter 7, the CEO must work to mould the firm's institutional structure and the relationship among shareholders, directors and top management. The principles of good corporate governance ensure that the distribution of decision-making power and the rights of each decision maker are clearly defined in a consistent framework. The CEO must see to it that corporate governance rules concerning the board of directors and the board of management, and the allocation of decision rights on important matters are clearly defined and consistent with the company's mission and values so that they assist the company in developing, surviving and becoming a respected institution.

4.4 Leading by example

A CEO develops people and talent not only by employing sophisticated techniques, but mainly by learning and becoming a positive model for others, without directly seeking this effect. In order to create an environment that encourages learning, relationships between people must be based on professional and personal trust. Professional trust arises first when people responsible for each task or function are competent – that is, capable of efficiently dealing with problems and finding solutions. Personal trust also demands a moral behaviour – and ethical values. Ethics, as fashionable in many companies as it is neglected and circumvented with sophisticated arguments, is more than just a condition of survival or a prerequisite for making money. Ethics is a vital ingredient of professional competence and one of the pillars on which the CEO's character is built. An executive who adheres to certain stable ethical values is predictable and capable of generating trust among the company's people, and ensuring the long-term future of the enterprise as a whole.

A CEO with a strong sense of integrity and ethical values does not just talk about ethics; he tries to put it into practice in every business problem or challenge. A responsible CEO must strive to live by the core virtues that facilitate personal growth and development, like fortitude, justice, prudence and temperance. In this he bears a great responsibility. He cannot help the people who work with him grow and contribute to the company's development unless he first sets an example.

A chief executive works in a glass house, and every action and omission sends signals to the rest of the organization. Positive, consistent messages naturally make the company stronger, while negative messages reveal inconsistency, cause confusion, weaken the company's internal cohesion and jeopardize its long-term viability.

A senior executive must make every effort, within his natural limitations, to be a positive reference point with his life – partly, of course, to further his own personal growth. It is in the CEO's heart and mind that the various dimensions of professional, and personal life flow together and converge. Each of these dimensions influences other people more or less directly, so a CEO cannot be a reference to his subordinates if any aspect of his life is less than exemplary. Like any other person, a CEO deserves respect and forgiveness for mistakes, but a CEO cannot be a reference and motivate those who work with him if his conduct is not exemplary in other areas of his life. As with an alcoholic who says he drinks only outside working hours, experience shows that certain mental barriers or deeply rooted behaviours are intractable obstacles to certain undertakings.

This suggests that the CEO's job shares many attributes and characteristics of a vocation – an undertaking that is more than just a way of earning a living. It is a call to perform a task in the service of others, a task that has an enormous impact on the CEO and on others.

4.5 People development, talent building

For a company to survive in the long term, it must help develop the next generation of managers, build efficient teams and develop people's professional capabilities. Companies are made up of people and companies are, essentially, what their people are; it is reasonable to say that a company's long-term viability will depend largely on the professional and personal qualities of the people who work in it. Consequently, a CEO must ensure that the company has not only the managers it needs today but also the necessary plans and processes for developing the next generation of managers from within, without excluding the possibility of hiring managers from outside.

A company will face a variety of challenges at different points in its life. Those in the positions of greatest responsibility must be prepared to meet those challenges successfully. Sometimes, these people may come from other companies. One indicator of a company's strength as an institution, however, is its ability to generate, attract and retain talent. Good professionals expect appropriate financial rewards, but to varying degrees they also expect more from a company: professional challenges, constant opportunities to learn and improve, and a working atmosphere in which they can grow and be part of an enterprise that has a sense of mission extending well beyond the job of each individual.

Creating such a work environment, one in which people are able to integrate and realize their potential, is the CEO's direct responsibility. A core requirement of any such environment is that the company has a mission to accomplish, a reason for existing and making a profit. Profitability is necessary, but is not the cornerstone of the firm but a necessary condition for the firm to exist. What abides is the mission: the will to create a different type of organization, to offer goods or services that are useful to someone and meet a need, or to anticipate possible future needs. Nokia, for instance, aims to connect people through technology. Apple wants to help create the future by encouraging its people and customers think differently in the personal computer world. Novartis aspires to cure diseases. And Medtronic's goal is to alleviate pain, restore health and extend life. Companies with an explicit or implicit mission that justifies their existence as institutions are more respected and, in the long run, better able to attract and retain talent.

4.6 Willingness to learn

What counts as success for a CEO and what is learned from success or failure are vital to the company's long-term survival. It is easy enough to identify indicators of failure; these include the inability to build a strong management team, a lack of operational efficiency, persistent losses, low staff morale and poor customer relationships.

Measures of success are more elusive. Many of the factors that influence a company's earnings and share value are beyond the company's or the CEO's control. Earnings and share value are important indicators, but they should not be the only ones – otherwise the notion of success would become an intolerable burden for the CEO. In his classic management book *Management: Tasks, Responsibilities, Practices* (1974), Drucker said that the CEO must set goals, organize, communicate and monitor goal achievement. No company can survive without such managerial effectiveness.

For the development of an organization that lasts, management indicators must include not only economic and financial variables but also variables that encourage people to learn from their successes and failures. Companies must achieve adequate financial results, but they must also achieve other goals relating to the way they function, their ability to attract and retain excellent professionals, and their success in creating a working environment in which personal development comes first.

In his efforts to develop the firm as an institution, the CEO must not neglect to foster ongoing professional and personal learning and improvement. He must show the same commitment to self-improvement as he expects of those who work with him. Otherwise, his credibility will be eroded, and his professional development will go into reverse. It is important to remember also that the development of new competencies in an organization depends to a significant extent on the continuous improvement of the professional competencies and moral qualities of the organization's CEO and top management team.

5. SOME FINAL THOUGHTS

The growing importance of the firm in our society has led to an upsurge of interest in leadership and the qualities of a good leader. There are no simple answers to these questions, which have been discussed at great length in management literature.

In this chapter, we have proposed some thoughts on CEOs' qualities and attributes in light of the goal of creating and developing respected institutions – that is, firms that are recognized by society as having an economic dimension but that also have other dimensions. If we try to define the qualities of a good CEO, we run the risk of focusing on attributes whose importance changes over time, such as charisma or emotional intelligence.

The greatness of a CEO's work lies not in his supposedly decisive influence or the spectacular scale or impact of his decisions, but in his ability to promote the development of effective professionals and, respected and enduring institutions. His legacy will be the nurturing of firms that combine efficiency with humanity, organizations that are efficient and also help and encourage people to grow and develop professionally and personally.

KEY LEARNING POINTS

- CEOs should have a few basic professional competencies and capabilities: business knowledge, people management, finance, marketing and operations among others. They must also be team players, deploy good cross-cultural abilities and be good at execution. But a CEO should also have some personal attributes and qualities that are indispensable to developing a firm as a respected social institution.
- Beyond the basic business capabilities, we have explored the dimensions around six attributes that a CEO needs to help build a respected company: a long-term perspective, a global and integrative view of the firm, humanistic qualities, leading by example, developing people and willingness to learn. Though these qualities require that CEOs have excellent business expertise, they go beyond it. They are attributes that could help transform a company into a respected institution.

Bibliography

Alchian, A. A. 1950. 'Uncertainty, evolution and economic theory'. *Journal of Political Economy* 58(2): 211–21.

Aldama, E. *et al.* 2003. *Informe de la Comisión Especial para el fomento de la transparencia y seguridad en los mercados y en las sociedades cotizadas.* Madrid.

Argandoña, A. 1991. 'Ética y economía de mercado'. *Información Comercial Española* 691: 45–53.

Argandoña, A. 2006. 'Economía de mercado y responsabilidad social de la empresa'. *Papeles de Economía Española* 108: 2–9.

Argandoña, A. 2008. 'Integrating ethics into action theory and organizational theory'. *Journal of Business Ethics* 78(3): 435–46.

Arrow, K. J. 1951. *Social choice and individual values.* John Wiley, New York.

Arrow, K. J. 1974. *The limits of organization.* Norton, New York.

Arrow, K. J. 1986. 'Rationality of self and others in an economic system'. *Journal of Business* 4(2): S385–S400.

Barnard, C. 1938. *The functions of the executive.* Harvard University Press, Cambridge, MA.

Bebchuk, L. 2004. 'The case for increasing shareholder power'. The Harvard John M. Olin Discussion Paper Series no. 500, Harvard Law School, Cambridge, MA.

Bebchuk, L. and Fried, J. M. 2004. *Pay without performance: the unfulfilled promise of executive compensation.* Harvard University Press, Cambridge, MA.

Benioff, M. with Southwick, K. 2004. *Compassionate capitalism. How corporations can make doing good an integral part of doing well.* Career Press, Franklin Lakes, NJ.

Bennis, W. G and Thomas, R. J. 2002. 'Crucibles of leadership'. *Harvard Business Review,* September: 39–45.

Berle, A. A. and Means, G. C. 1932. *The modern corporation and private property* (1991 edition). Transaction, New Brunswick, NJ.

Bishop, M. and Green, M. 2008. *Philanthro-capitalism.* Bloomsbury Press, New York.

Bogle, J. C. 2008. 'Reflections on CEO compensation'. *The Academy of Management Perspectives* 22(2): 21–5.

Bouton, D. 2002. *Promoting better corporate governance in listed companies.* Paris.

Bower, J. L. 2007. *The CEO within.* Harvard Business School Press, Boston.

Cadbury, A. 1992. *Codes of best practice: report from the committee on financial aspects of corporate governance.* Gee Publishing, London.

Cadbury, A. 2002. *Corporate governance and chairmanship.* Oxford University Press.

Canals, J. 1997. *Universal banking.* Oxford University Press.

Canals, J. 2000. *Managing corporate growth.* Oxford University Press.

Canals, J. 2003. 'Gobierno corporativo. Más allá de las reformas legales'. *Revista del Instituto de Estudios Económicos* 1: 19–33.

Cardona, P. and Wilkinson, H. 2008. 'Bertelsmann Media Worldwide: worldwide culture?', IESE case no. 2–408–016.

Carroll, A. B. 1999. 'Corporate social responsibility'. *Business and Society* 38(3): 268–95.

Carter, C. B. and Lorsch, J. 2003. *Back to the drawing board.* Harvard Business School Press, Boston.

Chandler, A. 1977. *The visible hand.* Harvard University Press, Cambridge, MA.

Child, J. 1972. 'Organization structure, environment and performance: the role of strategic choice'. *Sociology* 6: 1–22.

Collins, J. 2001. 'Level 5 leadership'. *Harvard Business Review*, January: 67–76.

Collins, J. and Porras, J. 1994. *Built to last.* HarperCollins, New York.

Committee for Economic Development 1971. 'Social responsibilities of business corporations'. New York.

Conference Board, The 2003. 'Findings and recommendations'. Commission on Public Trust and Private Enterprise, New York.

Conger, J. A., Lawler III, E. E. and Finegold, D. L. 2001. *Corporate boards.* Jossey-Bass, San Francisco.

Core, J. E., Guay, W. R. and Thomas, R. S. 2005. 'Is US CEO compensation broken?', *Journal of Applied Corporate Finance* 17(4): 97–104.

Corrales, A. and Melé, D. 2005. 'Medtronic Inc: from corporate mission to organizational culture'. IESE case no. 0–305-066.

Davis, G. F. (2009). *Managed by the markets.* Oxford University Press.

Davis, K. 1960. 'Can business afford to ignore corporate social responsabilities?' *California Management Review* 2(1): 70–6.

Debreu, G. 1959. *The theory of value.* John Wiley, New York.

Demb, A. and Neubauer, F. F. 1992. *The corporate board.* Oxford University Press.

Diamond, D. W. 1984. 'Financial intermediation and delegated monitoring'. *Review of Economic Studies* 51: 393–414.

Donaldson, G. and Lorsch, J. 1984. *Decision making at the top.* Basic Books, New York.

Drucker, P. 1954. *The practice of management.* Harper & Row, New York.

Drucker, P. 1974. *Management: tasks, responsibilities, practices.* Harper & Row, New York.

Edwards, J. S. S. and Fischer, K. 1994. *Banks, finance and investment in Germany.* Cambridge University Press.

Elkington, J. and Hartigan, P. 2008. *The power of unreasonable people: how social entrepreneurs create markets that change the world*. Harvard Business School Press, Boston.

European Commission 2001. 'Corporate social responsibility', Green Paper, Brussels.

Fama, E. 1970. 'Efficient capital markets: a review of theory and empirical work'. *Journal of Finance* 25(2): 383–417.

Fama, E. and Jensen, M. 1983. 'Separation of ownership and control'. *Journal of Law and Economics* 26: 301–25.

Ferraro, F., Pfeffer, J. and Sutton, R. 2005. 'Economics language and assumptions: how theories may become self-fulfilling'. *Academy of Management Review* 30(1): 8–24.

Fox, J. 2009. *The myth of the rational market*. Harper Business, New York.

Freeman, R. E. 1984. *Strategic management: a stakeholder approach*. Pitman, Boston.

Friedman, M. 1970. 'The social responsibility of business is to increase its profits'. *New York Times Magazine*, 13 September.

Friedman, M. and Friedman, R. 1962. *Capitalism and freedom*. University of Chicago Press.

Fukuyama, F. 1995. *Trust*. Free Press, New York.

Gallo, M. A. 1980. *Responsabilidades sociales de la empresa*. EUNSA, Pamplona.

Garriga, E. and Melé, D. 2004. 'Corporate social responsibility theories: mapping the territory'. *Journal of Business Ethics* 53(1): 51–72.

George, B. 2003. *Authentic leadership*. Jossey-Bass, San Francisco.

George, B. 2007. *True north*. Jossey-Bass, San Francisco.

Ghemawat, P. 1991. *Commitment*. Free Press: Boston.

Ghoshal, S. 2005. 'Bad management theories are destroying good management practices'. *Academy of Management Learning and Education* 4(1): 75–91.

Ghoshal, S. and Bartlett, C. A. 1997. *The individualized corporation*. Harper Business, New York.

Gilson, R. J. 2000. 'The globalization of corporate governance: convergence of form or function?'. Columbia Law School, Working Paper No. 174.

Gintis, H. and Khurana, R. 2006. 'Corporate honesty and business education: a behavioral model', in P. J. Zak (ed.) *Moral markets: the critical role of values in the economy*, Princeton University Press.

Greenwald, B. and Stiglitz, J. E. 1986. 'Externalities in economies with imperfect information and incomplete markets'. *Quarterly Journal of Economics* 101(2): 229–64.

Grove, A. 1997. *Only the paranoid survive: how to exploit the crisis points that challenge every company and career*. HarperCollins, New York.

Hambrick, D. C. and Fukutomi, G. 1991. 'The seasons of a CEO's tenure'. *Academy of Management Review* 16: 719–42.

Hamel, G. and Prahalad, C. K. 1994. *Competing for the future*. Harvard Business School Press, Boston.

Hart, O. 1995. *Firms, contracts and financial structure*. Oxford University Press, Oxford.

Hausman, D. and McPherson, M. S. 1993. 'Taking ethics seriously: economics and contemporary moral philosophy'. *Journal of Economic Literature* 31(2): 671–731.

Heckscher, C. and Adler, P. S. 2006. *The firm as a collaborative community*. Oxford University Press.

Hellwig, M. 1991. 'Banking, financial intermediation and corporate finance', in A. Giovannini, C. Mayer (eds.), *European financial integration*. Cambridge University Press, Cambridge.

Henderson, A. D., Miller, D. and Hambrick, D. C. 2006. 'How quickly do CEOs become obsolete? Industry dynamics, CEO tenure, and company performance'. *Strategic Management Journal* 27(5): 447–60.

Higgs, D. 2003. *Review of the role and effectiveness of non-executive directors*. UK Department of Trade and Industry, London.

Holmstrom, B. and Kaplan, S. N. 2003. 'The state of US corporate governance: what's right and what's wrong?', *Journal of Applied Corporate Finance* 15(3): 9.

Hosher, L. T. 1995. 'Trust', *Academy of Management Review* 20(2): 379–402.

Jensen, M. 2000. 'Value maximization, stakeholder theory and the corporate objective function', in M. Beer and N. Nohria (eds.) *Breaking the code of change*. Harvard Business School Press, Boston.

Kaplan, R. and Norton, D. 1996. *The balanced scorecard*. Harvard Business School Press, Boston.

Kaplan, S. N. 1997. 'Corporate governance and corporate performance: a comparison of Germany, Japan and the US'. *Journal of Applied Corporate Finance* 9(4): 86–93.

Kaplan, S. N. 2008. 'Are US CEO's overpaid?', *The Academy of Management Perspectives* 22(2): 5–20.

Khanna, T. and Palepu, K. G. 2004. 'Globalization and convergence in corporate governance: evidence from Infosys and the Indian software industry'. *Journal of International Business Studies* 35: 484–507.

Khurana, R. 2002. *Searching for a corporate savior*. Princeton University Press.

Khurana, R. 2007. *From higher aims to hired hands*. Princeton University Press.

Knight, F. 1921. *Risk, uncertainty and profit* (1965 edition). Harper & Row, New York.

Kreps, R. 1984. 'Corporate culture and economic theory'. Mimeo, Stanford University.

La Porta, R., López de Silanes, F., Shleifer, A. and Vishny, R. 1997. 'Legal determinants of external finance'. *Journal of Finance* 52: 1131–50.

Leibenstein, H. 1966. 'Allocative efficiency versus X-efficiency'. *American Economic Review* 56: 392–415.

Levine, R. 2002. 'Bank-based or market-based financial systems: which is better?' *Journal of Financial Intermediation* 11: 398–428.

Levitt, Jr., A. 2005. 'Corporate culture and the problem of executive compensation'. *Journal of Applied Corporate Finance* 17(4): 41–3.

Llano, C. 2004. *Humildad y liderazgo*. Ed. Ruz, Naucalpan, México.

Logan, D., Roy, D. and Regelbrugge, L. 1997. *Global corporate citizenship*. The Hitachi Foundation, Washington, DC .

Lucier, C., Schuyt, R., Tse, E. 2005. 'CEO succession 2004: the world's most prominent temp workers'. *Strategy + Business*, Summer.

March, J. 1994. *A primer on decision making: how decisions happen*. Free Press, New York.

Marshall, A. 1885. *The present position of economics*. Reprinted in A. C. Pigou (ed.) (1925), Memorials of Alfred Marshall, Macmillan, London.

Mayer, C. 1998. 'Financial systems and corporate governance: a review of the international evidence'. *Journal of Institutional and Theoretical Economics* 154(1): 144–65.

McGregor, D. 1960. *The human side of enterprise*. McGraw-Hill, New York.

Melé, D. (ed.) 1998. *Ética en la actividad financiera*. Eunsa, Pamplona.

Melé, D. 2008. 'Integrating ethics into management'. *Journal of Business Ethics* 78(3): 291–7.

Merck, G. W. 1950. 'Speech at the Medical College of Virginia at Richmond'. Merck & Company historical archives (quoted by J. Collins and J. Porras, 1994).

Micklethwait, J. and Wooldridge, A. 2003. *The company*. Weidenfeld & Nicolson, London.

Milgrom, P. and Roberts, J. 1992. *Economics, organization and management*. Prentice Hall, Englewood Cliffs, NJ.

Miller, M. and Modigliani, M. 1961. 'Dividend policy, growth and the valuation of shares'. *Journal of Business* 34: 411–33.

Mirlees, J. A. and Stern, N. H. 1972. 'Fairly good plans'. *Journal of Economic Theory* 4: 268–88.

Mohn, R. 1996. *Success through partnership*. Doubleday, New York.

Nestlé 1998. *The Nestlé corporate business principles*. Vevey.

Nonaka, I. and Takeuchi, H. 1995. *The knowledge-creating company*. Oxford University Press, New York.

Noria, N. and Khurana, R. 2008. 'It's time to make management a true profession'. *Harvard Business Review*, October: 70–77.

Noria, N., Joyce, W. and Roberson, B. 2003. 'What really works'. *Harvard Business Review*, July: 43–52.

Ouchi, W. G. 1981. *Theory Z: how American business can meet the Japanese challenge*. Addison-Wesley, Reading, MA.

Packard, D. 1960. 'Training session'. Hewlett-Packard Company archives (quoted by J. Collins and J. Porras 1994).

Palepu, K., Khanna, T. and Kogan, J. 2002. 'Globalization and similarities in corporate governance: a cross-country analysis'. Working Paper 02–31, Harvard Business School, Boston.

Pérez López, J. A. 1993. *Fundamentos de dirección de empresas*. Rialp, Madrid.

Perry, T. and Peyer, U. 2005. 'Board seat accumulation by executives: a shareholder's perspective'. *Journal of Finance* 60(4): 2083–2106.

Pfeffer, J. 1978. 'The ambiguity of leadership', in M. McCall, W. Morgan and M. M. Lombardo (eds.) *Leadership: where else can we go?* Duke University Press, Durham, NC: pp. 13–34.

Pfeffer, J. 2005. 'Working alone: what ever happened to the idea of organizations as communities?'. Stanford University.

Porter, M. E. 1980. *Competitive strategy*. Free Press, New York.

Porter, M. E. 1985. *Competitive advantage*. Free Press, New York.

Porter, M. E. 1996. 'What is strategy?' *Harvard Business Review*, November–December: 61–78.

Raheja, C. G. 2005. 'Determinants of board size and composition: a theory of corporate boards'. *Journal of Financial and Quantitative Analysis* 40: 283–306.

Rappaport, A. 1986. *Creating shareholder value*, Free Press, New York.

Roberts, J. 2004. *The modern firm*. Oxford University Press.

Roe, M. 1990. 'Political and legal restraints on ownership and control of public companies'. *Journal of Finance Economics* 27: 7–41.

Roe, M. 1994. *Strong managers and weak owners: the political roots of American corporate finance*. Princeton University Press.

Rosanas, J. M. 2008. 'Beyond economic criteria: a humanistic approach to organizational survival'. *Journal of Business Ethics* 78(3): 447–62.

Rosanas, J. M. 2009. 'A humanistic approach to organizations and to organizational decision making'. IESE Working Paper, Barcelona.

Ross, D. and Westernfield, R. 1988. *Corporate finance*. Time Mirror, St Louis.

Salas, V. 2002. *El gobierno de la empresa*. La Caixa, Barcelona.

Schwenk, C. 1988. 'The cognitive perspective on strategic decision making'. *Journal of Management Studies* 25(1): 41–55.

Scott, W. R. 1995. *Institutions and organizations*. Sage, Thousand Oaks, CA.

Sen, A. 1987. *On ethics and economics*. Blackwell, Oxford.

Selznick, P. 1957. *Leadership in administration*. Harper & Row, New York.

Shivdasani, A. 2004. 'Best practices in corporate governance: what two decades of research reveal'. *Journal of Applied Corporate Finance* 16: 29–41.

Shleifer, A. and Vishny, R. 1997. 'A survey of corporate finance'. *Journal of Finance* 52: 737–83.

Shook, R. L. 1990. *Turnaround: the New Ford Motor Company*. Prentice Hall, New York.

Simon, H. 1947. *Administrative behaviour*. Macmillan, New York.

Simon, H. 1964. 'On the concept of organizational goals'. *Administrative Science Quarterly* 9(1): 1–22.

Simon, M. 1986. 'Rationality in psychology and economics'. *Journal of Business* 4(2): S225–S250.

Smith, A. 1776. *An inquiry into the nature and causes of the wealth of nations* (1976 edition). Oxford University Press, Oxford.

Snider, J., Hill, R. P. and Martin, D. 2003. 'Corporate social responsibility in the 21st century: a view from the world's most successful firms'. *Journal of Business Ethics* 48(2): 175–87.

Stiglitz, J. E. 1994. *Whither socialism?* MIT Press, Cambridge, MA.

Stiles, P. and Taylor, B. 2001. *Boards at work*. Oxford University Press, Oxford.

Swartz, J. 2005. 'The purpose of profit'. Mimeo, Tomorrow's Company, London.

Tett, G. 2009. *Fool's gold*. Free Press, New York.

Tichy, N. M. 1997. *The leadership engine*. Harper Business, New York.

Tichy, N. M. and Devanna, M. A. 1986. *The transformational leader*. John Wiley, New York.

UN Global Compact. 2004. *Learning to talk: corporate citizenship and the development of the UN Global Compact*. Greenleaf Books, New York.

Velamuri, R. and Mitchell, J. 2005. 'Infosys Technologies: powered by intellect, driven by values'. IESE case no. 0–605-021.

Walras, L. 1874. *Elements d'Economie Politique pure* (English version, *Elements of Pure Economics*, 1954, trans. R. Irwin, Homewood, IL).

Williamson, O. 1975. *Markets and hierarchies*. Free Press, New York.

Index